T0305108

Transport Project Evaluation

To Julien van den Broeck

Transport Project Evaluation

Extending the Social Cost–Benefit Approach

Edited by

Elvira Haezendonck

University of Brussels (VUB) and
University of Antwerp (UA), Belgium

BELGIAN-DUTCH ASSOCIATION FOR INSTITUTIONAL AND POLITICAL ECONOMY

Edward Elgar
Cheltenham, UK • Northampton, MA, USA

Published by
Edward Elgar Publishing Limited
The Lypiatts
15 Lansdown Road
Cheltenham
Glos GL50 2JA
UK

Edward Elgar Publishing, Inc.
William Pratt House
9 Dewey Court
Northampton
Massachusetts 01060
USA

Reprinted 2015

A catalogue record for this book
is available from the British Library

Library of Congress Cataloguing in Publication Data

Transport project evaluation : extending the social cost–benefit approach / edited by Elvira Haezendonck.
p. cm.
Includes bibliographical references and index.
1. Transportation and state—Europe. 2. Transportation—Cost effectiveness.
I. Haezendonck, Elvira, 1973–
HE242.T74 2007
388.068′4—dc22

2007001393

ISBN 978 1 84720 379 3

Printed and bound in Great Britain by T.J. International Ltd, Padstow

Contents

Figures

Tables

Contributors

Chris Coeck, Antwerp Port Authority, Antwerp, Belgium

Klaas De Brucker, VLEKHO Business School, Brussels, Belgium

Martin de Jong, Delft University of Technology, the Netherlands

Michaël Dooms, University of Brussels (VUB), Belgium

Harry Geerlings, Erasmus University, Rotterdam, the Netherlands

Elvira Haezendonck, University of Brussels (VUB) and University of Antwerp, Belgium

Cathy Macharis, University of Brussels (VUB), Belgium

Eric Molin, Delft University of Technology, the Netherlands

Enrico Musso, University of Genoa, Italy

Theo Notteboom, ITMMA, University of Antwerp, Belgium

Rafael Saitua, Centraal Planbureau, the Netherlands

Simona Sanguineti, Italian Excellence Center on Integrated Logistics, University of Genoa, Italy

Cécile Sillig, University of Genoa, Italy

Toon Tessier, Antwerp Port Authority, Antwerp, Belgium

Eric Van Hooydonk, University of Antwerp, Eric Van Hooydonk Lawyers, Belgium

Bert Van Wee, Delft University of Technology, the Netherlands

Alain Verbeke, University of Calgary, Canada and University of Brussels (VUB), Belgium

Roger Vickerman, Centre for European, Regional and Transport Economics, University of Kent, UK

Willy Winkelmans, ITMMA, University of Antwerp, Belgium

Acknowledgements

TO JULIEN VAN DEN BROECK

I am very pleased to have the opportunity to acknowledge the importance of the contribution of Julien van den Broeck to the development of the Belgian-Dutch Association for Institutional and Political Economy (AIPE). Julien was President of the predecessor of AIPE, namely *The Association of Post-Keynesian Studies*, and has been an active board member of AIPE for more than twenty years. He has organized a number of its annual conferences and he has edited AIPE volumes such as *Public Choice* and *The Economics of Labour Migration* and co-edited *Changing Economic Order*. AIPE has benefited a lot from Julien's extensive international network, especially with universities and research institutes in Eastern Europe. The importance of Julien's role was also internationally recognized with the title of Doctor Honoris Causa of the National Technical University of Charkov, Ukraine. We very much hope that Julien, after his retirement from academia, will continue to share his insights in institutional economics with us.

John Groenewegen, President of AIPE

Introduction: transport project evaluation in a complex European and institutional environment

Elvira Haezendonck

INTRODUCTION

As society has evolved over time, it has increasingly become more complex. This complexity affects all aspects of society and has a particular relevance for public decision-making, especially regarding decisions with a substantial budgetary impact. For example, with respect to large transport infrastructure investments, stakeholders are also evaluating the economic and social return expected to arise from these investments and, as a result, stakeholders are becoming a more demanding and active group. Hence, transport project appraisal is becoming more complex as well.

Incomplete information on, for example, the environmental impact of certain investments, uncertainty of exact traffic evolutions and pay-offs, an increasing set of regulations and regulatory bodies and controversy on the methodology to be used for the valuation of environmental and social impacts are just a few of the aspects that complicate the investment decision-making process for transport infrastructure.

Decision-makers are confronted with the difficult problem of evaluating potential outcomes and choosing policies to achieve the desired outcomes in the presence of this intense complexity. Decisions that are well intended can lead to losses in social welfare as a result of unexpected outcomes, or outcomes with unexpected consequences. Decision-makers therefore have a great need for a framework that structures information in such a way that the complexity is more manageable, but still takes into account the implications of the complexity and the need for incorporating the different views of stakeholders involved in a particular transport investment project.

At the same time that society has become increasingly complex (and perhaps because society has become increasingly complex), policy-making has entered an era in which social benefits of governmental actions are increasingly questioned. As society has evolved and fears for unintended outcomes and unexpected consequences resulting from public policy have appeared, there has been an increased call to subject all important infrastructure investment decisions to a rigid evaluation process. Here, a systematic comparison of the value of outcomes with the value of resources achieving the outcomes is required, including all involved stakeholders and their views. Hence, a legitimate basis for investment decisions would be created.

This book describes how transport project evaluation has recently evolved towards a comprehensive evaluation framework. This framework takes into account the complex institutional environment and views of multiple and diversified stakeholders involved in, for example, transport infrastructure investment decision-making. Moreover, the book includes a number of empirical cases on transport project evaluations in Europe and provides insights into the institutional drivers and impediments related to project assessment.

The contributors are state-of-the-art experts on project evaluation methodologies and share in this book their latest research on the complexity of transport project appraisal in theory and practice. Although the chapters in this book concentrate more on theoretical views and empirical exercises within the transport and port sector, the concepts and ideas put forward in this book are also useful for other research domains or empirical settings. Here, it is indicated that the concepts proposed in this book can also be used for overall project evaluation, outside the context of traditional transport project evaluation. Further, the different terms which are used in the book to depict evaluation, that is project evaluation, transport project evaluation and project assessment or appraisal, have to be considered as synonyms.

The aim of the book is twofold:

- to share the result of recent research efforts on project evaluation methodologies in the light of a very complex environment such as an increasing environmental awareness, restricted public funds, the need for legitimacy of decisions towards multiple stakeholders, incomplete information, uncertainty, and so on;
- to indicate in what way project evaluation is carried out in practice and how an integrated 'system approach' could be useful for transport project appraisals and decision-making, that is based on project outcomes or results.

AIPE (the Association for Institutional and Political Economy) strongly supports the integration of institutional aspects, influencing the complex environment, into economic decision-making. As such, this book is the result of the discussions that took place during their annual meeting and conference in Antwerp (26 November, 2004).

TOWARDS AN INCREASED NEED FOR TRANSPORT INFRASTRUCTURE POLICY AND EVALUATION GUIDELINES

Decision-making on infrastructural projects is a political and administrative process. Despite the complex environment, important construction decisions have to be taken. These decisions are sometimes associated with great risks due to uncertainty over future developments and effects. The great responsibility associated with these decisions encourages policymakers and public agents to ascertain for themselves the best available information and techniques as an input to the decision-making process.

The demand for transport has dramatically increased over recent years and several studies suggest that traffic will continue to grow exponentially during the next two decades. Especially with regard to maritime container traffic in major seaports, even the most careful forecasts by internationally renowned experts indicate a tremendous cargo growth, which is substantially higher than what can be expected from GDP evolutions or industrial production trends. Given the restricted means and limited investment budget of, for example, EU governments today, it is unlikely that infrastructure investments will be undertaken at the same pace as transport growth. The possible imbalance between cargo handling capacity and cargo demand stresses the importance of sound, careful and just-in-time investment decisions. In the case of port investment projects, timing is crucial and anticipating maritime transport developments is necessary for a port to be able to cope with the fierce competition in the industry. This explains why, for example, ports take every available opportunity to influence or accelerate government action or public funding.

Indeed, the nature of large infrastructural projects necessitates and justifies active government intervention, public involvement and public policy. A public policy aiming to allocate limited public resources is efficient if it maximizes the absolute total net benefits available to society. Here, potential Pareto improvements are often used by economists as the criterion that determines the welfare impact on society as a whole. Government policy also aims to improve equity among members of society. Improving equity implies determining whether costs and benefits are systematically reallocated in ways that do not discriminate between groups. In other words, public policy should guarantee a fair distribution of net benefits among all members of society. Taking these two objectives of public policy into account, it can be concluded that the evaluation of the desirability of large infrastructure projects encompasses more than a simple economic assessment.

In the context of an increased need for well-founded investment decisions, the Dutch and Flemish governments[1], but also French authorities, for example, have paid special attention to creating project evaluation guidelines and regulation of the selection criteria and techniques that should lead to solid investment decisions. These techniques should take into account long-term consequences, and need to include the point of view of a large set of stakeholders. Hence, investment decisions need not be based on short-term political compromises, but should fit within a long-term strategic transport infrastructure vision.

THE EVOLUTION OF TRANSPORT PROJECT EVALUATION: SOCIAL COST–BENEFIT ANALYSIS AND OTHER EVALUATION TECHNIQUES

Decision-making in transport infrastructure projects in the EU and the methods used to underpin these decisions have changed remarkably in recent years. In the 1980s, cost–benefit analysis (CBA) was used most frequently for transport project evaluation. The instrument is based upon perfect markets in which market prices reflect the marginal willingness-to-pay of society for a certain good or service. In reality, however, substantial market failures do exist and need to be included in a project evaluation instrument. During the 1990s, both academics and practitioners in policy analysis claimed that the traditional policy analysis methods were 'out of fashion' because of their prime focus on economic efficiency and the lack of adaptability to the requirements of multi-actor settings of integrating different stakeholder opinions or choices. However, CBA has experienced a sudden resurgence since the year 2000, in the form of a renewed version of the well-known CBA method, also called social cost–benefit analysis (SCBA), for example as a result of the Dutch OEEI guideline (see note 1). Despite all the theoretical studies performed on the types of information policy-makers can process, the need for transparency and for an active multi-actor involvement in the evaluation and decision process has become politically essential and explains why SCBA became successful.

Theoretical and practical contributions in this book analyse social cost–benefit analysis more in depth. Social cost–benefit analysis can be summarized as a systematic means to include all benefits and costs, much like a private sector investment. Because this type of evaluation instrument deals with issues of public policy, it should consider types of benefits and costs that go beyond business decisions, focusing merely on net profit maximization.

To a certain degree, CBA can potentially identify a number of imbalances in the distribution of costs and benefits. However, CBA cannot measure multi-dimensional aspects of project desirability, such as sustainability, ethics and other social values. As a result, CBA provides information for the decision-making process, but it does not provide sufficient information to take decisions that necessitate multi-actor views. Therefore, the most efficient project from an economic point of view (determined by a CBA) should not automatically be pursued, without considering other important criteria that can affect overall social desirability.

In recent literature, it is recognized that formal economic evaluation analyses (based on net present values such as cost–benefit analysis) tend to be inadequate, for example for public expenditure analyses, as the anticipated objectives (for example generation of employment) are often broader than pure economic or market concerns. Social cost–benefit analysis, together with some extensions suggested in this book, is the approach which enables these additional (often non-market) goals and effects to be quantified. It is often considered as the public expenditure equivalent of the net present value methods when evaluating private investments. Besides economic and financial appraisal, social appraisal is one of the three main components of SCBA. This component examines both the distributional consequences of project choices over a period of time, and concerns between groups in society at a specific point in time. Including this element is essential in a multi-actor setting.

Social CBA could well serve a decision-maker during the analytical phase of the process. Multi-criteria analysis could then complement a CBA in the decision phase, as it better takes into account the political feasibility and social acceptability consensus. Here, it is important to mention that the methodology used should enable analysis as well as synthesis. Results should be represented in such a way that the decision-maker is perfectly informed and transparency is realized. Contrary to many transport project evaluation studies in the past, a sound, clear and policy-relevant conclusion or synthesis should also be part of the proposed method of transport infrastructure evaluation.

EMPIRICAL EVIDENCE FROM EVALUATION TECHNIQUES

Next to theoretical propositions for an optimal transport policy evaluation, throughout the book several case studies on transport evaluation are described that provide practical evidence for the use of different evaluation techniques.

A large number of cases indicate the necessity of a multi-actor approach. Indeed, the major shortcoming is the neglect of societal and environmentally based elements in the conventional project appraisal techniques.

Only by the explicit integration of the objectives of relevant stakeholders involved and by allowing the stakeholders (be they representatives of business firms or governmental agencies) to reflect their ideas and views, can an overall and successful evaluation procedure be created.

THE 'INTEGRATED SYSTEM APPROACH' FOR TRANSPORT PROJECT EVALUATION

The different contributions in this book indicate that most traditional CBA methods are both too limited in scope and too partial in nature to reflect the necessities of modern economy. Vickerman (see Chapter 2) argues in this respect: 'we need to identify clearly what factors are included and what not, to be able to interpret the outcome (. . .). The development of a more appropriate and full CBA can be seen as a set of step-changes'. Here, an important distinction can be made between the theoretically optimal CBA and a best practice CBA such as an extended SCBA. Including a multi-actor approach in CBA evaluations enhances the effectiveness and efficiency of the government action and as such increases societal benefits in favour of specific stakeholders. Different strategically positioned stakeholders may try to get an advantage over other parties and influence project evaluation and decision-making. Here, government should act as a party that neutralizes the excessive bargaining strength of powerful, strategically positioned stakeholders.

Throughout the book it is indicated that a number of shortcomings in traditional CBA techniques exist. An 'integrated system approach' to transport project evaluation or an extended SCBA will attempt to overcome these problems. This includes a number of new evaluation procedures but also the integration of additional participation techniques to include all relevant points of view of stakeholders in the decision-making process. Only in this way can the evaluation techniques match the increased complexity and institutional change of society.

The described analyses can never replace the political decision-making itself. However, the evaluation procedure can try to ensure that political decisions are taken on the basis of complete and relevant information, using unequivocal terms and a solid and reliable base for evaluations.

This position is clearly represented by Musso, Sanguineti and Sillig (Chapter 4):

> Some degree of participation should be introduced in order to be aware of the cultural and institutional context in which the project is to be implemented, and to relate its evaluation to that context as much as possible, so that the final project, if implemented, can match the real needs and will of the people for whom it has been planned. This can be made possible only if all stakeholders take part in the process.

In addition, the 'integrated system approach' that is developed in this book in the framework of large transport projects, can, in principle, also be used for the analysis of large and small projects in other economic domains.

STRUCTURE OF THE BOOK

This book provides an overview of a wide array of aspects related to transport project appraisal and can be considered as a benchmark in the transport project evaluation literature. The book is structured along the systematic application of socio-economic evaluation instruments for assessing the design, effects and implementation of investment projects.

Two major parts can be distinguished in the book. The first part concentrates on general perspectives for evaluation procedures and transport project appraisal methodologies. The second part provides an overview of a number of empirical applications and case studies of transport evaluation in practice.

The methodological part of the book consists of six chapters. Saitua and De Brucker and Verbeke, in Chapters 1 and 3 respectively, provide the institutional drivers of transport infrastructure evaluation and analyse the characteristics of social cost–benefit analysis as a tool for decision-making, together with alternative multi-criteria-based instruments. Vickerman provides a critical examination of the evaluation of transport projects in Chapter 2. Emphasis is put on transport appraisal in the UK. Chapter 4, by Musso, Sanguineti and Sillig, focuses on socio-economic impact assessment and its relation to institutional aspects, and discusses some of the institutional and socio-economic limits of most common evaluation tools. This chapter also describes the negative consequences of the fact that these techniques fail to consider institutional aspects properly. In Chapter 5, Macharis builds on elements of former chapters and describes in what way multi-criteria analysis can be used as a tool to include multiple stakeholders in project evaluation. Finally, part 1 of the book is concluded by Van Hooydonk in Chapter 6. This author stresses the limits of traditional legislative procedures for transport infrastructure evaluation. It is argued that transport development is benefited often by an ad hoc procedure that is project-specific but also in line with the public interest and importance of the proposed project.

Part 2 of the book consists of four chapters. The examples and cases in this part are mostly of Belgian, Dutch, German and Danish origin. Chapter 7 concentrates on the use of social cost–benefit analysis for transport infrastructure investments in the Netherlands. More in particular, it examines the reasons for implementing a new guideline for *ex ante* evaluation of large infrastructural projects. In Chapter 8, Coeck and Tessier describe evidence and experiences of the Deurganckdock case in the port of Antwerp. The procedures used for evaluating this major port container project reveal a number of shortcomings. Chapter 8 provides a number of possible opportunities for adapting port project evaluation in this respect. In Chapter 9 Dooms, Macharis and Verbeke describe an application of stakeholder analysis to infrastructural development and the use of multicriteria analysis in the DHL project. Here, they analyse what kind of stakeholders should be included, in the decision-making process. Chapter 9 also discusses the different steps that need to be taken in the decision-making process. Finally, Chapter 10 provides an expert valuation of the various institutional structures for infrastructure decisions in Denmark, Germany and the Netherlands. This chapter concentrates on a search towards the ideal structure for decision-making on transport infrastructure.

Coeck and Haezendonck conclude the book and suggest that transport project appraisal is evolving towards an integrated systems approach and that important extensions to SCBA are considered necessary for sound and legitimate transport investment decisions.

NOTE

1. In 1998, a research programme on the economic effects of infrastructure (named 'OEEI', Overview of Economic Effects of Infrastructure) was commissioned by the Dutch Ministry of Transport, Public Works and Water Management and the Ministry of Economic Affairs. The results of several studies within this programme have led to a comprehensive guide including definitions and methodologies for appraising infrastructure projects in the Netherlands. The guide (appraisal system and recommendations) was approved by the Dutch Cabinet in 2000 and positively evaluated in 2002. Following the Dutch initiative, the Flemish government introduced a project in 2005 for developing a standard method for project appraisal and investment decisions (named 'Standaard Methodiek MKBA'). This project reflects the Flemish need for an integrated appraisal framework.

Institutional drivers and impediments in the context of current transport projects

Theo Notteboom and Willy Winkelmans

INTRODUCTION

Mobility is considered to be a human right. Ensuring mobility of persons and goods is, or at least should be, at the heart of any transport policy. A coherent transport policy should aim at achieving integrated systems, combining the use of different modes where appropriate on the same journey (combined or multi-modal transport) and with special attention to the use of environmentally-friendly transport modes. Two basic principles have to be kept in mind when designing a coherent transport policy aimed at sustainable mobility: the principle of the coverage of infrastructure costs and external costs and the principle of fair competition among all transport modes (level playing field).

The constant increase in mobility puts high pressure on the daily management of traffic flows. Densely populated areas are suffering from an increasing lack of space and associated functional competition for space, while increasing traffic goes hand in hand with challenges in the field of safety, energy consumption and environmental comfort. All over the world, transport infrastructure supply increasingly faces a hard time in meeting transport demand both in terms of quantity and quality. The mounting tensions are the result of the interplay among actors and factors. The resulting mobility problems can not be narrowed down to transportation problems.

A strong correlation exists between economic development and transport, but this relation is rather ambiguous, especially in relation to freight transport. Over the last ten years, growth rates in freight transport have been consistently higher than the growth rates of relevant determinants, such as industrial production and gross domestic product (GDP). Transport is more than just a derived activity. The process of globalization of production and consumption makes transport a fully-fledged and independent industry, an active partner in the business and logistics world. Transport growth not only depends upon production of goods. Technological evolutions follow and/or trigger changes in the economic system. The relocation of industries, particularly for goods with a high labour input, implies a spatial dispersion of production sites (global production networks) up to thousands of kilometres away from the final assembly plant or from the end users. The result of global sourcing and complex logistics networks is a disproportional increase in ton kilometres compared to related productions in value (for example GDP and industrial production) and as such an intensified use of transport infrastructures.

Mounting tensions between transport demand and supply accentuate the fact that mobility can not be taken for granted. A coherent and consistent internal mobility policy requires a multi-faceted approach to transport infrastructures in which organizational, economic and technological evolutions are considered in combination with intelligent regulation and stimulation as a function of assessments of the various socio-economic and external effects linked to transportation. Only then will sustainable development be attained.

This contribution deals with current issues in the role and the appraisal of transport infrastructure projects. The first part addresses the need for transport infrastructure investments and the low adaptability of transport infrastructure in responding to user and market dynamics. The appraisal and evaluation of transport infrastructure projects forms the core of the second part. It will be demonstrated that the decision-making process regarding transport infrastructure projects is becoming more complex, both in terms of procedural aspects and the appraisal and evaluation tools used.

TRANSPORT INFRASTRUCTURE UNDER SCRUTINY

The primary aim of the White Paper of the European Commission 'European Transport Policy to 2010: time to decide' was sustainable mobility in the long run (European Commission, 2001). Most proposed measures in the White Paper involve choices and actions at a national level, in the context of subsidiarity, nevertheless requiring new forms of regulation. One of the key concepts relates to putting the user back at the heart of transport policy, implying a renewed policy focus on aspects such as road safety, reliability and flexibility. This renewed focus on the user is also reflected on transport infrastructures. The White Paper states:

> One of the important reasons why imbalances and inefficiencies have arisen is because transport users have not been adequately confronted with the full costs

> of their activities (. . .) If prices do not reflect the full social cost of transport, demand will be artificially high. If appropriate pricing and infrastructure policies were to be pursued, these inefficiencies would largely disappear over time. (European Commission, 2001: 71)

From a theoretical point of view prices are instruments to stimulate equilibrium between demand and supply, but in view of a more sustainable mobility the existing gap between both may be too wide to solve the problem of imbalance only by changing the transport price(s). Achieving sustainable mobility is not only a question of fair and efficient pricing, but also of country and city planning and of guaranteeing a fair and sustainable balance between supply and demand. In many industrialized countries the relative weight of investments in transport infrastructure has decreased significantly. The average degree in Europe in the 1970s was around 3 per cent of the GDP; since the 1980s, however, the average went down to about 1 per cent (European Commission, 2001). This has contributed to the observed discrepancy between the demand for more mobility and the available supply in transport infrastructure.

A wide range of actions can be taken and are being taken to optimize the use of existing transport infrastructures including for example tidal flows, peak lanes, separated lanes, van and carpooling zones and variable taxation of car use and car possession. These measures may improve the quality of existing mobility, but the question remains whether they represent long-term solutions for the growing transport demand. Only structural measures can bring forward long-lasting solutions. Structural improvements aim at re-establishing the equilibrium between demand and supply of transport, by developing new transport capacities, improving existing capacity through elimination of missing links and bottlenecks and by stimulating integrated and multi-modal transport systems. Capacity extensions can take various forms: new transport infrastructures in nodes and along corridors, the introduction of larger vehicles and the disconnection of passenger transport from freight ways (for example through dedicated freight railways).

Transport infrastructures should valorize the intrinsic accessibility of a region or location. At the same time, transport infrastructure should meet user requirements (demand pull). A major tension can be observed in the adaptability/responsiveness of transport infrastructures to changes in transport demand and associated flows (passengers and goods). Given long planning periods, infrastructures typically show a low adaptability (expressed in time) in facing user and market changes. For example, the planning and construction of major port and inland infrastructures (infrastructural level) typically takes many years. The duration of the planning and implementation of shuttle trains on specific railway corridors (transport operator level) usually varies between a few months up to one year. At the logistical level, freight forwarders and multi-modal transport operators are able to respond almost instantly to variations in the market by modifying the supply chain design, that is the routing of the goods through the transport system. The differences in responsiveness on the proposed levels leads to considerable time lags between proposed structural changes on the logistical and the transport operator level and the necessary infrastructural adaptations needed to meet these changes adequately. This issue becomes particularly acute given the paradigm shift towards supply chains. This phenomenon partly explains both the existing congestion and overcapacity situations in transport infrastructures.

The tensions between the infrastructural layer and the transport and logistics layers are a mixed result of a number of factors. First, there is the issue of time-consuming planning and project appraisal processes involving a large number of stakeholders (market players, community groups, environmental organizations, and so on). Unfortunately, quite a number of stakeholders take transport infrastructure for granted. Transport infrastructures are considered by many as abundantly available and as tools in satisfying the hunger for mobility. Second, environmental legislation at EU level does not always guarantee legal certainty to infrastructure. In the port industry, the application of the Bird and Habitat Directives of the European Commission serves as a good example (see for example Van Hooydonk, 2006). Third, legal complications with financial institutions or building contractors can result in a construction halt that can last for months. Fourth, the political aspect related to the provision of most large transport infrastructures further complicates and lengthens the decision-making process.

The limited and slow adaptability of transport infrastructures to changes in transport demand and associated flows has its impact on transport policy initiatives. The implementation of modal shift policies of governments at the local, regional, national and supranational level is often hampered by the existence of infrastructural bottlenecks and a low interoperability and interconnectivity between modal transport systems (both point and line infrastructures). As the dynamics in the economic system is high, long delays in the realization of physical infrastructures could ultimately lead to a misallocation of means. Hence, user requirements and market conditions might change considerably in the time span between the planning phase and the actual realization of an infrastructure. So, an infrastructure investment which at the time of its conception seemed feasible and market-driven, could end up as an investment in the wrong place, at the wrong time, for the wrong market and using the wrong technology. Such mis-steps can have serious impacts on markets in terms of pricing, user costs and competition levels.

Because of the above factors, transport infrastructures are on the verge of becoming scarce goods. For example, port congestion along the US West Coast and in many European ports in the summer of 2004 demonstrated how scarcity of port facilities and intermodal throughput capacity can impact a broader economic system. Scarcity in markets can lead to more efficient use of resources, which is a good thing. But accepting a continuous high level of scarcity as the 'new normal' might in the longer term have adverse effects on the whole logistics system and eventually also on global production and consumption networks. Therefore, it is a joint responsibility of infrastructure managers, policy-makers and other stakeholders to foster transport infrastructures and the broader networks of which they are part and to safeguard their future development potential.

KEY ISSUES IN TRANSPORT INFRASTRUCTURE PROJECT APPRAISAL

Transport infrastructure projects are under scrutiny due to government budget constraints, increased competition for land, environmental awareness and the need for integrated transport systems. These considerations are also mirrored on appraisal and evaluation procedures applicable to transport infrastructure project proposals.

Governments have to ensure that public funds are spent on activities that provide the greatest benefits to society, and that they are spent in the most efficient way. Decisions taken at the appraisal stage can and mostly do affect the whole life cycle of new policies, programmes and projects. Similarly, the proper evaluation of previous initiatives is essential in avoiding past mistakes and to learn from experience.

Governments all over Europe have developed guidelines and tools to encourage a more thorough, long-term and analytically robust approach to appraisal and evaluation of transport infrastructure projects. France, the Netherlands and the United Kingdom are examples of countries where formal decision-making frameworks for large infrastructure projects have been put in place. The term 'formal' does not necessarily imply the framework is backed up by actual legislation. Even when a legal foundation is present, as is the case for the '*Loi d'orientation sur les transports intérieurs*' in France (LOTI-law of 30 December 1982), the legal stipulations are merely referring to the general principles. The formal frameworks typically refer to internal arrangements and working procedures for a specific ministry. An example is the MIT framework (*Spelregels van het Meerjarenprogramma Infrastructuur en Transport*) of the Dutch Ministry of Transport (Ministerie van Verkeer en Waterstaat, 2004).

In the remainder of this contribution some current issues and developments in project appraisal of large transport infrastructure projects are discussed. As other contributions in this book will zoom in on methodological issues and practical applications, this section does not intend to provide a detailed analysis of all issues raised.

Guidelines on Project Appraisal and Evaluation are becoming Widespread

Decision-making frameworks on large infrastructure projects are typically complex, both in terms of the procedural aspects and the appraisal and evaluation tools used. The EU-funded research programme Developing Harmonised European Approaches for Transport Costing and Project Assessment (HEATCO) provides a thorough analysis of the methods used in socio-economic appraisal of transport infrastructure projects in the EU and Switzerland (HEATCO, 2005). The main conclusions can be summarized as follows.

First, most countries have developed guidelines on the socio-economic evaluation of road and rail infrastructure projects. The use of standard methodologies is less common for other modes.

Second, projects that get partial funding by the European Investment Bank (EIB) or the European regional funds have to follow specific guidelines, for example the guidelines of the Directorate-General Regional Policy of the European Commission (European Commission, 2002).

Third, the social cost–benefit analysis is an integral part of decision-making trajectories. In most cases SCBA is combined with other methods including multi-criteria analysis, quantitative impact analysis and qualitative impact analysis. The latter methods are typically deployed to evaluate effects which one cannot or does not want to express in monetary values. The economic impact study or economic effects analysis is used nowhere as a formal and separate appraisal method. In some cases, input–output analyses, which form the basis of economic impact studies, are being used in view of the assessment of indirect economic effects. As such, the economic impact study, where used, is one of the quantitative impact analysis methods that can be used in combination with the SCBA.

Fourth, a considerable stream of literature has developed over the years on the identification, management and realization of costs and benefits. This increased focus on methodologies to estimate the effects of infrastructure projects has led to a multiplication of the kind of effects that are being considered in an SCBA. Direct and external project effects that are commonly considered in an SCBA relate to construction costs, costs of maintenance and management, different types of transport benefits (time savings, vehicle costs, benefits for goods transportation) and the impact of the project on traffic safety. The picture is less straightforward in the case of some other external effects such as noise pollution, air pollution and visual intrusion. In quite a number of countries these latter effects are expressed in monetary values using a set of valuation techniques. Other countries opt for separate quantitative or qualitative analyses in view of assessing these effects, without monetary valuation. Valuation techniques for visual intrusion, vibrations and community severance have proven to be less robust and less broadly accepted than the methodologies for evaluating noise and air pollution.

Managing Procedural Aspects of the Decision-making Process

The procedural aspects of the decision-making on large infrastructure projects are designed in such a way that (a) the procedure can be finalized within an acceptable timeframe, (b) the involvement of relevant stakeholders throughout the process is guaranteed and (c) the quality of the project appraisal results can be guaranteed. We will discuss each of these points.

The time factor

The time factor plays an important role in any infrastructure project appraisal. First there is the timing of the trajectory from conception of a project to the final decision-making. The whole procedure should be finalized within an acceptable timeframe. Guidelines on project appraisal generally do not contain clear stipulations on the timing for completion of the SCBA and other studies. The timing of the SCBA is determined by the broader decision-making trajectory. Deadlines are often put forward for formal steps in the decision-making process.

Second, there is the tension between the long-term focus in infrastructure planning/realization on one hand and the short-term developments in business cycles and market developments on the other. Markets change almost overnight, so companies typically use a short planning horizon of a few years. The shorter business cycles and economic cycles means that it becomes increasingly difficult to develop a long-term focus in the framework of transport projects. For example, ten years ago nobody anticipated that the Chinese economy would boom in such a way that it would considerably impact markets. Long time series about flows are at the core of any transport infrastructure appraisal, but the uncertainty of long-term developments becomes more apparent. Scenario building and risk analysis have therefore gained in importance when considering transport infrastructure appraisal.

Iterative processes are gaining ground as they are generally considered as the way forward in view of providing a reasonable understanding of whether, in the light of changing circumstances, the project proposal is likely to remain good value for money. Iterations in a project evaluation procedure often involve a stepwise approach. The detail and accuracy of the data provided increases as the evaluation progresses from the initial steps of identifying and appraising the project alternatives to the final steps in the procedure.

Given rising budget constraints, procurement routes are increasingly considered, including the role of the private sector in the financing of the project (public–private partnerships). This trend poses great challenges to the transport project appraisal procedures as potential partnering arrangements and their implications on costs and benefits sharing should be identified early in the process.

Streamlining stakeholders' involvement

The interest in stakeholder approaches to strategic management is growing around the world (Mills and Weinstein, 2000). The dynamics of investments in transport infrastructure is not taking place in a vacuum, but is articulated by the strategic and operational decisions of the stakeholders involved. Consultation is important. The times when governments could unilaterally decide on large transport infrastructure projects without involvement of stakeholders are long gone. At present, a large part of the financial and human resources linked to a project appraisal procedure is linked to consultation with and between stakeholders.

Streamlining the involvement of stakeholders throughout the appraisal and decision-making procedure is a painstaking process. The classification of stakeholders depends on the purpose. This inevitably leads to a wide diversity in interpretations of who can be classified as a stakeholder (see, for example, Donaldson and Preston, 1995). In the broad view, stakeholders are described as any individual or group having interest in or being affected by the project. The narrow view only recognizes stakeholders whose relationship is primarily of an economic/contractual kind (Shankman, 1999).

Stakeholder relations management (SRM) aims at holding the balance between various groups and taking due note of their rights (Argenti, 1997). Governments are well aware of the fact that socially responsible behaviour is a must. SRM applied to transport infrastructure projects requires simultaneous attention for the legitimate interests of all appropriate stakeholders, both in the establishment of procedures and general policies and in case-by-case decision-making. However, this principle does not imply that all stakeholders should be equally involved in all processes and decisions.

Decision-making procedures on transport infrastructures in France and the United Kingdom explicitly include public hearings. The results of the

SCBA are made public in most countries and serve as input for a community-wide discussion. Formal processes typically describe how and when consultation of stakeholders should take place.

Government departments have to decide about the role attributed to each stakeholder in the decision-making processes (Notteboom and Winkelmans, 2003). In a first step, they could try to discriminate between those stakeholders with genuine legitimate interests in the process considered and those who only claim to have a legitimate interest. This exercise can turn out to be very difficult, because the simple act of classifying a group as not relevant for a specific process (for example, the planning of a new highway) in itself can become a major source of conflict. For instance, a party with no direct legitimate interest can have a large political influence (for example, a party who has the capacity to mobilize the press can have an impact on the political level). In order to avoid such situations, governments often opt for a maximum approach, in which both the legitimate groups and the non-legitimate groups are invited to take part in the process. In many cases, the active role of the latter groups is limited to information exchange.

Governments also have to decide on the role attributed to each stakeholder in the decision-making processes. Stakeholders should be classified based on their involvement in the process/decision and their possible impact on the process/decision.

Designing a well-balanced time planning for the structuring of stakeholders' participation throughout the trajectory of the project proposal is one of the key actions in SRM (Brooke, 2002). A government department can decide to involve all stakeholders right from the start. The advantage is that no stakeholder will feel neglected. However, a slow start due to long pre-negotiation rounds in the early phases of the project is an important disadvantage of this approach. Alternatively, a government department might decide to draw up detailed plans in-house. Stakeholders will only be involved in the process once these plans have gained maturity. The strength of this approach is that stakeholders are confronted with rather concrete development plans, so there is less room for them to introduce unrealistic alternatives. However, some stakeholders might not feel at ease: such a top-down approach might give the impression that the decisions have already been taken, thereby reducing the stakeholders' participation process to a formality or a diversion. Conflict and suspicion among stakeholders will stimulate formal bargaining resulting in time delays and increased costs. Formal bargaining often appears when stakeholders demand compensation for incurred risks or harms. Compensation claims are often subject to highly politicized negotiation rounds, characterized by a lack of trust and an absence of solid deals/arrangements among the stakeholders. Under these circumstances government departments might be tempted to use compensation as a tool to neutralize (at least temporarily) some community groups, whereas community groups might use the negotiation rounds as a tool to consolidate their position as legitimate interlocutors in port development debates.

At the appraisal level, there is a greater emphasis on assessing the differential impacts of project proposals on the various stakeholders, where these are likely to be significant. In other words, project evaluation techniques are geared towards making the distribution of costs and benefits among the relevant groups/stakeholders in the society more transparent.

Quality assurance

Transport project appraisal and evaluation procedures and guidelines attach more and more importance to quality management. Quality tests can take various forms ranging from assessing compliance with the guidelines on project appraisal to the evaluation of the basic scenarios and forecasts used. Interim and final results of SCBAs are often screened by an external expert commission, typically consisting of members of central planning authorities and academics. SCBAs are often too specific and the number of SCBAs is often too low to justify a permanent status of such an expert commission. Government departments and agencies are increasingly encouraged to consider establishing formal evaluation or assessment units and formalizing access to internal and external auditors.

There is an increasing trend in dealing with systematic optimism in project evaluation. There is a demonstrated, systematic tendency for project appraisers to be overly optimistic (Flyvbjerg, 2002). Optimism bias has played a major role in, for example, the underestimation of construction costs or the overrating of indirect benefits of a project. Dealing with optimism is slowly being internalized in the evaluation process, for example via an explicit adjustment procedure to redress the systematic optimism. Sensitivity analyses are now broadly used to test assumptions about operating costs and expected benefits. Project proposals are typically reviewed more than once in terms of impact of risks, uncertainties and inherent biases.

CONCLUDING REMARKS

Mobility is a basic need in modern society. Institutional measures are required to make mobility as efficient and sustainable as possible. The need for a comprehensive, integrated and socially-based transport policy has made the decision-making process on large infrastructure projects more complex, both in terms of the procedural aspects and the appraisal and evaluation tools used. Procedures are geared towards meeting an acceptable timeframe, a fair level of involvement of relevant stakeholders and a high level of quality assurance.

The ultimate outcome of any transport infrastructure appraisal is a decision whether or not to proceed with a transport project proposal. The presentation of the conclusions and recommendations to decision-makers and key stakeholders is a very important part of the decision-making process. Remarkable progress has been made in the last five years in the field of making project appraisal results more transparent towards helping the decision. These improvements relate to the transparency as regards evidence and assumptions, forecasts, costs and benefits and sensitivity and scenario analyses. The output of an SCBA no longer provides single point estimates of expected values (for example net present value), but a whole range of indicators. This is to help the decision-makers in interpreting the ranges of potential outcomes as a function of future uncertainty.

REFERENCES

Argenti, J. (1997), 'Stakeholders: the case against', *Long Range Planning*, **30**(3), 442–5.

Brooke, J. (2002), 'Stakeholder participation in port development decision making: how? where? And when?', *Proceedings PIANC 2002, 30th International Navigation Congress*, Sydney, September 2002 (proceedings on CD-Rom).

Donaldson, T. and L.E. Preston (1995), 'The stakeholder theory of the corporation: concepts, evidence and implications', *Academy of Management Review*, **20**(1), 65–91.

European Commission (2001), 'European Transport Policy to 2010: time to decide', White Paper, COM(2001) 370 final, Brussels: European Commission.

European Commission (2002), *Guide to Cost–benefit Analysis of Investment Projects*, DG Regional Policy, Evaluation Unit, Brussels: European Commission.

Flyvbjerg, B. (2002), 'Underestimating costs in public works projects', *Journal of the American Planning Association*, **68**(3), 279–95.

HEATCO (2005), 'Deliverable 1. Current practice in project appraisal in Europe: analysis of country reports', Brussels.

Mills, R. and B. Weinstein (2000), 'Beyond shareholder value – reconciling the shareholder and stakeholder perspectives', *Journal of General Management*, **25**(3), 79–93.

Ministerie van Verkeer en Waterstaat (2004), *Spelregels van het Meerjarenprogramma Infrastructuur en Transport*, The Hague: Ministerie van Verkeer en Waterstaat.

Notteboom, T. and W. Winkelmans (2003), 'Dealing with stakeholders in the port planning process', in W. Dullaert, B. Jourquin and J. Polak (eds), *Across the Border: Building upon a Quarter Century of Transport Research in the Benelux*, Antwerp: De Boeck, pp. 249–65.

Shankman, N.A. (1999), 'Reframing the debate between agency and stakeholder theories of the firm', *Journal of Business Ethics*, **19**, 319–34.
Van Hooydonk, E. (2006), *The Impact of EU Environmental Law on Ports and Waterways*, Antwerp-Apeldoorn: Maklu Publishers.

PART I

Perspectives on transport project evaluation and methodologies

1. Some considerations on social cost–benefit analysis as a tool for decision-making

Rafael Saitua

WHAT IS SOCIAL COST–BENEFIT ANALYSIS?

Social cost–benefit analysis (SCBA) seeks to evaluate all the expected impacts of an option or a project on *all* the individuals of a society, not just the parties directly involved as consumers or producers. The word *social* is used in the literature mainly to refer to this aspect of an SCBA. The analysis intends to be comprehensive. Every project effect that has a value for the individuals of the community concerned and that is related to scarcity, is systematically estimated and, wherever possible, given a monetary value. These valuations are rooted in the welfare theory and have a large tradition. In this theory it is assumed that individuals are the best judge of their own welfare (Brent, 1996: 29).

Projects are compared with a so-called 'do minimum' alternative that implies the best possible solution of the problem with a minimum use of resources. In a cost–benefit analysis, welfare effects are estimated either on the basis of market prices or elicited from the behaviour of economic agents in the market system. Benefits are based on the individual's willingness-to-pay for a certain good or service. Costs are based on what economic agents are willing to receive as compensation for the supply of resources. Basically, a project is desirable if the benefits exceed the costs, with both benefits and costs suitably discounted over time. In this case, the winners will be able to compensate the losers and, potentially, everybody will be better off after realization of the project. However, if distribution is an issue, there are some qualifications on this statement, as we will see below.

If markets were working perfectly, market prices would express the marginal willingness-to-pay for the individuals of a society for a certain good or service. At the same time, market prices would express the marginal cost for the society in producing the good or service under consideration. In this case, a calculation with market prices yields a result that automatically expresses the desirability of a project provided that distribution is not an issue and that all effects are priced.

Because market failure often occurs in the real economy, it is not always possible to use market prices in evaluating projects. In this case, the concept of social prices or shadow prices is of the highest importance. The social (or shadow) price of a commodity can be defined as its social opportunity costs, that is the net loss (gain) for the society associated with having one unit less (more) of it (Drèze and Stern, 1994: 59–99). The determinant for the social price is the restriction that has to be relaxed to dispose of 'one unit more'.

SCBA deals with social prices instead of market prices in clear cases of market failure. In doing so, an SCBA intends to deal with the problems related to market failure or to non-existing markets. The preferences of individuals as expressed directly or indirectly in the market system, or other information on preferences of individuals, with the necessary corrections to get social prices, are the starting point for valuation of a certain effect. In some cases, notably when markets don't exist, other relevant markets are used or surrogate markets are created. But the methodology mainly rests on individual preferences as expressed in individual behaviour and in this sense it rests on the so-called methodological individualism (Arrow, 1994).

We will illustrate the difference between social prices and market prices by briefly analysing one market where market failure occurs. A good example is the knowledge market. Investors in knowledge do not obtain all the yields because there is a leak to other parties of the gains of the knowledge created. Therefore, the private benefits related to producing knowledge do not reflect the social benefits of disposing of 'one unit more'. Private knowledge producers will continue to produce until their marginal benefits equal their marginal costs. In this case, the social price of new knowledge will be higher than the private price because part of the benefits will leak to third parties. To put it in other words, the loss incurred of disposing of 'one unit less' is larger than the producer's loss.

More generally, typical cases of market failure are:

- A monopolistic market structure in which prices are set above marginal costs. In this case, the social price of the product produced by the monopoly depends on what restriction has to be relaxed. If a new activity replaces the use of the monopoly's product by another already existent activity, the monopoly price is the right social price. If the new activity is using 'one unit more' produced by the monopoly, then the social price reflects the marginal costs of the monopoly (Anderson and Settle, 1979: 37–9).[1] Government's *ad valorem* taxes can be seen as a special case of a monopoly.

- Segments of the labour market with structural unemployment, for instance because wages have been determined above its equilibrium value. In this case, the social labour price is lower than the actual wage and, in absence of cyclical unemployment, payments will be equal to the reservation wage of additional labour.
- External effects, like pollution, congestion, disruption, landscape quality. In a positive sense, possible 'cluster effects', like scale economies, or technology diffusion. A social price of a product has to take the costs of external effects of producing 'one unit more' of the product concerned into account.

THE SPECIFIC CHOICE OF INDIVIDUALS AS A STARTING POINT

Through their specific choices in the market system, individuals express their preferences for goods or services. The importance of this information cannot be stressed enough, because it emerges from the specific choice of individuals in situations of limited resources. And this is what project evaluation is about. Therefore, individuals' willingness-to-pay is clearly a very robust starting point for the valuation of most projects' effects. On the other hand, as we shall see later on, it has also its limits. In addition, valuation on the basis of the preference of individuals as expressed in the market system, limits the otherwise long lists of diverse subjectively determined advantages and disadvantages which complicate rather than simplify a comprehensive analysis of project effects. The debate will then be concentrated on the really important issues. For example, do the gains of a project compensate for the loss of a unique landscape? Or does a favourable effect on a region justify a loss of national welfare?

Valuation on the basis of choice of individuals in the market system also has a disciplining effect. It prevents double-counting, as it requires insight into the relationship between the various impacts affecting the choice of individuals.

PROJECT ALTERNATIVES

In an SCBA, we compare the returns of a project with alternative investments for the community. This can only be determined after the benefits have been compared to the alternative returns. This is precisely what takes place in an SCBA when performed properly.

This search for alternatives is also very important within the project. In this case, alternatives should relate to the scale of the project and to the timing. When we think about the scale of a project, the most relevant comparison is not with a 'do nothing' alternative but rather with a 'do minimum' alternative. When we think about the timing of a project, the most relevant alternative is a 'do later', rather than a 'do nothing' alternative. By considering both the scale and the time dimension, one seeks to optimize the project, determining planning phases in it. Alternatives could also relate to different locations or competing modes of transport. SCBA is well suited for comparing various project alternatives systematically and for providing information in terms of which the various alternatives can be assessed.

RISK AND UNCERTAINTY

Decisions about the project have been made now but the effects will often only be visible in the long term. A long-term perspective is thus inherent in many infrastructural projects. A project is not only assessed on the basis of the average expected outcome, but also on the spread of the outcomes, because in the preferences of the people there is an element of risk aversion. Because of this aversion a project with a low certain yield may be just as valuable as a project with a high but uncertain yield. This *insurance premium* can serve as the basis for the risk assessment. The costs of the risk will increase over time, because uncertainty generally increases in the future. Risk aversion may therefore have implications for the choice of the discount rate. This is particularly the case for projects for which the risk cannot be diversified with the outcomes of other projects because the outcomes correlate with the macro-economic development of the country (Dixit and Williamson, 1989).

It is also very important to take into account that the future holds many fundamental uncertainties. Using one prognosis only provides the illusion of certainty. Therefore, in this case, the proper approach will first of all be to determine the critical success factors and then to formulate various developments for these factors. If there is a connection between these factors, it is advisable to work with scenarios. Various developments are often also plausible within the context of one scenario. In this case, it is advisable to consider different alternatives. With a proper sensitivity analysis, it is possible to test the robustness of the analysis for the variation of some basic parameters, or the state of the world in different scenarios. In this way, it is possible to take aspects such as risks and uncertainty into account and to test the robustness of the evaluation.

EXTERNAL EFFECTS

External effects are unintentional, non-priced effects on the welfare of others. For these effects market prices don't exist, because they are not mediated through the market. A well-known example is environmental effects. Economists have developed special methods to deal with these types of effects. These methods are based on behaviour of economic agents in markets that are in some way related to the environmental good (revealed preference), or on direct information by use of questionnaires to elicit preferences (stated preferences). For instance, the price of noise nuisance can be evaluated by looking at differences in house prices in locations with and without noise nuisance. This is the so-called Hedonic method. An overview of different methods to evaluate environmental effects can be found in Freeman (1993), Taylor (2001) and Bateman et al. (2002). Lindberg (2003) gives an overview of the recent progress in the measurement of external costs in Europe. Despite the enormous progress achieved, the application of these methods doesn't always lead to unambiguous results. In some cases, the method itself is under discussion among theorists but it is often possible to obtain estimation margins for many of these effects.

Unfortunately, for some external effects, it is almost impossible to express them properly in monetary terms. For instance, what is the value of a change in a unique landscape, or the so-called existence value of nature (for instance, the preservation of wildlife)? Contingent valuation methods, often used to evaluate these issues, are open to question on good reasons (Sen, 2000). When answering questionnaires, individuals have great problems evaluating issues for which they have no experience in their daily life. In some cases, and for such an effect, it might be possible to take the implicit value that can be deduced from other projects or decisions performed by the state. This information strives to achieve some coherence in the decision-making process concerning these effects, but it does not give a hard valuation of the effect. It is also possible to estimate the costs of preventing the damage or restoring the original situation, or to indicate the 'break-even point' for the value of the effect beyond which the project is no longer profitable. But again, these methods don't necessarily express the real preferences of the people.

Another problem is that it is open to question whether all relevant choices can be taken on an individualistic basis, since some choices could be by their nature intrinsically collective. Therefore, it could be misleading to approach them by the individual willingness-to-pay. This could be the case for some environmental effects or the provision of some collective goods. For example, the individual willingness-to-pay to preserve a unique landscape of historical value could depend on the willingness-to-pay by others, because of the so-called 'free rider' problem. It is also possible that people don't have enough information, or cannot form a clear opinion until there has been a public debate on the issue. In this case, a decision by public organs after an informed public debate could be better than a valuation obtained through questionnaires (contingent valuation). The limits of the methodological individualism, which is at the basis of the welfare theory, become apparent.[2]

DISTRIBUTION ISSUES

Each infrastructural project has winners and losers. It is therefore important in the context of an SCBA to give an overview of distributional effects of a project for different social groups or regions. However, the SCBA analysis yields no objective criterion to evaluate these effects. This concerns questions such as: is it fair that some people benefit greatly from the project while others are disadvantaged by it? And if it is not fair, what is to be done? Issues such as fairness and social support play an important role in society. Concerning these matters, the limitations of SCBA become apparent, because it is impossible to determine the individual valuation of redistributive impacts (the most important basis of an SCBA).

An SCBA aims at distinguishing all effects and at expressing them in monetary terms as well as possible. If this is successful, and all sums, positive for winners and negative for losers, are added up and the total result is positive on balance, then the project would lead to an improvement in welfare.[3] In SCBA terminology, this is the so-called Hicks–Kaldor criterion. This implies that the gains have to be high enough to compensate for those who are disadvantaged by the project. According to this criterion, this transfer does not actually have to be paid. It intends to give an efficiency guide. When using this criterion, two problems seem to arise: distributional issues are not taken into account and insufficient attention is paid to the differences between potential and actual compensation. Because the marginal utility of income decreases with the income, a project generating gains for a high income group and disadvantages for a low income group can cause a decrease in welfare even if the winners can compensate the losers.[4] Of course, the winners can *potentially* compensate the losers and everybody would be better off, but in practice, compensation often does not occur for several reasons, for instance, because compensation through negotiations between beneficiaries and victims could be inefficient and/or difficult due to the involvement of too many parties. Anyway, it is important that compensation actually takes place as much as possible.

In addition, it could be a good case for the realization of a project even if the benefits, measured by the willingness-to-pay, are lower than the costs. This may be so if decision-makers assign a crucial value to a desirable distributional effect, for instance, higher consumption of a merit good by a vulnerable social group or a backward region. In this case, the consumption of the merit good is supposed to have a positive external effect beyond the specific group that is benefiting from it, or to respond to some ethical consideration. To evaluate distributional effects properly in an SCBA, it may be necessary to have a welfare function combining the utilities of all individuals of society at one's disposal. This requires information that is not available. Because such a welfare function depends on the weight attached to the different individual utilities, and these weights depend on ethical and political preferences, there are no welfare functions free of ethical or political considerations.[5] Moreover, there may be interdependence between the utilities of different individuals because things like compassion and envy play an important role on how individuals experience welfare. In practice, explicit evaluation of distributional effects is unusual, if only because politicians want to determine how different effects should be evaluated. Of course, for this purpose it is important that the distributional effects, for instance for income groups and regions, are clearly visualized anyway.

SCBA AND DECISION-MAKING

Let us now analyse what the role of SCBA should be in the decision-making process. We illustrate this with a description of the role of SCBA in this process in the Netherlands. Finally, we briefly address the place of multi-criteria analysis as evaluation technique proposed by some authors.

An SCBA, if properly carried out, can provide a balanced analysis of a project, but an SCBA does not replace the decision-making process, which is a political process. In this process, we should distinguish the analysis stage from the decision stage. In the analysis stage, the analyst intends to make an objective valuation of all the relevant aspects of the project.[6] Sometimes the valuation is complete, sometimes some aspects cannot be properly evaluated or can only be evaluated with a method open to questions. All the relevant valuations, including their possible limitations, should be presented transparently. Those aspects whose valuation depends on ethical or political preferences should be visualized as much as possible anyway. Only the decision-makers decide if the limitations are important or not and what value has to be assigned to the aspects that couldn't be assessed, or were not assessed unambiguously. In this way, the decision-making process is concentrated on the really important alternatives of the decision, centred around the real trade-offs.

In addition, as we have already mentioned, it is possible that the decision-makers decide to perform a project on reasonable grounds even if the losses are larger than the gains. This doesn't mean that an SCBA is less relevant for decision-making. In a democratic process decisions are taken by specially elected public organs or by organizing a referendum after a public debate in the case of an important project. As Sen (1999) states, 'public policy has a role not only in attempting to implement the priorities that emerge from social values and affirmations, but also in facilitating and guaranteeing fuller public discussion'. It makes a great deal of difference on which information this debate has been based. It is important that the public debate and the decision emerging from this debate are anchored on a broad informational base. An objective analysis on the expected benefits and losses, as much as possible expressed in monetary terms, and an identification of the winners and the losers are essential parts of this 'broad informational base'.

A second opinion on the analysis could also be important, at least for large projects. An advisory board of specialists should judge and comment on the scientific quality of the analysis before it goes to the next stage, that of the political decision.[7] As mentioned earlier, the decision-makers will often not only consider the balance sheet of the SCBA analysis but also other relevant aspects like distributional effects, ethical considerations, political support, and so on. To make this process well-ordered, they could use techniques of multi-criteria analysis, if the number of alternatives and criteria is large. However, if the SCBA is performed properly, the discussion at the decision-making stage can be limited to the real trade-offs. In that case, a lot of subjective valuations can be prevented. Decision-makers could take decisions that seem to contradict the results of the SCBA, but this is their responsibility, not that of the analysts. In a democracy, the elected political organs have to give account of their choices to the electorate, not the analysts. Eventually, the elected organs have to explain why they take their decisions, and not the analysts. If their decision seems contradictory to the results of the SCBA, they have to produce very convincing arguments.

We can illustrate these considerations with the development of the role of SCBAs in the Netherlands. The use of social cost–benefit analysis has been institutionalized in the Netherlands since 1999. Many Dutch economic research institutes have worked on the 'Research programme on the economic effects of infrastructure' (OEI) in 1998 and 1999. This programme has been initiated by the Ministries of Transport and Economic Affairs after discussions on the benefits of various major transport infrastructural projects. This large-scale research programme has produced about ten reports that have been integrated into a guide for cost–benefit analysis published in 2000 (Ministry of Transport, Public Works and Water Management, Ministry of Economic Affairs, 2000). These guidelines present directives for the realization of CBAs. According to a government decision, the use of these guidelines is obligatory for large infrastructural projects. The use of the guidelines was evaluated in 2002.

The conclusions of this evaluation were translated in an agenda. This agenda aimed at filling up some gaps and at stimulating further developments in areas such as the assessment of the macro-economic risk, the quantification of indirect effects of projects on welfare, guidelines for the assessment of environmental effects, the valuation of time and reliability in passenger transport and transport of goods, clarification of the role of SCBA in the decision-making process and the role and organization of an advisory board. This research has resulted in a set of documents to complement earlier mentioned guidelines.

MULTI-CRITERIA ANALYSIS

Some authors argue that the effects of transport policy should be measured by multiple criteria, which should take into account the interests of the different stakeholders of the policy in question. Multi-criteria analysis is a technique in which decision-makers attach weights to a number of criteria to evaluate policy alternatives. By definition, it is a subjective valuation, depending on the subjective preferences of decision-makers. These subjective preferences do not necessarily reflect the preferences of the people as they are expressed when making choices under the restriction of limited resources. There is nothing censurable in this qualification, because it is inevitable that decision-makers take decisions partly on subjective grounds. However, the dependence on subjective preferences by decision-makers means that multi-criteria analysis should not be part of the analysis stage of a project. This analysis should be kept free of value judgements and subjective preferences of analysts or decision-makers as much as possible. Multi-criteria analysis should certainly not be applied if the valuations of effects can be reasonably performed by the pool of methods and techniques developed for SCBA.

Quinet (2000) mentions that the application of multi-criteria analysis to evaluate projects in France in the late 1980s and the beginning of the 1990s 'led to a waste of public funds and to clearly irrational decisions, which could only be explained by a very high weight on subjective items'.

Multi-criteria analysis could well play a role in the decision stage as a tool for the decision-makers to systematize the weights of their preferences and value judgements, concerning the trade-offs which are beyond the scope of the SCBA.

CONCLUDING REMARKS

An SCBA yields a very relevant analysis and provides broad information for the decision-making process in a systematic way. The analysis principally relies on the preferences of individuals as expressed in the market system. This is a very robust starting point for the valuation of project effects. The valuation of every project effect in monetary terms is not a simple matter. However, SCBAs draw on a pool of experience of methods and actual values to complete their analysis. By indirect methods as 'revealed preferences' or using questionnaires as in 'stated preferences' methods, it is often possible to obtain reasonable estimation margins for the value of most effects. However, some environmental effects cannot be properly evaluated in monetary terms. Some choices could be by their nature intrinsically collective, so that valuation on the basis of individual preference makes no sense.

SCBAs can yield insight into the distributional effects of a project for different social groups but cannot evaluate these effects 'objectively'. In the decision-making process of infrastructural projects, it is desirable to distinguish the analysis stage from the decision stage. The first stage intends to provide all the relevant information for decision-making. The best way to do this is to perform an SCBA that is as complete and objective as possible, free of value judgements and subjective preferences of analysts or decision-makers. Analysts don't take decisions. These are within the competence of decision-makers designated through our democratic political process. Because SCBAs are sometimes not complete and also other considerations could be relevant, the final decision will often involve aspects other than the SCBA.

Multi-criteria analysis could be a technique in addition to SCBA to help decision-makers in their task, but because it is based by definition on subjective valuation and because it is not free of value judgements, it should not be part of the analysis stage. Analysts must try to put their own preferences aside.

NOTES

1. In the first case, the opportunity cost is the price of the activity that has been crowded out by the new activity and this value in equilibrium equals the value of the monopoly's

product. In the second case, the opportunity costs are given by the marginal costs of the monopoly.

2. The essence of the methodological individualism is the view that human social behaviour can be explained as a function of only individualistic, non-social motivations of the member's group. Arrow (1994) argues that this is sometimes too narrow a point of view. He states: 'More generally, individual behavior is always mediated by social relations. These are as much part of the reality as is individual behavior'.
3. Posner (2000) stresses that in this case the most appropriated term is wealth maximization rather than utility or welfare maximization.
4. For a theoretical critique of the Hicks–Kaldor criterion, see Layard and Walters (1994).
5. Konow (2003) shows how complex the perception of justice by individuals is. Most individuals have an idea of justice based on a combination of three principles: equity/merit, efficiency and need. The weights of these principles depend on individual preferences for each individual and on the context.
6. With 'objective valuation', we refer to a valuation based on the preferences of the people expressed in their specific behaviour under the restriction of limited resources.
7. In the Netherlands, this procedure has been adopted for large infrastructural projects, such as the expansion of the port of Rotterdam, Schiphol Airport or the deepening of the waterway of the Scheldt.

REFERENCES

Anderson, L.G. and R.F. Settle (1979), *Benefit–Cost Analysis: A Practical Guide*, Lexington, Toronto: Lexington Books.

Arrow, K. (1994), 'Methodological individualism and social knowledge', *American Economic Review*, **84**(2), Papers and Proceedings of the 106th annual meeting of the American Economic Association.

Bateman, I.J., R.T. Carson, B. Day, M. Haneman, N. Hanley, T. Hett, M. Jones-Lee, G. Loomis, S. Mourato, E. Ozdemiroglu, D.W. Pearce, R. Sugden and J. Swanson (2002), *Economic Valuation with Stated Preferences Techniques: a Manual*, Cheltenham, UK and Northampton, MA, USA: Edward Elgar.

Brent, R. (1996), *Applied Cost–Benefit Analysis*, Cheltenham, UK and Brookfield, USA: Edward Elgar.

Dixit, A. and A. Williamson (1989), 'Risk-adjusted rates of return for project appraisal', *Working Papers, Agriculture and Rural Development*, The World Bank.

Drèze, J. and N. Stern (1994), 'Shadow prices and markets: policy reform, shadow prices and market prices', in R. Layard and S. Glaister (eds), *Cost–Benefit Analysis*, Cambridge: Cambridge Univeristy Press, pp. 59–99.

Freeman, A.M. (1993), *The Measurement of Environmental and Resource Values: Theory and Methods*, Washington DC: Resources for the Future.

Konow, J. (2003), 'Which is the fairest one of all? A positive analysis of justice theories', *Journal of Economic Literature*, **XLI**, 1188–239.

Layard, R. and A.A. Walters (1994), 'Income distribution: allowing for income distribution', in R. Layard and S. Glaister (eds), *Cost–Benefit Analysis*, Cambridge: Cambridge University Press, pp. 179–98.

Lindberg, G. (2003), 'Recent progress in the measurement of external costs and implications for transport pricing reforms', *European Journal of Transport and Infrastructure Research*, **4**, 387–400.

Ministry of Transport, Public Works and Water Management, Ministry of Economic Affairs (2000), *Evaluation of Infrastructural Projects: Guide for*

Cost–Benefit Analysis, AVV Transport Research Centre, Rotterdam, the Netherlands.
Posner, R.A. (2000), 'Cost–benefit analysis: definition, justification, and comment on conference papers', *Journal of Legal Studies*, **XXIX**, 1153–177.
Quinet, E. (2000), 'Evaluation methodologies of transportation projects in France', *Transport Policy*, **7**, 27–34.
Sen, A. (1999), *Development as Freedom*, Oxford: Oxford University Press.
Sen, A. (2000), 'The discipline of cost–benefit analysis', *Journal of Legal Studies*, **XXIX**, 931–52.
Taylor, L. (2001), 'The hedonic method', in P. Champ, K. Boyle and T. Brown (eds), *A Primer on Nonmarket Valuation*, Dordrecht: Kluwer Academic Publishers, pp. 331–94.

2. The boundaries of welfare economics: transport appraisal in the UK

Roger Vickerman

1. BACKGROUND AND INTRODUCTION

The methodology for transport appraisal in the UK has gone through a significant period of change in recent years. In this chapter we look at the extent to which the approach which has been used is based on the theoretical principles of welfare economics and how useful these principles can be in providing a justification for practical transport appraisal methods.

For a long period road projects have been appraised by the use of a formal computerized cost–benefit analysis model known as COBA (DMRB, 2002). We shall look at the elements of COBA in more detail in section 6 below, but in essence it is a conventional CBA analysis which deals only with those elements which can be both quantified and monetized (principally time and accident cost savings) in order to provide a consistent comparative treatment of all road projects. The key elements of this are that it does not deal with the environmental, social or wider economic impacts of a project and is confined to use in road projects.

Rail projects have largely been required to meet stricter financial viability criteria. One argument advanced to support this is that in rail the end user has to pay at the point of use and hence can be made to reveal his or her preferences directly. However, it is also the case that rail may be able to generate wider benefits which are not adequately accounted for in a situation where there is imperfect competition in the rail-using markets, such that the true value of benefits is not fully stated by the price paid.

Changes to the approaches adopted in appraising transport projects have been driven by three main forces. In the case of roads, the national road network is now largely complete, leading to an end to the general approach of 'predict and provide' which had dominated policy at least to the end of the 1980s. This meant that new projects were more about infilling, or the provision of bypasses to small towns, where time savings would be generally smaller, but concern over the environmental and social consequences would often be greater. Secondly, the privatization of the national rail network required a more robust approach to the way that government dealt with the need to provide financial support to privatized operators, including the track authority, to cover the difference between costs and revenues. Thirdly, and most significantly, the Labour Government, elected in 1997, was committed to the development of an integrated transport system which required the evaluation of alternative approaches to transport problems rather than the traditional separation of all decisions by mode. This necessitated a consistent approach to appraisal for each mode as well as a planning system which allowed for a multi-modal approach to the solution of a perceived transport problem.

Here we develop three main issues. First, in sections 2 to 5, we deal with the theoretical basis for CBA in transport, showing how that needs to be developed from the simplified textbook example to deal with social, environmental and wider economic effects and how alternative approaches such as Multi-Criteria Decision Analysis (MCDA), Land Use Transport Interaction (LUTI) and Computable General Equilibrium (CGE) models have a role to play in this. Secondly, in section 6, we look in more detail at practical implementation of this in the UK through the development of COBA into the New Approach to Appraisal (NATA). Finally, in section 7, we assess the scope for a genuinely integrated approach to transport appraisal, including the capture of wider economic benefits.

2. THE STANDARD COST–BENEFIT CASE[1]

It is worth recalling the standard textbook cost–benefit case as a reference point for the start of this discussion. Essentially this requires us to assess the change in consumer surplus resulting from a change in supply conditions. However, as we shall show, it is also necessary to allow for other changes such as general economic growth or the changing spatial distribution of economic activity, given the time period over which transport projects have to be evaluated due to both long gestation periods and long irreversible (at least costlessly) lifespans.

In the most basic case (Figure 2.1), given known demand conditions (D_0) and the cost conditions represented by the supply curve S_0, the consumer surplus is shown as the light shaded area. The supply curve incorporates all the known generalized costs of making a trip. In particular, it includes any direct monetary outlays and estimated values of time and accident costs. The upward slope of S_0 refers to the fact that as traffic flow increases on a section of road with given capacity, all of these costs will increase.[2]

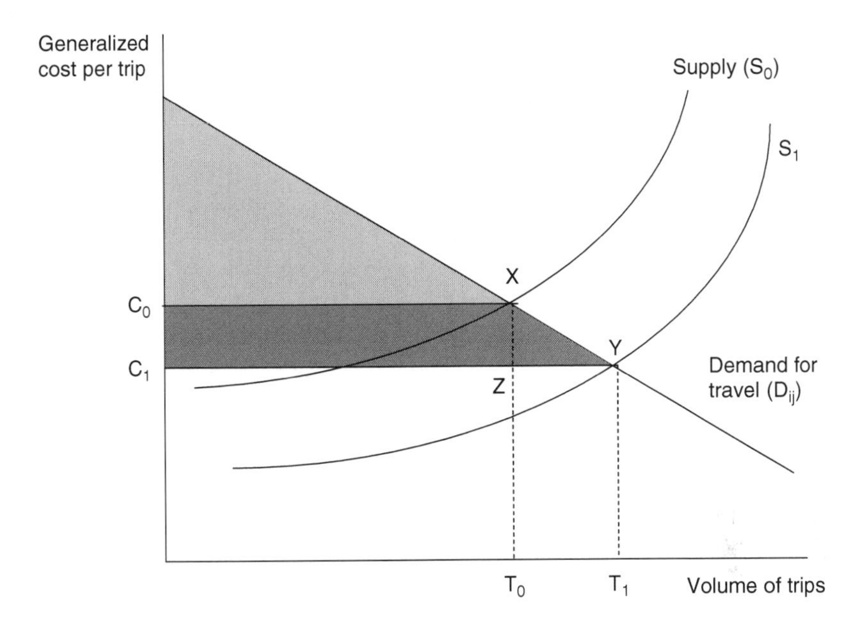

Figure 2.1 The basic cost–benefit model

If generalized costs fall from C_0 to C_1, the volume of trips increases from T_0 to T_1 and the increase in consumer surplus, indicating user benefit, is the darker shaded area C_0XYC_1.

The key to successful evaluation is to identify the base case, that without the proposed intervention, and the supply conditions resulting from the intervention. The same principle applies to the evaluation of measures such as traffic restraint which are designed to increase the direct costs to users, where the supply curve for the with-scheme case will lie above the base case curve, and to those which increase road capacity or decrease costs, where the new supply curve will lie below the base case curve. The task is to evaluate the move in Figure 2.2 from the base case equilibrium point A to the new equilibrium point B or B′.

Over time, however, exogenous factors – changes in economic growth and income, changes in the price of car ownership and travel, and changes in the numbers and disposition of people, households, jobs and other activities – will shift the demand curve. The problem is that we need to forecast that shift in the demand curve and to find the new equilibrium point (Figure 2.3) C which becomes the effective base case from which changes have to be evaluated. To appraise an intervention which will only take effect in the future, the task is to find the new equilibrium point D, where the new demand curve intersects the new supply curve (Figure 2.4). Transport

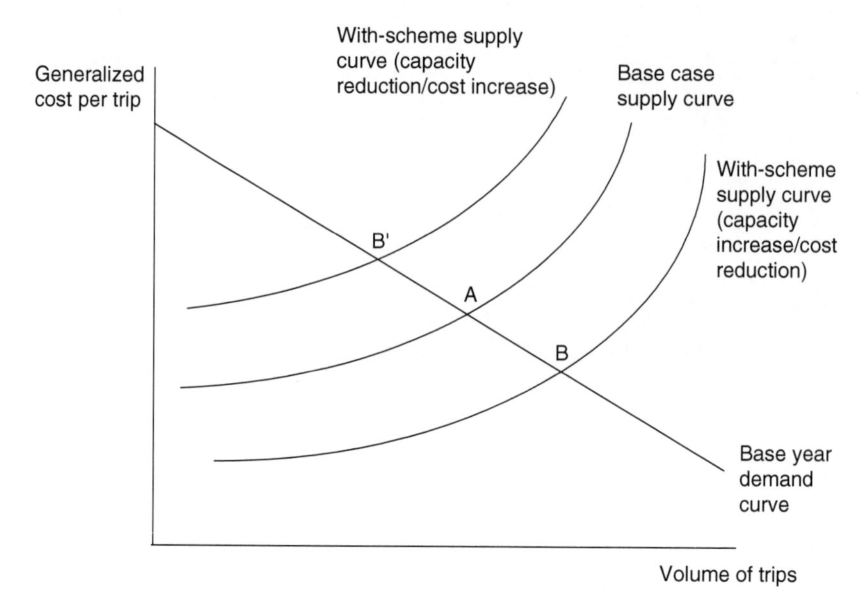

Figure 2.2 Base and with-scheme supply curves

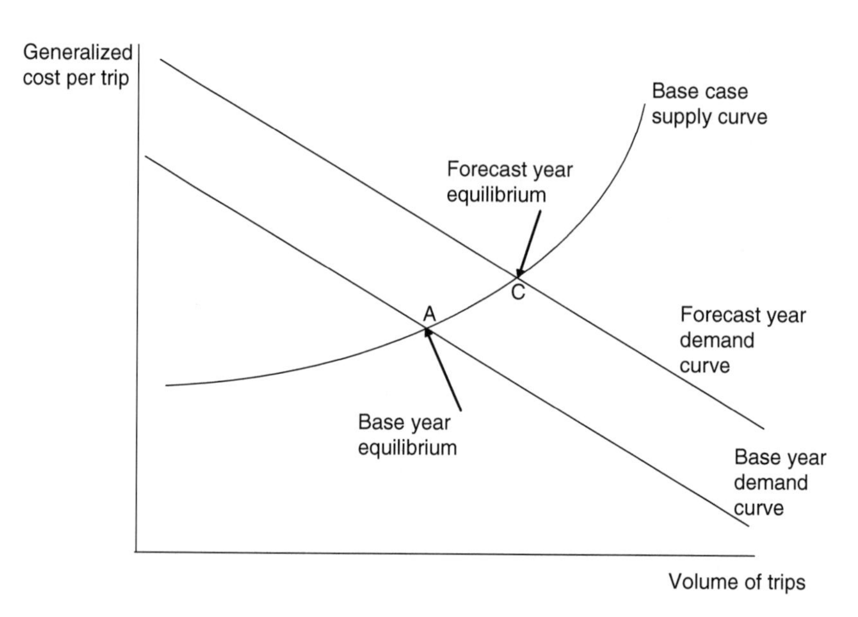

Figure 2.3 Forecast year equilibrium

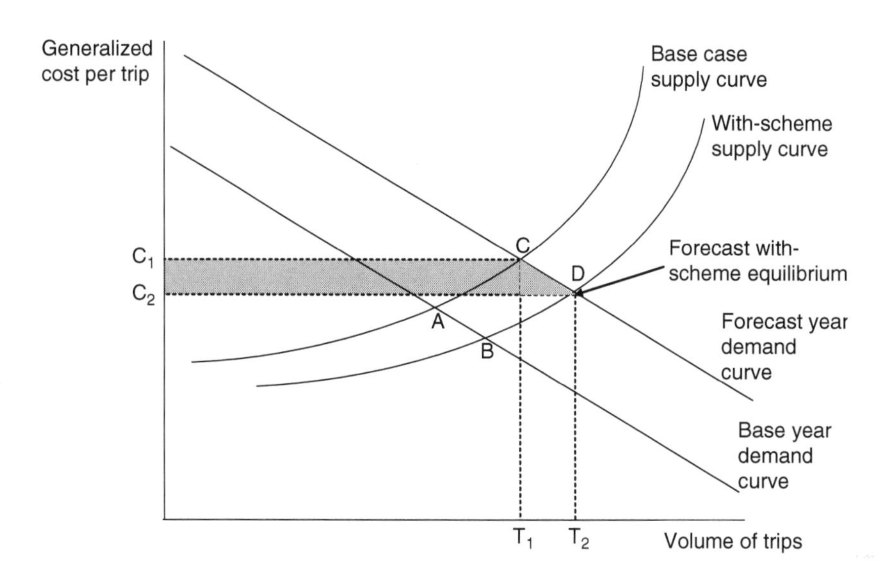

Figure 2.4 Benefits allowing for forecast demand and with-scheme supply

models thus need to forecast travel demands and costs for two situations: a base case or do-minimum case and a with-scheme case or do-something case. The transport benefits are given by the shaded area.

A conceptually correct transport CBA is thus very demanding: it requires a travel demand curve derived to incorporate the reorganization and output effects as travel costs change. This implies that it requires knowledge of the relevant conditions in all the markets likely to be affected by a transport scheme in order that the required demand curve can be correctly estimated and equilibrated with transport supply. In practice, simplifying assumptions are made, of which the most significant are that there is perfect competition in all transport-using markets, and that trip matrices are fixed. The first of these assumptions implies that in all transport-using markets, price equals marginal social cost, such that the demand curve completely measures all of the benefits associated with the use of transport. Thus any change in the perceived price of transport will be completely and directly reflected in decisions concerning the activities using transport. We return below to what happens if this does not hold. The second assumption of fixed trip matrices means that we assume that changes in transport costs only reassign traffic between links of a network, they do not change the total amount of trip-making in the network, its origins or destinations. This would imply that lower transport costs do not induce additional trip-making or cause the reallocation of trips between different destinations

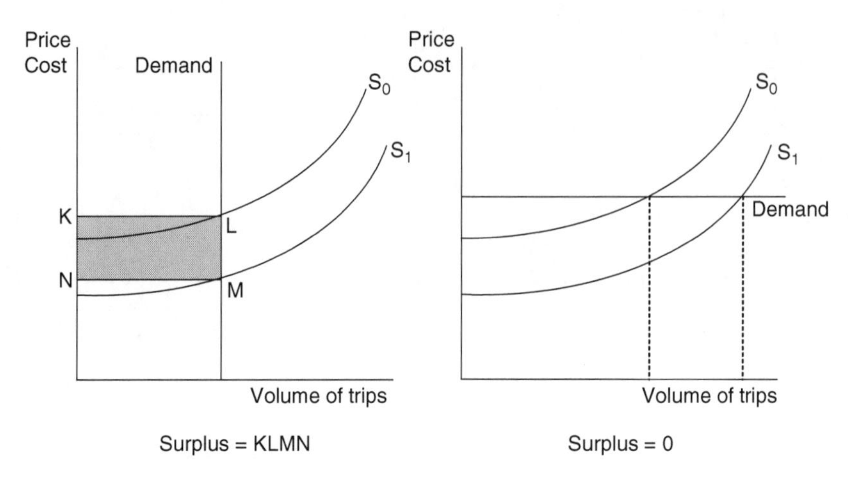

Figure 2.5 Benefits with fixed and variable trip matrices

(SACTRA, 1994). The implications of this are shown for the two extreme cases of the perfectly fixed and perfectly variable (infinitely elastic) cases in Figure 2.5. Note that in the case where demand is perfectly elastic all the additional benefits disappear and in certain cases (see Venables, 1999) it is possible to show that consumer surplus can be reduced to a level below that obtaining in the do-nothing situation.

In order to make the simple CBA come close to one which represents a more real world situation a number of changes would have to be made. Some of these are relatively straightforward, at least conceptually. It is relatively straightforward to move from modelling the traffic impacts as a single link to one of the whole network. This would also allow for a framework in which fixed trip matrices were replaced by variable trip matrices. These measures are simply ones of defining the traffic forecasting model appropriately rather than changing the principles of evaluating benefits. A further issue is that of whether the values which are included in a CBA should be based on economic resource values (factor costs), market price values or some synthetic generalized cost (Sugden, 1999).

The impact of transport changes on land use and location and how these should be included in a CBA is a major issue. Some of this we shall return to in more detail in the following section, but the issue here is essentially the one determining how far attempts to include detailed information on land use change are simply double-counting in a situation in which variable trip matrices have been allowed for, since these presumably reflect land use changes. As long as transport-using sectors are assumed to be in perfect competition, changes in land use will be completely picked up in the trip-making forecasts. This is a similar argument to that which shows that changes in land values should not be regarded as an additional benefit of transport changes since these will either simply reflect changing accessibility which determines the changed trip-making patterns or are simply a redistribution from one factor (or one group of individuals) to another. However, this is still assuming that transport-using activities are perfectly competitive; the implications of changing this assumption are much more profound as we shall explore in the following section.

3. TRANSPORT BENEFITS AND FINAL ECONOMIC BENEFITS

In this section we shall explore in more detail the linkages between the transport sector and the transport-using sector which give rise to the possibility of wider economic benefits (or costs). There are four basic parameters which affect this, but the extent to which they have an effect depends critically on the nature of competition in the transport-using markets.

The four basic parameters are: the responsiveness to a fall (or rise) in transport costs; the substitutability of transport and non-transport inputs; the price elasticity of demand for the final output of the transport-using sector; and the proportion of transport costs in total costs. Responsiveness to changing transport costs depends to a large extent on the other three factors, but we have to recognize the role which perception and a degree of path dependency play in this mechanism. Following long periods of declining real costs of transport it is not clear that there is any symmetry in the response to rises in these real costs (Goodwin, 1992; Hanly et al., 2002). The induced location effects of the long-run cost reduction have built in a degree of inertia to the system which may make it difficult to get significant shifts in transport behaviour in the short run. Given the transaction costs of adjustment, quite significant shifts in transport costs may be necessary to effect any major change in actual transport demand.

The substitutability of transport and non-transport inputs has typically been ignored in a model which has assumed that transport is simply the derived demand for some predetermined level of activity at a given location. Once transport is allowed to be substituted for the non-transport inputs, this recognizes the feasibility of the reorganization of all aspects of production (or consumption) to optimize with respect to changes in real transport costs. One of the most significant changes is the substitutability between land and transport as transport has become cheaper. This is seen, for example, in the advent of just-in-time production which allows for the reduction in expensive inventories using the increasing reliability of transport to deliver inputs when needed, or in the development of out-of-town shopping centres where cheaper land can be used, relying on the growth of personal transport to bring customers.

On the other hand, to the extent that transport remains a derived demand, and to the extent that changes in transport costs affect the final price of finished goods, whether changes in transport costs have any impact will depend on the price elasticity of demand for the finished product or activity. This interacts with the relative importance of transport costs in total costs or in total value added. For activities where transport costs are significant, final price elasticities may be quite small, for example the cases of cement or aggregates given the limited availability of substitutes. Where final price elasticities are higher, transport costs typically contribute a much smaller share to either total costs or value added. This may not, however, mean that changes in transport costs are unimportant as despite the small contribution to value added, transport costs may be seen as one of the potentially most variable costs and hence a significant contributor to variations in profitability.

This leads us to the consideration of how the degree of competition in transport-using markets determines the likely extent of any reorganization and output effects from any change in transport costs. Under perfect competition competitive pressures will force firms to respond fully to changes in transport costs: if costs rise for all firms, prices will need to rise to cover the increase; if costs rise for just one firm then it will be unable to compete and will be forced to leave the industry. Conversely, if costs fall, firms will make an abnormal profit which will encourage new entrants (Fujita et al., 1999; Brakman et al., 2001; Quinet and Vickerman, 2004). Under imperfect competition, how firms respond will depend more on their strategic decisions. Rises (or falls) in costs could be passed on or absorbed according to the attitude firms take towards profitability or market share.

If a reduction in transport costs enables firms to increase their market share then scale economies and agglomeration economies could produce wider economic benefits which are greater than those measured just by the direct reduction in costs. How large these additional benefits may be has been a matter of some speculation. This will depend on the size of the mark-up, the importance of transport costs in total costs and the elasticity of demand for the product (SACTRA, 1999; Venables and Gasiorek, 1999; Newbery, 1999). Estimates of these effects vary, but are dependent more on informed assumptions than detailed estimates: a typical range is of the order of 10 per cent to 40 per cent additional benefit to a local economy. However, it has also to be recognized that such gains are not guaranteed and in certain circumstances, for example where prices are less than marginal costs due to subsidies, such wider benefits can be negatives. In other words the direct transport benefits may both overestimate as well as underestimate final benefits.

This discussion suggests that transport benefits may not be the most reliable estimate of the final economic benefits resulting from any change. How good the estimate is will depend on the specific circumstances of the change to be appraised; this will include the characteristics of the area where the change is implemented, the nature of the local economy in terms of its sectoral and market structure and the ability of transport users to change in response to the transport change.

Most CBA analyses are both limited in scope and partial in nature. We need to identify clearly what factors are included, and what not, to be able to interpret the outcome and consider how far any changes involve a more general equilibrium. The development of a more appropriate and full CBA can be seen as a set of step-changes which we shall consider in more detail in the following section. However, it has to be decided whether it is possible (or desirable) to try and incorporate all these changes in a single decision variable. A range of approaches may provide a richer set of information which would result in better decisions.

4. A TYPOLOGY OF CBA

The above discussion suggests that a number of stages can be identified in developing CBA from the simple first step which has formed the basis for much previous appraisal, through successive steps which incorporate the various modifications discussed above.

There are essentially three steps (SACTRA, 1999):

- The pure transport CBA (CBA*):
  - assumes perfect competition in transport-using sectors
  - assumes transport costs and benefits are acceptable approximations of final costs and benefits
- The best practice CBA (CBA**):
  - takes account of all indirect and direct responses by economic agents under conditions of perfect competition in the economy as a whole
  - includes all dimensions of travel choice, repercussions on land use and economic activity, all externalities including environmental impacts
- The theoretically optimal CBA (CBA***):
  - all direct and indirect responses by economic agents taken into account

- assumption of perfect competition relaxed (price not assumed equal to marginal social cost)
- imperfections or failures in both goods and factor markets: imperfect competition in product markets, wages exceeding the opportunity cost of labour, taxation effects, external costs and benefits including all environmental and social impacts.

Most practical applications of CBA, such as the COBA model in the UK and its urban equivalent URECA, are, when applied correctly, only equivalent to the pure transport CBA*. If allowance is made for induced traffic it is possible that it can come close to the best practice CBA**. However, in both of these cases application in the UK has not made full economic allowance for environmental and similar external effects of transport projects and so tends to remain largely a transport CBA* with some allowance for directly related land use and transport demand effects. Moving to the theoretically optimal CBA*** requires a much fuller analysis of the linkages discussed in the previous section and hence some more detailed modelling outside the strict CBA framework; it is to this possibility which we now turn.

5. TRANSPORT BENEFITS AND FINAL ECONOMIC BENEFITS: NEW APPROACHES

Even the theoretically optimal CBA*** defined above depends on the ability to identify the likely impacts outside the transport sector and the feedback which these will have for travel demand and transport. Hence implementation of an ideal appraisal model depends critically on the modelling which lies behind it.

The adoption of Multi-Criteria Decision Analysis (MCDA) has been a partial solution which allows the incorporation of a wider set of impacts. Although it provides a useful and sophisticated decision model it has only a limited role in assessing the wider economic impacts. MCDA models have been useful in allowing for the inclusion of effects which can be measured physically fairly precisely, but on which there is greater uncertainty of the monetary value.[3] The advantage of MCDA is that it allows the use of explicit weights to be put on a range of possible impacts and thus achieve a greater degree of transparency. It allows for consistency with economic impact measures because the methods of determining weights imply the use of a form of utility function (Keeney and Raiffa, 1976; Bogetoft and Pruzan, 1991). It shows clearly whether different overall assessments depend on differences in outcomes or differences in preferences. However,

MCDA depends on being able to assess the impacts unambiguously. In the case of wider economic impacts it will depend, as we have seen, on the possible range of responses of different economic actors and, whilst MCDA can generate a series of 'what-if' outcomes, it cannot by itself evaluate these in such a way as to secure robust planning of the outcomes. In this way it is as limited as CBA.

Modelling of the wider impacts requires a more comprehensive approach such as can be provided by either advanced Land Use Transport Interaction (LUTI) models or Computable General Equilibrium (CGE) models. LUTI models have been used by urban planners in particular for some time as extended travel demand models which allow for the interaction of transport and land use (Simmonds, 1999). In this way they are close to the best practice CBA**. More recently LUTI models have been extended to deal with regional and inter-regional impacts of transport development (Wegener and Bökemann, 1998; Bröcker et al., 2004). These models vary in the precise way they operate but essentially comprise a series of linked detailed models covering travel/transport, production and GDP, labour markets and population and land use. At the heart of the model is the transport sector which, through changes in accessibility which change the cost of transport, impacts on both production and the labour market. The production sector is typically modelled through a set of input–output relationships which define the need for transport to move goods into and out of a defined spatial area. This includes the need for labour inputs which interact with the available labour force (and hence local population) to determine commuting and migration patterns. Land use acts as a constraint on the development of the economy since production and the resident labour force have minimum requirements for land.

The main problem with LUTI models arises from the assumptions implicit in each of these constituent models. Hence input–output models are often static in nature, dependent on existing patterns of behaviour, and are solved by ensuring that equilibrium is reached in each relevant market. Similarly the links between population, labour force and labour demand also depend on assuming that existing patterns of behaviour do not change, when the evidence from major changes in the transport network is that behaviour can actually change quite significantly. Furthermore, the models make assumptions about the land use requirements which do not allow for changing capital and labour intensities and tend to treat different sectors equally. The output of the LUTI model is typically a measure of GDP change for each spatial area which raises the question of the validity of GDP as a measure of the consumer welfare which a typical CBA seeks to estimate. LUTI models assume perfectly competitive markets in which the market outcome is a valid measure of the welfare change.

CGE models, by their nature, also assume equilibrium and are based on the fundamental input–output relationships in the economy, but in this case they allow for more interaction between constituent markets in order to achieve a general equilibrium of all sectors through a process of numerical iteration. The key difference is that CGE models have at their core the possibility of assuming that consumers display preferences over differentiated goods which are produced by imperfectly competitive firms (Bröcker, 2001; 2004; Bröcker et al., 2004). Because of this use of a utility function, CGE models can make a direct estimate of the welfare effects resulting from a change.[4] But CGE models do still have major drawbacks: assumptions about equilibrium, the need for large data inputs from existing sources and the 'black box' nature of large models all limit their usefulness and ease of application. Thus far CGE models have tended to be used for cases where there are thought to be significant non-transport impacts; their use as part of the regular appraisal of minor transport projects would be difficult to justify (SACTRA, 1999).

6. UK ROAD APPRAISAL: COBA TO NATA

In this section we turn from the abstract discussion of principles to look at the way in which practical appraisal methods for road projects have developed in the UK from the simple use of the COBA (COst–Benefit Analysis) model to the rather wider New Approach to Appraisal (NATA) approach and the Appraisal Summary Table (AST) which lies at its core.

Although road appraisal has traditionally seen the COBA model as its core component, COBA is in fact only one element in a 28-step decision procedure which runs from identifying problems, through determining and evaluating alternative solutions to public inquiries and final decisions. COBA involves a computer-based assessment which undertakes a rigorous evaluation of those elements which can be unambiguously defined and monetized. It provides a common treatment to evaluate and rank all projects and is accepted as a recognized element in official public inquiries. COBA comprises a rigorous traffic model which can be defined with either fixed or variable trip matrices. The main elements included are the value of time savings and the benefits from reductions in accidents. Not directly included are any environmental costs or benefits from a project or any wider economic impact. All costs and benefits are discounted at a standard rate (currently 3.5 per cent) over a 30-year period and the resulting benefit–cost ratio (BCR) is used to rank projects (HM Treasury, 2003).

Although COBA has a clear pedigree based solidly in welfare economics, it has been increasingly seen as rather too limited for the changing nature of the decisions required. In a 'predict and provide' world, what was needed was a robust way of ranking alternatives in terms of the main contribution they would make to the primary objectives of making transport more efficient (time savings) and safer (accident reduction benefits). In the newer world of increased environmental concern and the need to compare alternative modal solutions to perceived problems in a more budget constrained situation, a rather broader approach was needed and one which could be applied equally to new investment in any mode, traffic restraint or alternative methods of supply.

The New Approach to Appraisal (NATA) set out to provide the basis for this, initially with respect to road appraisal, with the stated objective to 'develop a clear and open framework to appraise and inform the prioritization of trunk road investment proposals'. NATA is based on five criteria: environmental impact, safety, economy, accessibility and integration as detailed in Table 2.1 (see DETR, 1998a; 1998b; Prince, 1999; Glaister, 1999; Vickerman, 2000).

Table 2.1 NATA criteria

Criteria	Nature of measure	Indicators
Environmental impact	Physical	Noise Local air quality Landscape Biodiversity Heritage Water
Safety	Money value	Accident reduction (value of statistical life saved)
Economy	Money value	Vehicle operating costs Scheme costs
	Physical and money value	Journey time reduction Reliability
	Qualitative	Regeneration impacts
Accessibility	Qualitative	Access to public transport Community severance Impact on pedestrians and others
Integration	Qualitative	Contribution to integrated transport
COBA score	Money value	BCR

Source: DETR (1998c)

The key point to note in Table 2.1 is that there is no attempt to place a monetary value on environmental impacts. The traditional sources of monetary evaluation, safety and time reduction are still included, although the latter now has an attempt to include reliability on which the evaluation evidence is less robust. The new areas included, economic regeneration, accessibility and integration, are all handled by qualitative evidence. Significantly here there is no attempt to quantify or evaluate the impact on economic regeneration, which is a key objective in the wider economic impacts; it is simply measured in terms of an assessment of the degree of regeneration impact that a project will produce. Similarly, despite the availability of sophisticated measures of accessibility, the definition used here is about access to alternative modes of transport measured qualitatively. Integration is also assessed in terms of the contribution of a measure to the overall policy of integrated transport, but again assessed purely qualitatively. The BCR produced by COBA from the money values in the economic impacts section is also included.

From the assessment of the NATA criteria the decision-maker is presented with an Appraisal Summary Table (AST). The AST brings together all the relevant information, but there is no attempt to impose any predetermined weighting on the various elements as in a formal MCDA approach. For an example see Table 2.2. This scheme was accepted despite a relatively low, although positive, NPV under COBA of £14m giving a BCR of 1.5 and some negative environmental effects. The decisive factors here were probably the positive scores for improved reliability and the contribution to regeneration. Of course, increasing experience with the use of the AST means that, at least for a given decision-making body, its decisions will begin to reveal an implicit set of weights on the various criteria.

7. BEYOND NATA

The problem with COBA was always that it separated decisions on road investment from other public investment decisions, including in other modes of transport. The use of a consistent CBA framework did imply that NPVs or BCRs of road projects could be compared with investment decisions in other areas for which public investment competed in accordance with procedures laid out in the Treasury's Green Book (HM Treasury, 2003). However, COBA excluded many of the increasingly important aspects of a road investment given that the efficient supply of road capacity is not tested in the market in terms of directly priced services. Most other transport services could be appraised in terms of a more direct financial test using revenues as a more comprehensive measure of project value. It can

Table 2.2 Example Appraisal Summary Table

Scheme	A2 Bean-Cobham Phase 1: 1996 Scheme – 6km D4 on-line widening. Cost £44m	
Criterion	Indicator	Assessment
Environmental impact	Noise	0 properties win or lose
	Local air quality	+12 PM10 +27 NO_2
	Landscape	Slight negative
	Biodiversity	Slight negative
	Heritage	Neutral
	Water	Moderate negative
Safety	Accident reduction (value of statistical life saved)	PVB £2.0m
Economy	Journey times and vehicle operating costs	PVB £41m
	Scheme costs	PVC £29m
	Reliability	Moderate/High rel. to PVC
	Regeneration impacts	Yes
Accessibility	Access to public transport	Neutral
	Community severance	Neutral
	Impact on pedestrians and others	Neutral
Integration	Contribution to integrated transport	Positive
COBA score	BCR	1.5

Source: DETR (1998c)

still be argued that in the case of imperfectly competitive markets for both transport and transport-using activities, user revenues will not be a perfect measure of user values, and in particular may misestimate wider economic benefits and costs, and above all environmental impacts will not be adequately accounted for. There is a strong case therefore for extending the developing NATA framework to all modes of transport, as was done through a series of multi-modal studies which aimed to consider a range of solutions to perceived transport problems, including comparing alternative modal solutions or developing genuine multi-modal solutions for given corridors (Department for Transport, 2003).

There was also a need to provide a robust method of evaluating alternative urban solutions such as the comparison of rail or light rail with guided busways. Reliance on financial appraisal, especially where complex private finance or public–private partnerships were to be used, could omit some of the key environmental and wider economic impacts. Multi-modal studies have been developed for a number of situations where serious transport problems existed, but there was no clear solution. These included a number of key inter-urban corridors experiencing serious congestion, and towns where poor accessibility was perceived to be a constraint on economic development. Delivering multi-modal solutions to multi-modal problems has, however, proved to be a greater problem since non-road solutions have typically depended on the need for private sector finance raising problems of traffic forecasting and risk transfer. As Flyvbjerg et al. (2003) have shown in a critique of forecasting problems, there has been a consistent tendency towards the overestimation of traffic and underestimation of costs, especially in rail-based projects.

This raises the question of how far the public sector should be paying for the possibility of capturing wider benefits from a scheme largely financed by the private sector. The danger is that some of these effects may already have been captured in user benefits which are paid for by users. Additionally, as we have seen, depending on the nature of competition wider impacts can be negative as well as positive. Some may also simply involve redistribution between one area and another.

What implications does this have for appraisal? At the heart of any transport appraisal the primary concern is to ensure that the transport benefits and direct external costs are both measured and evaluated correctly. No attempt to include wider indirect benefits and costs can overcome inaccuracies in the estimation of the basic transport user benefits. Thus, first, the situation depicted in Figure 2.4 has to depend on the accurate measurement of the traffic impacts of a scheme, taking into account the position expected to obtain at the date of its introduction. As Flyvbjerg et al. (2003) and others have shown it is poorly executed forecasting of both demand and costs which has often undermined the appraisal process.

Beyond this it is desirable to include directly the measurable elements of directly attributable external costs. The uncertainty surrounding precise valuations of environmental impacts has often led decision-makers to be reluctant to incorporate these directly into CBA and instead use MCDA or the even less ambitious AST which avoid placing monetary values on these effects. The disagreements between analysts of the precise monetary values to be placed on greenhouse gas emissions or local air pollution have often been used as an excuse for avoiding methods which require such valuations. However, not placing a monetary value on such factors does implicitly place such a value in the overall appraisal and it is more satisfactory to include a value (or range of values) which can demonstrate the sensitivity of the overall appraisal to each factor in turn. More difficult are such factors as landscape impacts and visual intrusion where the physical measure is also less objective. The danger of excluding factors which are difficult to evaluate is that they may finish up being accorded excessive weights in the more qualitative stage of appraisal.

What SACTRA (1999) and others have shown is that there is no simple rule for ascribing wider economic impacts to a particular value of transport user benefits. It is not possible for example simply to utilize a multiplier which aggregates user benefits by a factor of 1.1 or 1.2. It has been well established (Dodgson, 1973; Jara-Diaz, 1986) that in a perfectly competitive environment the user benefits will be a sufficient and complete measure of all the benefits. More significant is the situation in an imperfectly competitive environment. As Venables and Gasiorek (1999) have shown in a theoretical model, reinforced by attempts to apply a working model to specific situations (for example Bröcker, 2000; Oosterhaven and Elhorst, 2003), a wide range of different outcomes can be obtained according to the precise nature of both the sectoral and geographic situations.

The problem is whether it is feasible to develop and use large-scale CGE models for every appraisal exercise. If these are only thought to be effective for the appraisal of major changes to networks, what constitutes the minimum size of a project, and how would we know if a particular project might have wider impacts which are worthy of more detailed analysis without having first carried out the analysis? As theoretical analysis in the new economic geography (Fujita et al., 1999) has shown, the impact of a given change in transport costs can differ in different situations; small changes can in some cases have disproportionately large impacts and vice versa. Even changes which have a large impact on transport costs and accessibility may have a very small impact on regional economies; Bröcker et al. (2004) show that the EU's TENs programme may produce changes in accessibility of up to 40 per cent but the overall economic impact is typically between one-twentieth and one-tenth of this.

The great advantage of the CGE approach is that it directly produces a measure of the overall change in welfare; as long as the appropriate direct external effects are included in the model structure it can give us an overall appraisal evaluation. But the big question is how far decision-makers are prepared to accept this essentially black box approach to appraisal. The great advantage of the AST approach is its apparent transparency where each element is spelled out, but it then requires great consensus amongst the various interested parties to accept the implicit weighting attached to each value. After nearly eighty years of CBA we clearly still have a long way to go in resolving the questions over its acceptability as an objective method of analysis firmly rooted in economic theory.

NOTES

1. This section draws heavily on the analysis provided in SACTRA (1999) of which the author was one of the members. See also Quinet and Vickerman (2004) for a more formal analysis.
2. Although we can conceive of a case where the supply curve at current levels of use would effectively be perfectly elastic, there would be little need for any evaluation of new investment for a road where usage was so far below capacity.
3. For a comprehensive guide to the use of MCDA in public decision-making see ODPM (no date).
4. Moreover this is of the technically more correct equivalent variation in income resulting from a change rather than the (Marshallian) consumer surplus of the traditional CBA model.

REFERENCES

Bogetoft, P. and P. Pruzan (1991), *Planning with Multiple Criteria: Investigation, Communication, Choice*, Amsterdam: North Holland.

Brakman, S., H. Garretsen and C. van Marrewijk (2001), *An Introduction to Geographical Economics*, Cambridge: Cambridge University Press.

Bröcker, J. (2001), 'Trans-European effects of trans-European networks', in F. Bolle and M. Carlberg (eds), *Advances in Behavioural Economics*, Heidelberg: Physica, pp. 141–57.

Bröcker, J. (2004), 'Computable general equilibrium analysis in transportation economics', in D.A. Hensher, K.J. Button, K. Haynes and P. Stopher (eds), *Handbook of Transport Geography and Spatial Systems: Handbooks in Transport Volume 5*, Oxford: Elsevier, pp. 269–92.

Bröcker, J., R. Capello, L. Lundquist, T. Pütz, J. Rouwendal, N. Schneekloth, A. Spairani, M. Spangenberg, K. Spiekermann, R. Vickerman and M. Wegener (2004), *Territorial Impact of EU Transport and TEN Policies*, Final Report of Action 2.1.1. of the European Spatial Planning Observation Network ESPON 2006, Kiel, Institut für Regionalforschung, Christian-Albrechts-Universität.

Department of the Environment, Transport and the Regions (DETR) (1998a), *A New Deal for Transport: Better for Everyone*, London: The Stationery Office.

Department of the Environment, Transport and the Regions (DETR) (1998b), *A New Deal for Trunk Roads in England*, London: DETR.

Department of the Environment, Transport and the Regions (DETR) (1998c), *A New Deal for Trunk Roads in England: Understanding the New Approach to Appraisal*, London: DETR.

Department for Transport (2003), *Multi-Modal Studies: Introduction to the Guidance on the Methodology for Multi Modal Studies. TAG Unit 1.2.1* (www.webtag.org.uk/webdocuments/1_Overview/2_Multi-Modal_Studies/1.2.1.pdf).

Design Manual for Roads and Bridges (DMRB) (2002), *Economic Assessment of Road Schemes: The COBA Manual*, DMRB Vol.13, Department for Transport,

Scottish Executive Development Department, Welsh Assembly Government, Department for Regional Development Northern Ireland.
Dodgson, J.S. (1973), 'External effects in road investment', *Journal of Transport Economics and Policy*, **7**, 169–85.
Flyvbjerg, B., N. Bruzelius and W. Rothengatter (2003), *Megaprojects and Risk*, Cambridge: Cambridge University Press.
Fujita, M., P. Krugman and A.J. Venables (1999), *The Spatial Economy: Cities, Regions and International Trade*, Cambridge, MA: MIT Press.
Glaister, S. (1999), 'Observations on the new approach to the appraisal of road projects', *Journal of Transport Economics and Policy*, **33**, 227–33.
Goodwin, P. (1992), 'A review of new demand elasticities with special reference to short and long run effects of price changes', *Journal of Transport Economics and Policy*, **26**, 155–69.
Hanly, M., J. Dargay and P. Goodwin (2002), 'Review of income and price elasticities in the demand for road traffic', Report to Department for Transport, London: ESRC Transport Studies Unit, University College London.
HM Treasury (2003), *The Green Book: Appraisal and Evaluation in Central Government*, London: Stationery Office.
Jara-Diaz, S.R. (1986), 'On the relations between users' benefits and the economic effects of transportation activities', *Journal of Regional Science*, **26**, 379–91.
Keeney, R.L. and H. Raiffa (1976), *Decisions with Multiple Objectives: Preferences and Value Trade-offs*, New York: Wiley (Reprinted, Cambridge University Press, 1993).
Newbery, D.M. (1999), 'Measuring the indirect benefits of transport cost reductions', Report to Marcial Echenique and Partners, Cambridge.
Office of the Deputy Prime Minister (ODPM) (no date), 'Multi-criteria analysis manual', (www.odpm.gov.uk/stellent/groups/odpm_about/documents/page/odpm_about_608524.hcsp).
Oosterhaven, J. and J.P. Elhorst (2003), 'Indirect economic benefits of transport infrastructure investments', in W. Dullaert, B.A.M. Jourquin and J.B. Polak (eds), *Across The Border. Building Upon a Quarter Century of Transport Research in The Benelux*, Antwerp: De Boeck, pp. 143–62.
Prince, A. (1999), 'The new approach to the appraisal of road projects in England', *Journal of Transport Economics and Policy*, **33**, 221–6.
Quinet, E. and R. Vickerman (2004), *Principles of Transport Economics*, Cheltenham, UK and Northampton, MA, USA: Edward Elgar.
SACTRA (Standing Advisory Committee on Trunk Road Assessment) (1994), *Trunk Roads and the Generation of Traffic*, London: HMSO.
SACTRA (Standing Advisory Committee on Trunk Road Assessment) (1999), *Transport and the Economy*, London: Stationery Office.
Simmonds, D. (David Simmonds Consultancy in collaboration with Marcial Echenique and Partners) (1999), 'Review of Land Use/Transport Interaction Models', Report to Standing Advisory Committee on Trunk Road Assessment, London: DETR.
Sugden, R. (1999), 'Developing a consistent cost–benefit framework for multimodal transport appraisal', Economics Research Centre University of East Anglia, report to Department of the Environment, Transport and the Regions.
Venables, A.J. (1999), 'Road transport improvements and network congestion', *Journal of Transport Economics and Policy*, **33**, 319–28.

Venables, A. and M. Gasiorek (1999), 'The welfare implications of transport improvements in the presence of market failure part 1', Report to Standing Advisory Committee on Trunk Road Assessment, London: DETR.

Vickerman, R.W. (2000), 'Evaluation methodologies for transport projects in the UK', *Transport Policy*, **7**, 7–16.

Wegener, M. (2004), 'Overview of land use transport models', in D.A. Hensher, K.J. Button, K. Haynes and P. Stopher (eds), *Handbook of Transport Geography and Spatial Systems: Handbooks in Transport Volume 5*, Oxford: Elsevier.

Wegener, M. and D. Bökemann (1998), *The SASI Model: Model Structure*, SASI Deliverable 8. Berichte aus dem Institut für Raumplanung 40, Dortmund: Institut für Raumplanung, University of Dortmund.

3. The institutional theory approach to transport policy and evaluation. The collective benefits of a stakeholder's approach: towards an eclectic multi-criteria analysis

Klaas De Brucker and Alain Verbeke

1. INTRODUCTION: DIFFERENT VIEWS ON THE 'INSTITUTION' CONCEPT

Two competing paradigms can be adopted when assessing transport policy measures and large infrastructure projects, namely the neoclassical and the neo-institutional approach. The neoclassical paradigm is summarized in Robbins' (1932: 15) definition of economics: 'Economics is the science that studies human behaviour in terms of a relationship between ends and scarce means which have alternative uses'. In this definition, the individual consumer is viewed as having insatiable wants ('ends'), which are usually quantified using the concept of willingness-to-pay. Thus, consumer sovereignty plays a central role in this approach. 'Means', however, are limited ('scarce'). Therefore choices need to be made. The neoclassical approach assumes that the individual engages in a comparison between marginal benefits (as measured by willingness-to-pay) and marginal costs (as measured by opportunity cost). In principle, full rationality and complete information prevail. The individual, therefore, does not need to rely on habits, routines or complex decision rules ('institutions') when making choices.

In contrast, the institutional theory approach is based on the concept of 'institutions'. Various views exist on this concept in the economics literature. Steunenberg (2001: 15ff) and Van Hees (2000: 55–9) discuss three key perspectives on the concept. First, the behavioural view on institutions can be traced back to the original definition given by the 'old institutionalism' scholar T. Veblen, who defined institutions as 'settled habits of thought common to the generality of men' (Veblen, 1919: 239). Here, institutions are patterns of behaviour, shared and accepted by the members of a group or society. Second, institutions can be defined as conventions or as 'the rules of the game in a society' (North, 1990: 3). With this approach, institutions are considered as rules that regulate human behaviour (that is, the behaviour of the players) in a society. Individuals and organizations are the 'players' of the game. Third, institutions can be considered 'decision procedures', that is, procedures (or sets of rules) that enable a group or society to transform individual preferences into collective preferences. This third view (and, to a lesser extent, also the second one) is in line with the old institutionalism view of J. Commons, who argued that society is a complex entity of multiple actors with partly conflicting and partly converging interests. The various 'trade or social relations' involving the actors or stakeholders often lead to conflicts, given problems of economic scarcity. The essence of economics is then to solve – or at least manage – these social conflicts. Effective conflict management increases economic welfare. This can be achieved through 'collective action' and 'collective democratic planning' or an 'evolving system of rules', that is institutions (Commons, [1934]1959: 73ff, 108ff; Klein, 1984; Mitchell, 1969: 719). This last view bears some similarity with the contractarian view on institutions (Buchanan, 1975: 26–7). Schotter (1981: 5) provides a definition of economics consistent with both the second and third views above: 'Economics is the study of how individual economic agents pursuing their own selfish ends evolve institutions as a means to satisfy them'. This definition emphasizes both intentional design and the pursuit of distributional advantage. It assumes that individuals and organizations develop institutions or influence them in the pursuit of their own self-interest, that is to obtain a strategic advantage. Below, we describe a variety of mechanisms instrumental to overcoming this advantage-seeking or rent-seeking behaviour.

The common element in the three above views is that institutions constrain human behaviour. Whether institutions are defined as habits (that is behaviour), as conventions or as decision rules, they limit the options available to an individual or an organization, and thereby create a situation of socio-economic stability and order. Socio-economic stability and order can be interpreted as a public good or the collective benefit of institutions. Conflicts of interest and the way in which institutions contribute to solving or controlling these conflicts, play a central role in the third (and, to a lesser extent, also in the second) view on institutions.

Institutions can be formal or informal in nature. The former include laws and regulations. The latter include social customs and norms. Institutions can emerge spontaneously, as in Darwinian biology, with its variety generation and natural selection processes (Menger, [1883]1985; Hayek, 1973). Institutions can also be created by man through a process of intentional design, that is, an artificial selection process (Commons, [1934]1959). In this contribution, we will not focus on the behavioural (or Veblenian) view on institutions, but rather on formal institutions created through intentional design. As noted above, this third view considers institutions as decision rules or procedures to transform individual or stakeholder preferences into group preferences. We shall pay specific attention to the application of this third view through the use of social cost–benefit analysis (SCBA) or multi-criteria analysis (MCA) in project evaluation.

In the next section of this chapter, we examine more closely the institutional foundations of both the neoclassical and the institutional approach, and their implications for project evaluation, in the form of SCBA and MCA. In the third section, we analyse in more detail the drivers of – and impediments to – the application of the institutional approach. More specifically, we ask the question whether or not the institutional approach can contribute to achieving a social optimum. In the fourth section, we report on the development and application of a new method allowing SCBA and MCA to be integrated into an overall or 'eclectic' framework, which we have named 'eclectic multi-criteria analysis' (EMCA). The fifth section concludes.

2. INSTITUTIONAL ASPECTS CRITICAL TO THE NEOCLASSICAL AND THE INSTITUTIONAL APPROACH, AS APPLIED TO PROJECT EVALUATION

2.1. Institutional Aspects Underlying the Neoclassical Approach versus the Institutional Approach

Below, we demonstrate that both the neoclassical and the institutional approaches to project evaluation are grounded in specific institutions. In the next section, we investigate how these institutional aspects reappear in the project evaluation methods, with a focus on SCBA and MCA.

The traditional neoclassical approach to economics largely ignores the impact of institutions. An institution-free state is implicitly assumed in the neoclassical approach. A closer look at this approach, however, suggests that the neoclassical approach builds implicitly on a set of important institutions, namely (1) private property rights; (2) markets where supply meets demand; (3) competition at the supply side (and competition law); (4) the price mechanism; and (5) a unit of account (a 'numéraire'). This set of institutions can itself be viewed as a public good. SCBA is based on the concept of willingness-to-pay and this concept assumes the presence of both property rights and markets. Indeed, willingness-to-pay can be interpreted as willingness to acquire the property rights (or at least some component of the property rights) of a specific good. Full property rights can be decomposed into three elements, that is, the right to use a good (*jus utendi*), the right to claim the income generated by this good (*jus fruendi*) and the right to dispose of this good and to change its nature (*jus abutendi*). In turn, property rights can only be traded in a market. The neoclassical approach assumes the market as given, but in specific circumstances such markets (institutions) need to be created artificially. For example, surrogate markets are created by government when evaluating specific external effects and public goods, thereby sometimes establishing real new markets to trade rights related to these effects (for example, tradable pollution rights). As regards competition and competition law (for example, the articles 81 and 82 of the European Community treaty, or the Sherman Anti-trust laws in the US), it should be noted that these institutions are critical to obtain a Pareto efficient equilibrium price, whereby social welfare (as measured by social surpluses) is maximized. The institution of a transparent and stable price mechanism is also crucial to the neoclassical approach, since prices act as signals for both consumers and producers. For consumers, relative prices should equal the ratio of the relevant marginal utilities. For producers, relative prices should equal the ratio of the relevant marginal costs. Finally, a unit of account or numéraire (usually a monetary unit such as the euro or the United States dollar) is necessary, since prices are expressed in monetary terms.

The neoclassical approach takes for granted the above institutions and focuses on utility maximizing behaviour of consumers, and profit maximizing behaviour of producers. In contrast, the institutional approach focuses explicitly on the functioning and impact of institutions. This means their emergence (whether spontaneous or intentional), their transformation and their distributional effects are carefully examined. The institutions discussed above remain in place, but they are complemented with additional ones. Moreover, specific stakeholders are identified and the interactions among these stakeholders are studied in great detail. Here, stakeholders are considered the critical actors in policy processes. They are viewed as the 'players of the game', whereas institutions are the 'rules of the game', that is the procedures to be followed. Policy processes are not considered black boxes. On the contrary, black boxes must be opened and attention is devoted to the processes through which individual or stakeholder preferences are transformed into a social preference function. Specific outcomes of policy processes may result from particular interaction patterns among stakeholders. Some stakeholders may have a greater impact on the final outcome than others. Policy processes may be path dependent. The initial institutional context and the relative bargaining power of stakeholders may therefore be instrumental to the specific outcome and to the transformation of the institutions considered. Some solutions may be 'locked-in', given the options chosen in the past. Stakeholders' interests may converge but most often there is at least some level of conflict.

2.2. Institutional Aspects Inherent in Project Evaluation

Whereas the previous section focused on the general institutional aspects underlying both the neoclassical and the institutional paradigm, this section will focus on the institutional aspects underlying project evaluation. This means that the institutional foundations identified in the previous section remain relevant, but need to be complemented with additional elements.

The most important difference between public sector and private sector investment analysis is that in the former, the benefits and costs considered relevant accrue to different individuals or stakeholders in society. Business organizations (companies) can also be viewed as being composed of different constituencies, such as shareholders, managers, personnel, and so on. This implies that in private sector investment analysis, the utility accruing to (or the interests of) the various constituencies could, in principle, also be evaluated, or at least weighted. The difference with public sector investment analysis, however, is that private sector investment analysis is usually conducted within a single company and that all stakeholders inside the firm are in principle compensated for the costs they incur. In a private sector investment analysis, all internal costs (including the opportunity cost of money) are effectively compensated for and the project's surplus or net benefit – as measured by its net present value (NPV) – fully accrues to one specific group of stakeholders, namely the shareholders. The NPV can be interpreted as a measure for shareholder income. The NPV represents a *dividendum* (which in Latin means: something that should be divided), but this *dividendum* is divided only among the shareholders. A stakeholders' approach may also be relevant in the case of project evaluation in a private sector company, but only insofar as objectives other than sole profit maximization are viewed as relevant, for example, the firm's market share, growth, reputation, and so on.

In public sector project evaluation, benefits and costs accrue to different individuals or stakeholders, so that institutional aspects become crucial. In fact, economic evaluation from a socio-economic point of view requires interpersonal utility comparisons. Benefits (gains) accruing to one party (the winners) need to be compared with costs (losses) incurred by another party (the losers). A set of rules, that is an institution, is therefore necessary to aggregate the personal utility changes across all members of society affected by a project. It is this set of rules which allows a collective choice to be made. This collective choice would not only be different if another set of rules was used, but the distributional effects of this choice would also be different. The reason is that the application of these decision rules entails interpersonal utility comparisons. Effective compensation of the losers usually does not take place, and as far as the winners are concerned, some winners may win much more than others. As in private sector investment analysis, projects that pass the decision rules result in a net *dividendum*, but it is not clear a priori how this net *dividendum* is divided, either among the winners (as far as the benefits are concerned), or among the losers (as far as the costs are concerned). The choice of a set of decision rules is therefore critical and the study of the related choice process extends beyond simple economic analysis, and enters the realm of philosophy and ethics.

In the past, a number of eminent philosophers and economists have suggested various specific decision rules. Bergson and Samuelson have formulated a general welfare function (formula 3.1), stating that social welfare is a function of the individual utility levels (U) of the members (i) of that society (Samuelson, 1947: 228).

$$W = W(U_1, U_2, \dots, U_i, \dots, U_n) \tag{3.1}$$

Several other economists have tried to specify this function further. For example, the Cambridge economists (Bergson, 1938: 324) proposed a utility function stating that social welfare is the sum of the individual utility levels (formula 3.2).

$$W = \sum_{i=1}^{n} U_i \tag{3.2}$$

Concave welfare functions (formula 3.3) take into account the distribution of the individual welfare functions. They express the idea that replacing two unequal utility levels by their arithmetic mean, and in that way making the income distribution less uneven, will result in an increase in social welfare.

$$W = \sum_{i=1}^{n} U_i - a.\mathrm{var}\,U \tag{3.3}$$

Rawls (1971: 153–4) proposed the 'maximin' criterion, which states that government should aim to increase ('maximize') the utility levels of its poorest members (that is those with minimal utility levels) (as illustrated by formula 3.4).

$$W = \min(U_1, U_2, \ldots, U_i, \ldots, U_n) \tag{3.4}$$

According to Rawls, the members of a society would automatically agree to such a criterion if, before entering this society, they would have to agree (in a meeting) upon the rules that would govern this society. The reason why the future members would spontaneously agree to this decision rule is that they would hold an 'original position', behind a 'veil of ignorance', meaning they would not know which position they would eventually occupy in that future society. From an income distribution policy perspective, this criterion is controversial, since people would no longer have an incentive to work (that is, to produce) and society would end up with lower levels of aggregate income (consumption possibilities), worsening even the position of the least fortunate person in society. Mankiw (2004: 439) argues that the people behind the veil of ignorance would not be particularly risk averse, but rather they would be likely to treat all outcomes equally when designing public policies. In that case, the best policy behind the veil of ignorance would be to maximize the average utility of the members of society instead of the lowest utility levels.

Pareto (1927: 354) established the Pareto criterion. According to this criterion, social welfare increases when a Pareto improvement is possible, that is, a situation whereby the utility level of at least one individual is raised without decreasing the utility levels of any other individual; conversely, social welfare decreases when the utility level of one or more individuals is reduced, without increasing the utility levels of any other individual. Policy measures or projects that simultaneously increase the utility level of some individuals and decrease the utility level of others are said to be 'Pareto efficient', since a pure Pareto improvement is not possible. At first sight, the Pareto criterion seems to be value neutral, but a high increase of the utility level of one or more individuals or stakeholders, combined with unchanged utility levels of all the other individuals or stakeholders in society might make the income distribution substantially more unequal, thereby casting some doubt on the contribution to societal welfare of the policy measure or project considered.

Since policy measures or projects that lead to a pure Pareto improvement are virtually non-existent, Hicks (1939: 711) and Kaldor (1939: 550) introduced a compensation principle. This principle states that social welfare increases when the individuals whose utility levels have increased (that is, the 'winners') *can* compensate the individuals whose utility levels have decreased (that is, the 'losers') and still attain a higher utility level than was the case prior to the implementation of the policy measure or project. If the compensation were actually to take place, a pure Pareto improvement would result. If such compensation does not occur, the outcome is a 'potential Pareto' improvement. A justification for the compensation principle can be found in Posner's (1987) analysis, which asserts that common law (that is judge-made) rules are often best explained as efforts, whether intended or not, to bring about Pareto or Hicks–Kaldor efficient outcomes.

Condorcet (1785: lx[60]ff) formulated a principle that was initially related to democracy. But translated into project evaluation (or multi-criteria) terms, this principle states that one action (project) outranks another if it is 'better or at least as good as' this second action in terms of the majority of criteria ('voters') (that is the 'concordant criteria') and 'not much worse' than the latter for a minority of criteria ('voters') (that is the 'discordant criteria'). The application of Condorcet-based decision rules results in an ordinal ranking of projects.

2.3. Institutional Aspects Underlying Project Evaluation Methods: Social Cost–benefit Analysis versus Multi-criteria Analysis

A. Social cost–benefit analysis

The decision rule that allows making interpersonal utility comparisons in standard SCBA is the criterion of a potential Pareto improvement, or the Hicks–Kaldor compensation test. Expressed in simple terms, this decision rule implies that a project will increase social welfare if the increases in utility levels (that is, the benefits) for those who gain are higher than the decreases in utility levels (that is, the costs) for those who lose. Put even more simply, the Hicks–Kaldor compensation test underlying SCBA requires that winners should win more than losers lose. This decision rule is not more objective or less controversial (or more convincing) than the classic utilitarian rule (Cambridge social welfare function). However, if the compensation were actually to take place, a pure Pareto improvement would result and there would be no need for a compensation criterion. Sen (1987: 33) therefore concludes that compensation criteria (such as the Hicks–Kaldor compensation criterion) are either unconvincing (that is, controversial if compensation does not take place) or redundant (if the compensation actually does take place). Self (1975: 5) uses the term 'econocracy' to qualify the behaviour of public policy makers engaging in the weighing of policy objectives and effects and making their own views on policy subordinate to analytical tools such as SCBA (De Jong and Geerlings, 2003: 282). In his view, assuming the existence of a fundamental economic test or yardstick (such as the Hicks–Kaldor compensation criterion) according to which policy decisions can and should be made is the equivalent of shirking. Johansson-Stenman

(1998: 282–3), in defence of the Hicks–Kaldor rule, argues that as long as the distributional consequences are relatively small, such a compensation rule may be justified in real-world policy decisions. In addition, if government is able to address more important equity issues at a 'higher level', then the project evaluation process can focus on efficiency issues only. The problem with this approach, however, is that inertia and transaction costs in policy processes may prevent affected parties from being compensated effectively. In any case, interpersonal utility comparisons are necessary (no policy recommendation would be possible without making interpersonal utility comparisons), but not sufficient, since we need some social choice rule to determine how we should act, given the above information on changes in utility. In practical applications, however, the evaluation procedure often only includes an SCBA, limited to the effects which can be easily expressed in monetary terms, and the necessary supplement (the so-called 'social choice rule') cannot be applied given the presence of a number of 'pro memory' items on the balance sheet, or some plus or minus signs in a limited MCA. As an example, this occurred in the guidelines of the research programme 'Economic Effects of Infrastructure in the Netherlands' (*Onderzoeksprogramma Economische Effecten Infrastructuur*, the so-called 'OEEI-guidelines') conducted by the Ministry of Transport, Public Works and Water Management/Ministry of Economic Affairs (Eijgenraam et al., 2000).

Bearing in mind the decision rule underlying SCBA (that is, the Hicks–Kaldor compensation test), it is clear that SCBA is more than a simple tool of economic analysis, as it also aims to replace part of the political decision process. This feature of SCBA is often overlooked by policy makers and sometimes even by analysts. Political decision-makers are in fact not involved in the decision process and often they do not even understand the decision rule underlying SCBA. Mostly, they only look at the 'bottom-line outcome' of the SCBA (showing the NPV or the profitability index), and no further analyses are performed. The same ignorance often characterizes the public and even the stakeholders with an interest in the SCBA outcome. In addition, the exact meaning of the final SCBA score, that is the net present value (NPV), is usually not properly understood, either by the political decision-makers, or by the public or stakeholders. Most of the time, these actors interpret the NPV of a public investment project without taking into account the differences with private sector investment analysis. The similarity with private sector investment analysis is that in both cases the NPV criterion is associated with extra wealth (increases in utility levels), which needs to be divided. The differences are that in public sector investment analysis (1) this extra wealth does not typically take the form of monetary transfers accruing to a specific group of stakeholders (such as the shareholders); (2) the 'dividends' are unevenly divided among multiple stakeholders or members of society; (3) interpersonal utility comparisons are made, according to the principle that winners should win more than losers lose; and (4) effective compensation of the losers usually does not take place (at least not fully).

Important institutional aspects prevail in the decision-making process before the SCBA is conducted, especially the stage in which the relevant effects need to be identified and quantified. As regards the identification of effects, stakeholders are usually not involved, at least not in a formal and structured way in contrast to the case of MCA (which we shall discuss later). As regards the quantification of effects, it should be noted that this quantification is performed exclusively through attaching a monetary value to the effects. The monetary value of the effects reflects the willingness-to-pay on the part of consumers for the output or effects produced by the project, as well as for the inputs needed. This means that the consumers, that is, the market, rather than policy makers, assign implicitly monetary values to the project's effects. The higher the monetary value (given by consumers) in the SCBA, that is the higher the Dupuit–Marshall surplus (Dupuit, 1844: 332ff; Marshall [1890]1922: 175–7), the better a project is considered to be from a societal point of view. Nevertheless, three problems are associated with the use of such market values. First, it is assumed implicitly that individual preferences should prevail. This implies that consumers know what is good for them, and what is bad (Anderson and Settle, 1979: 11) and that their preferences are consistent over time. This assumption may be contested, since there are so-called 'merit goods' and 'merit bads' (or 'demerit goods') for which the preferences may be inconsistent over time. In the real world, consumers exhibit a high willingness-to-pay for items such as narcotics, tobacco, alcohol and sex, though (excessive) consumption of these items may reduce the welfare of both the individual and society. Consumption of merit bads does result in an immediate, but temporary award. It may result in a permanent, large cost or sacrifice in the future as well, which is often underestimated at the time the decision is made. In contrast, consumers often exhibit a low willingness-to-pay for goods such as education and medical care, though these goods may increase the welfare of both the individual and society. Consumption of these merit goods requires a sacrifice in the present, for a reward in the distant future, often underestimated at the time the decision is made (Mankiw, 2004: 493). In other words, actual choices by consumers may be inconsistent over time. Ignorance and the neglect of long-term effects may undermine the willingness-to-pay concept in general. Second, when market values derived from the consumers' willingness-to-pay are used as the basis for making policy decisions, this means that a normative (or prescriptive) statement (a policy recommendation) is derived from a positive or descriptive statement. More specifically, an 'ought situation' is derived from an 'is situation'. Hume (1739: 469) argued that this cannot be done. More recently, a number of economists have claimed that positive and normative statements may often be intertwined (Myrdal, 1932: 1–18; Blaug, 1992: 114; Hodgson, 1999: 24–9). The point is that in SCBA, this intertwining is often insufficiently visible and therefore mostly ignored. Third, revealed preferences (made explicit in the willingness-to-pay concept) may also be determined by external factors, especially for status goods (Frank, 1985; Veblen, 1899: 35–101; Galbraith, 1958: 312 and 161ff). Finally, the 'endowment effect' and sunk costs may also play an important role (Thaler, 1980: 43–50). Because of this, differences may exist between values obtained via willingness-to-pay methods versus willingness-to-accept methods.

B. Multi-criteria analysis

In contrast to SCBA, based on neo-Paretian welfare economics, MCA has its roots in a different discipline, namely operations research (Charness and Cooper, 1961). MCA does not necessarily rely on welfare economics concepts such as the consumer surplus, that is the Dupuit–Marshall surplus (Dupuit, 1844: 332ff; Marshall [1890] 1922: 175–7) but compares a number of actions or alternatives (for example, projects or policy measures) in terms of specific criteria. These criteria represent an operationalization of the objectives and sub-objectives of decision-makers and stakeholders participating in the decision-making process. In general terms, the process-related steps to be followed in an MCA have a structure as shown in Figure 3.1.

First, the nature of the problem is identified and analysed. On the basis of this analysis, actions or alternatives that may remedy the problem are formulated in the second step. In the third step, criteria are developed relevant to the evaluation of the actions or alternatives to be studied. A criterion is a function that makes it possible to provide a score (quantitative or qualitative) for each action, measuring the contribution of that action to a relevant specific objective. By giving scores, a partial evaluation is performed (that is an evaluation in terms of one or more specific objectives as measured by criteria). The objectives identified in the MCA may correspond to the objectives of specific stakeholders identified in the decision-making process. Alternatively, it is possible to define objectives (and hence criteria) directly on the basis of stakeholder analysis. This means that one first identifies the stakeholders and then looks at the effects that are considered relevant or important to these stakeholders. Criteria are then constructed on the basis of these effects to provide an evaluation in terms of specific stakeholder objectives (that is, a 'partial evaluation'). The second and the third step as shown in Figure 3.1 can also be reversed.

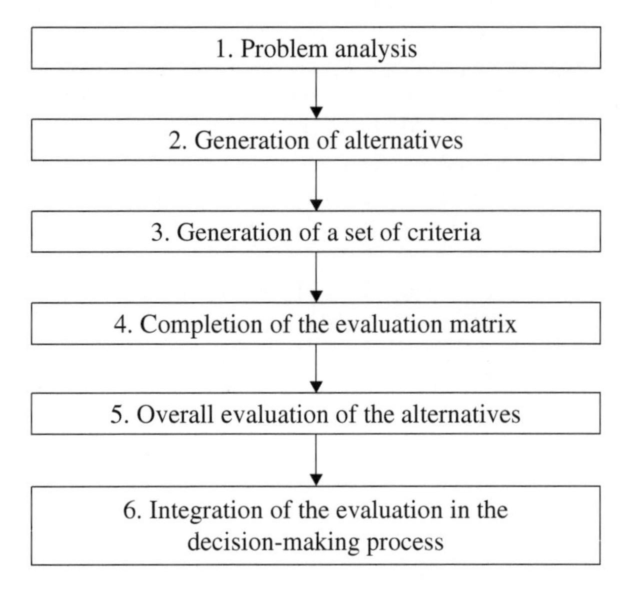

Source: Designed by the authors

Figure 3.1 Process-related steps in MCA

When criteria are developed first and actions thereafter, value-focused thinking is adopted (Keeney, 1996: 47ff). Values (to be measured by criteria) are made explicit from the outset. Only in the next step does one proactively attempt to identify actions that can contribute to these predefined values. The set of actions is thus 'constructed' instead of being determined externally. This approach contrasts sharply with the method of alternative-focused thinking, which is often applied in practice. According to Keeney (1996: 47ff), the latter approach reduces creativity and innovation, because the predetermined set of alternatives fundamentally constrains the evaluation process. The criteria are then typically selected based on thinking about the alternatives, not about the fundamental objectives (values) to be achieved.

The fourth step consists of constructing and completing the evaluation matrix. This is a matrix where all the actions are evaluated in terms of all the criteria (as shown in Table 3.1). Within the evaluation matrix, however, clusters of criteria can be distinguished. Criteria can be clustered in two ways. First, they can be clustered according to the type of effect or the way in which the effect was measured. Criteria may then be clustered into groups, such as a group that can be expressed in monetary units, another group related to non-monetary environmental or safety effects, still another group related to

Table 3.1 Evaluation matrix

	g_1	g_2	...	g_j	...	g_m
a_1	e_{11}	e_{12}	...	e_{1j}	...	e_{1m}
a_2	e_{21}	e_{22}	...	e_{2j}	...	e_{2m}
...	...	...	...	...	...	...
a_i	e_{i1}	e_{i2}	...	e_{ij}	...	e_{im}
...	...	...	...	...	...	...
a_n	e_{n1}	e_{n2}	...	e_{nj}	...	e_{nm}

Source: Schärlig (1985: 60), adapted by the authors

the non-monetary aspects of comfort, and so on. A second way to cluster criteria is according to specific points of view, corresponding to specific stakeholder objectives. Criteria can then be clustered into groups that represent, for example, the point of view of the logistics sector, the environmental point of view, a specific social perspective, and so on.

In the fifth step, the information in the evaluation matrix needs to be aggregated. The information represented in the evaluation matrix seldom makes it possible to select one alternative in an unambiguous fashion. In most cases, the scores obtained by the alternatives on the various criteria (partial evaluations) are conflicting, which means that they do not unanimously point to a single 'best' alternative, which would be superior in terms of all criteria. This situation is sometimes referred to as the 'multi-criteria imbroglio' (Schärlig, 1985: 4). An aggregation method is, therefore, needed in most cases to synthesize the conflicting information. Each aggregation method relies on specific assumptions regarding the comparability of the partial evaluations and the relations between criteria. In most cases, criteria should be given explicit weights by policy makers. Here, analysts can introduce an interactive tool to help policy makers when reflecting on relative weights, but ultimately it is the decision-makers themselves who must give the policy weights. This is in sharp contrast with SCBA whereby the scores on all criteria are supposed to be expressed in monetary values, and together constitute the NPV (Van Delft and Nijkamp, 1977: 24). These effects' monetary values, which act as scores and weights, are derived directly from the consumer's willingness-to-pay. Within each aggregation method, several MCA approaches can be used to aggregate the partial evaluations.

The method of complete aggregation is based on the multi-attribute utility theory (MAUT) of Keeney and Raiffa (1993), which is the American MCA-school. This method builds upon the axiom that a decision-maker implicitly or unconsciously always tries to maximize a cardinal utility function, aggregating all points of view (that is, all criteria) (Keeney and Raiffa, 1993: 68ff and 282ff). This function is given in formula 3.5.

$$U = U(g_1, g_2, \dots, g_m) \quad (3.5)$$

This function is not known in advance. It is the analyst who should 'identify' the function. He should identify the criteria and the linkages between the criteria by gathering relevant information from the decision-maker.

The method of partial aggregation, also called the outranking approach, was designed by the founding father of the French MCA-school (Roy, 1968; 1985) and his followers. They found that the synthesis achieved through MAUT was not sufficiently realistic. With complete aggregation methods, the final synthesis builds directly upon the information included in the evaluation matrix. But with the partial aggregation methods, a synthesis is achieved indirectly. In the first step, the information included in the evaluation table is further analysed through a concordance and discordance analysis. These two types of analysis constitute a set of rules to be fulfilled before it can be concluded that one action outranks another action (Roy and Bouyssou, 1993: 63). This analysis has a pairwise set-up and its result is shown in an outranking table. The analysis is based on a principle formulated by the French philosopher Condorcet (1785: 11–14) and was initially related to democracy. As noted above, this principle states that one action outranks another action if it is 'better or at least as good as' this second action in terms of the majority of criteria ('voters') (that is, the concordant criteria) and 'not much worse' than the latter for a minority of criteria ('voters') (that is, the discordant criteria). A synthesis is then made on the basis of the outranking relations and ultimately results in a ranking or selection of alternatives. Given the specific character of this aggregation method, this final ranking is neither necessarily complete nor transitive. This aggregation method also relies on weights to be given to the criteria. These weights should, however, not be interpreted in the same way as in the method of complete aggregation. With the latter approach, the criterion weights represent trade-offs between criteria. With the former, the weight of a criterion is to be compared to the number of votes in an election procedure (Vincke, 1989: 143).

Within the limited scope of this contribution, it is not possible to give an overview of the various MCA methods that have been developed in the recent past. High quality overviews are provided in Belton and Stewart (2002) (in English), and De Brucker et al. (1998) (in Dutch). We shall, however, briefly discuss one specific MCA method, namely the analytic hierarchy process (AHP) method of Saaty (1977, 1986, 1988, 1995) for three reasons. First, this method has actually been applied already in various real life applications. Second, it allows us to build ('construct') a solution step by

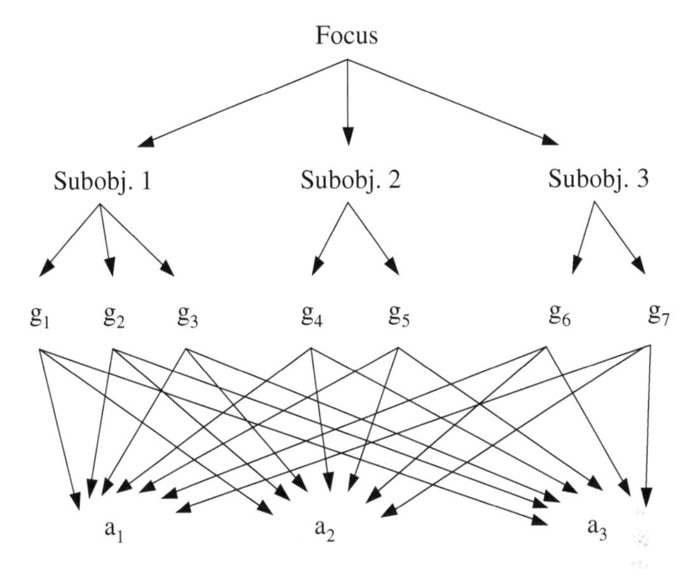

Source: Designed by the authors, based on Saaty (1995)

Figure 3.2 Example of a hierarchy in the AHP

step, taking into account conflicting stakeholder objectives. Third, it forms a core element in the eclectic approach developed by De Brucker (2000: 245ff), which will be discussed in section 4. The AHP method is based on three principles: (1) construction of a hierarchy, (2) priority setting and (3) logical consistency.

A hierarchy (as shown in Figure 3.2) is a complex system in which the constituent parts are hierarchically structured. The top of the hierarchy consists of a single element, which represents the overall objective or focus. The intermediate levels represent sub-objectives and their constituent parts (if possible, measured by operational criteria, that is $g_1 \ldots g_7$ in Figure 3.2). The lowest level consists of the final actions or alternatives considered. The arrows represent causal relationships within the hierarchy. Hierarchies can be constructed top-down or bottom-up.

The relative priorities given to each element in the hierarchy are determined by comparing all the elements at a lower level in pairs, in terms of contribution to the elements at a higher level with which a causal relationship exists, as illustrated in Table 3.2.

$Pg_j(a_i, a_{i'})$ represents the preference intensity for a specific pair of (sub-) objectives $(a_i, a_{i'})$ in terms of the higher level element (objective or criterion $[g_j]$) with which a causal relationship exists. This preference intensity is measured on a scale from 1 to 9 as illustrated in Table 3.3. A similar

Table 3.2 Pairwise comparison matrix in the AHP

g_j	a_1	. . .	. . .	$a_{i'}$	. . .	a_n
a_1	1					
. . .		[1]				
a_i			[1]	$Pg_j(a_i, a_{i'})$		
. . .				[1]		
. . .					[1]	
a_n						1

Source: Designed by the authors, based on Saaty (1995)

Table 3.3 Pairwise comparison scale in the AHP

Intensity of importance $Pg_j(a_i, a_{i'})$ Definition	Explanation
1 Both elements have equal importance	Both elements contribute equally to the criterion considered
3 Moderately higher importance of row element (RE) as compared to column element (CE)	Experience and judgement reveal a slight preference of row element (RE) over column element (CE)
5 Higher importance of RE as compared to CE	Experience and judgement reveal a strong preference of RE over CE
7 Much higher importance of RE as compared to CE	RE is very strongly favoured over CE, and its dominance has been demonstrated in practice
9 Complete dominance in terms of importance of RE over CE	The evidence favouring RE over CE is of the highest possible order
2, 4, 6, 8 (Intermediate values)	An intermediate position between two assessments
1/2, 1/3, 1/4, . . ., 1/9 (reciprocals)	When CE is compared with RE, it receives the reciprocal value of the RE/CE comparison
Rationals Ratios arising from the scale	If consistency were to be forced by obtaining *n* numerical values to span the matrix
1.1–1.9 For tied activities	RE and CE are nearly indistinguishable; moderate is 1.3 and extreme is 1.9

Source: Saaty (1988: 73), adapted by the authors

approach is followed for the constituent components within each objective and sub-objective (criterion).

Within each sub-system of the hierarchy, the relative priorities of the elements are determined through the pairwise comparison mechanism described above (Table 3.2 and Table 3.3). The relative priorities (weights) are given by the right eigenvector (W) corresponding to the highest eigenvalue (λ_{max}) as shown in formula 3.6. The pairwise comparison matrix is represented by the letter A. Its standard element is $Pg_j(a_i, a_{i'})$.

$$A.W = \lambda_{max}.W \tag{3.6}$$

Since in each pairwise comparison matrix, a number of pairwise comparisons are redundant, it is possible to neutralize possible estimation errors that may have occurred in the other pairwise comparisons of the same matrix on the one hand and to obtain a measure of consistency for the pairwise comparisons of the same matrix on the other hand.

In order to synthesize all local priorities, the various priority vectors are weighted by the global priorities of the parent criteria and synthesized. One starts this process at the top of the hierarchy. By doing so, the final or global relative priorities for the lowest level elements (that is the actions) are obtained. These final relative priorities indicate the degree to which the actions contribute to the focus. These global priorities form a synthesis of the local priorities, and thereby integrate the various inputs into the decision-making process. In that way, the various points of view of the different stakeholders are integrated into the final or global priorities, measuring the contribution of each action in terms of the overall objective or focus. In addition, one may as well perform a partial analysis (and synthesis) by doing the pairwise comparisons only from one specific point of view, that is taking into account only one sub-objective (or one stakeholder's point of view) (for example, sub-objective 1 in Figure 3.2). In addition, sensitivity analysis may play an important role in this type of MCA. Sensitivity analysis can be performed for each criterion separately, which means testing whether the final ranking would be different from the one obtained in the basic scenario when the weight of one specific criterion is increased or decreased. Sensitivity analysis can also take the form of scenario analysis or stakeholder analysis. In the latter two types of sensitivity analysis, the weights of several criteria are modified at the same time. These criteria are chosen to give special emphasis to specific policy scenarios or specific stakeholder interests. At that stage, it is possible to assess whether the ranking based on a specific point of view, corresponding to a specific stakeholder, is different from the ranking obtained in the basic scenario.

The AHP is a powerful decision-making tool. This method makes it possible to decompose decision-making problems into their constituent parts. According to a carefully designed decision-making process, a decision is constructed step by step, by making pairwise comparisons. This step-by-step process eventually results in a synthesis in the form of overall or global relative priorities for the final actions. In spite of the very structured process, there is ample room for learning, creativity and interactions among the analyst, the decision-maker and the stakeholders. In addition, it also allows for integrating qualitative and quantitative data (including monetized values), and the degree of conflict between various objectives or stakeholders can be analysed through sensitivity analysis.

3. DOES THE INSTITUTIONAL APPROACH GUARANTEE A SOCIAL OPTIMUM?

In the institutional approach, stakeholders are considered the main drivers of decision-making processes. Two critical comments should be made regarding the role of stakeholders in decision-making processes. First, stakeholder objectives are seldom converging. There may indeed be a substantial amount of conflict among stakeholder interests. For example, when a large transport infrastructure project is to be evaluated, the logistics sector may be interested in a number of criteria such as time-savings and economies of scale. But environmental pressure groups are interested in criteria regarding the environmental impact. Most often actions or project alternatives that obtain a good score on the former criteria obtain a bad score on the latter criteria. That is the reason why stakeholder objectives are said to be conflicting. But some stakeholder objectives may also be converging. The environmental pressure groups' objectives, for example, may converge with the interests of the people living in the neighbourhood of an infrastructure project. For that reason, the question can be asked whether a substantial amount of conflict may act as a driving force or an impeding force in decision-making processes. Second, some stakeholder groups may be more powerful than others. The more powerful stakeholders may then try to obtain a distributional advantage, either directly, through the implementation of specific projects, or more indirectly, through influencing the design and organization of the institutions meant to evaluate and decide on projects. We will address the two above issues in the next section. More particularly, we shall answer the question whether the problems above should be viewed as a serious impediment to the achievement of a social optimum.

3.1. The Control of Conflict in the Institutional Approach through Multi-criteria Analysis

Conflict is based on the incompatibility of goals and arises from opposing behaviours. It can be observed at the individual, group, organization and societal levels. A substantial body of management literature exists regarding conflict resolution at the organizational level (see for example, Mullins, 2005: 829ff). The economic theory literature regarding conflict and conflict resolution at the societal level, however, is not well developed, except for the Marxist paradigm in economics. Most of this literature is oriented towards sociology or political science. Nevertheless, a number of ideas about conflict and its relation to organizational effectiveness can be transferred to the societal context. From an organizational point of view, two diverging views on conflict exist. The traditional view is that conflict is bad for organizations. Conflict is perceived as disruptive and unnatural, and represents a form of deviant behaviour, which should be controlled and changed. More recently, conflict has also been seen as a constructive force, to be welcomed and even encouraged in some circumstances. Here, conflict acts as a catalyst for change. If managed effectively, conflict can help to minimize the destructive influences of a win–lose situation. A limited level of conflict, even in an organizational context, may result in better ideas being produced, people being forced to search for new approaches, the possibility of long-standing problems being brought to the surface and resolved, and interest and creativity being stimulated (Mullins, 2005: 904–5). In a societal context, conflicts among stakeholder objectives are quite natural and occur more often than in the organizational context. The reasons are that (1) the scope of the issues being discussed is much broader and the interests involved much wider and heterogeneous, and (2) the unifying or converging forces present in an organizational context are not that strong in a societal context. In the context of public sector project appraisal, a particular level of conflict may be beneficial, since it allows for creativity, value-focused thinking and learning. In addition, conflict resolution eventually leads to stability, that is an institutional equilibrium. These four benefit categories will be discussed below.

When there is a certain level of conflict among stakeholders' interests, this will enhance creativity, the act of looking for new, better or more efficient solutions. Through altering existing solutions, the disadvantages and weaknesses of these solutions may be alleviated.

Creativity may be enhanced when value-focused thinking is applied. This implies that values (to be measured by criteria) are made explicit from the outset. These values may be conflicting. In a next step actions are 'constructed'. This means that one proactively searches for actions that are good, or at least acceptable, to all stakeholders. This is done in an iterative, learning process. Therefore, actions are not considered as exogenous in this approach, since they evolve in the learning process. This learning process is driven by the concern for reducing conflict.

The resolution of conflict leads to stability, that is, an 'institutional equilibrium'. This is considered to be the collective benefit of an institution. This 'equilibrium' does not emerge spontaneously, but is the result of substantial conflict in an ongoing bargaining process among strategically positioned stakeholders seeking to obtain distributional advantage (or 'seeking to evolve institutions as a way of satisfying their own selfish ends', using the words of the Schotter definition mentioned in section 1 (Schotter, 1981: 5). Once the stakeholders have come to an agreement that is a situation acceptable to all, the bargaining process and its conflicts are halted. The strategically positioned (and therefore more powerful) stakeholders then no longer try to obtain extra distributional advantage, since they know the other stakeholders would counteract in a negative fashion.

Although the stability (the 'equilibrium') of the institution is seen as the 'collective benefit' of an institution, it is clear from the above observations that this equilibrium is not distributionally neutral. The institution may be more advantageous to some strategically positioned stakeholders and less advantageous to – or create losses for – other stakeholders. The mechanisms that allow counteracting or cross-cutting this rent-seeking behaviour will be discussed in the next section.

3.2. Emergence of Collective Benefits from an Institutional Approach to Project Evaluation

Although specific stakeholders' power may be counterbalanced when each stakeholder effectively participates in the decision-making process and this may eventually result in an institutional equilibrium (that is, a situation that none of the stakeholders involved wants to change, given the actions to be expected from the other stakeholders), this equilibrium is not necessarily distributionally neutral. Some stakeholders may have obtained a substantial advantage (or a 'rent') as compared to other stakeholders. The behaviour of stakeholders trying to obtain such an advantage or 'rent' is called 'rent-seeking behaviour', analogous to the similarly named concept in neoclassical welfare economics.[1] There are, however, a number of mechanisms that allow neutralizing or counteracting part of the potential distributional skewness of institutions or policy outcomes. Knight (1998: 40ff) identified a number of such mechanisms and these will be discussed below. He claims that the collective benefit or public good resulting from the equilibrium state is only a by-product of substantial conflict among stakeholders. The stakeholders do not have the intention to create a public good or collective benefit when trying to establish an institution. They are only striving for strategic advantage or 'rent' and it is only in the margin of this process that the collective benefit or public good emerges merely as a by-product. This by-product may arise because stakeholders may be constrained by barriers when trying to establish social institutions that produce a disproportionate distributional advantage to them.

First, there are *transaction costs*. Strategically positioned stakeholders who want to abuse their bargaining power and obtain a substantial distributional advantage know that they will be confronted with opposition from other stakeholders. Even if one specific group of strategically positioned stakeholders possesses substantial bargaining power and might successfully obtain a substantial distributional advantage, it knows it will only obtain this at a very high cost, that is, the transaction costs of offsetting the opposition from the other stakeholders (during the bargaining process, the enforcement stage later on, and withstanding the tensions for change afterwards).

Second, there is *uncertainty about future consequences and future preferences*. The former refers to the fact that some effects of the institution are not known with certainty in advance. The latter refers to uncertainty about relevant stakeholders' future status in the community and this induces greater concern about social efficiency. Stakeholders uncertain about the future forgo present distributional advantage in order to protect against the possibility of future harm (Brennan and Buchanan, 1985: 28–31). For example, the present owner of capital may try to design and influence an institution favouring capital owners, but may still be uncertain about his future position in society. Teachers, though they are unlikely to become students again themselves, may have children likely to become students, and this may affect their judgement on a variety of institutions in the educational sphere. The stakeholders in the two above examples operate behind a veil of ignorance; see Rawls (1971: 153–4).

Third, institutions may be conceived so as to have *cross-cutting effects*. An asymmetry is cross-cutting if 'each individual will sometimes find himself on one side of the asymmetry and sometimes on the other'. For instance, if one has two children and one has to divide a piece of cake (or land) between them, one can give the first child the right to cut the cake (the land) in two and the right of first choice to the second child. As a result, the first child can be expected to cut the cake nearly exactly in two equal parts. Also ongoing transactions in repeated interactions produce self-enforcing effects (cf. the tit for tat strategy in prisoners' dilemma situations), since the asymmetries may be cross-cutting. Once party A defects from an agreed upon strategy, party B will also defect. As long as party A plays the coordinated strategy (that is the optimal one), party B will also play the coordinated strategy.

Fourth, there is also competition among institutions and policy outcomes. Some authors, especially those who believe in a theory of spontaneous emergence, argue that institutions (sets of rules) may be subject to some sort of natural selection, following an evolutionary or Darwinian process, whereby only the most efficient solutions (institutions) survive. For example, firms wanting to invest in a new factory can freely decide in which state or region to settle, taking into account the set of institutions they consider to be optimal for their business. A person who wants to practise his profession can, in some cases, choose between alternative 'sets of rules', that is, he can decide to settle as a self-employed person or become employed by employer X as a salaried worker. In the context of project evaluation, one can decide to carry out an SCBA only, or an MCA only or an environmental impact assessment (EIA) only. Alternatively, one can also adopt a combined or 'eclectic' evaluation framework. As regards project implementation, there may be competition among various scenarios, such as implementation by the state, or various forms of public–private partnerships.

Fifth, if a (formal) *procedure for effective compensation* of the disadvantaged stakeholders exists, this may reduce the distributional advantage that powerful, strategically positioned stakeholders may obtain in practice. Under such conditions, the tendency of the latter to influence institutions, giving them a disproportionate advantage (before compensation), is likely to be neutralized.

Although a number of mechanisms constraining rent-seeking behaviour by powerful stakeholders have been identified above, some 'economic rents' or distributional skewness may still persist. The problem is that the mechanisms identified above often may not be sufficiently strong. For example, transaction costs may act as a two-edged sword and may even result in persisting distributional asymmetries. Since actors negatively affected by an existing institution also face transaction costs when attempting to change that institution, they may refrain from doing so, as long as the distributional disadvantage for them is not too high. This may explain the persistence of at least some economic discrimination against women, disabled persons and persons of colour in many advanced Western economies. As regards cross-cutting asymmetries, stakeholders enjoying a powerful position may be able to hold on to the related advantages (or 'economic rent') by applying the rules inconsistently. For example, some organizations act as both buyers and sellers, but when they act as a buyer they may require their suppliers to engage in competitive bidding, whereas they attempt to avoid competition when they act as the seller. One example is that of the banks, which simultaneously act as lender and borrower. In many countries, when they act as a lender, they are successful in charging interest for the whole duration of the loan, first day and last day included. However, when acting as borrowers, they do not pay interest for the first and last day of the period. As regards the competition argument, it should be noted that there are fundamental differences between ordinary goods competing for the consumer's favour and institutions, so that the process of natural selection is not straightforward in practice.

The problem of rent-seeking behaviour also occurs when adopting the neoclassical paradigm, particularly in SCBA applications. The difference with the institutional approach is that rent-seeking behaviour is less visible and more implicit in SCBA applications, given the intertwined monetization of effects, scores and weights, and the amalgamation of results into a single, synthetic (bottom-line) criterion, such as the NPV or the profitability index. This synthetic mono-criterion may be associated with 'false simplicity', whereas in the neo-institutional approach, especially in MCA, the decision hierarchy and its constituent elements (such as objectives, sub-objectives, criteria and actions), which need to be integrated using the pairwise comparison mechanism may be viewed as the expression of 'ordered complexity'. In the world of 'ordered complexity', distributional effects of institutional change (such as policy measures or projects) are easier to control, for example, through extensive sensitivity analysis, whereby specific points of view or stakeholder interests can be emphasized. Opponents of MCA could argue that the weighing of policy goals by policy makers is not sufficiently objective. However, this objectivity is not achieved in SCBA either, since the weighing of policy goals or effects in the latter method is based implicitly on compensation criteria, which are just as subjective as MCA-based weighing procedures, and scores used in SCBA are based on individual values as expressed by the consumer's willingness-to-pay. In fact, Forman and Selly (2001: 25), quoting Saaty, argue that objectivity is nothing more than 'agreed upon subjectivity'. Since every important decision has more than one objective and since the relative importance of the objectives is subjective, the only thing that is possible is 'agreed upon subjectivity' or 'subjectivity made objective'. In addition, in the neo-institutional approach, one extra element, a sixth constraint preventing distributional bias as a result of rent-seeking behaviour, is added, namely the presence of the state, which can act as a network hub (or forum) for institution building and change.

The *interests of the state* are indeed an important element in processes of institutional change, since the *state may act as a network hub for such change*. A centralized process or a process initiated by a central agency can simplify the collective-action selection problems as compared to a decentralized process. The final decision itself, however, is not necessarily centralized, only the process is initiated and coordinated by a centrally located agency. The state can act as a network hub to organize the various stakeholders engaged in collective action. In that way, the costs associated with achieving the stakeholders' goals can be reduced. The state can also enhance the bargaining power of the stakeholders disfavoured by prevailing institutions. But relying on the state is a two-edged sword. On the one hand, formal rules imposed by the state may constrain stakeholder actions. On the other hand, such rules may enhance stakeholder bargaining power, especially of weaker actors in the bargaining process, because they are given a place in the forum of stakeholders. The introduction of a third party (an enforcer or simply the state) in a process of establishment of rules can protect weaker stakeholders in various ways, namely through (1) protecting free association; (2) establishing rules or criteria for recognizing the bargaining rights of specific stakeholder groups (for example, unions in collective bargaining processes between management and workers); (3) establishing recognition procedures, and so on. J. Knight (1998: 203) argues that poorly organized stakeholders typically turn to the state for formal protection, whereas powerful stakeholders prefer to negotiate in an unconstrained market. This explains, *inter alia*, why states with lower union membership have more formal rules in this respect. In highly unionized countries, unions typically prefer more informal rules as the basis of labour negotiations. A similar argument is applicable in the context of large-scale infrastructure decisions in most developed economies. Here, the trade-off from the government's perspective is either to design very restrictive rules that protect local communities and ecosystems against the externalities created as a result of new infrastructure development or, alternatively, to let powerful environmental protection groups mobilize against project developers, thereby reducing the need for formal rules.

Although the state may be successful in enhancing the power of weak stakeholders, a number of problems may remain in this respect. First, the state itself consists of various constituencies, including politicians, civil servants, voters, members of political parties and pressure groups, each acting as a fully rational *homo oeconomicus*, that is, each maximizing to the fullest extent possible their individual self-interest, as described extensively in the public-choice literature (Buchanan, 1967; Niskanen, 1971: 36ff; 1975: 619ff; 1994: 273ff). Second, stakeholders representing a higher number of voters may command more influence on politicians, since they represent a larger part of the electorate. As an example, policemen, railway personnel, nurses and physicians often obtain extra compensation for work performed at night or during weekends, whereas teachers or educators seldom do. The reason is that in the former categories of workers, close to 100 per cent engage in night work and weekend work, whereas in the latter category the individuals affected represent a very small category. This phenomenon is known as the Matthew-effect. Third, median-voter interests are more likely to influence policy decisions than more extreme or atypical interests. Extreme or atypical proposals normally will not obtain a majority. Only when such proposals move towards the median proposal, may a majority be obtained, since the proposal close to the median proposal will then be supported by the median voters and by at least one of both extremums in the distribution. Because of the problems identified above, it is therefore of utmost importance to have a good and solid constitution, as well as universal freedoms protecting the rights of minorities, fostering pluralism and banning discrimination. The role of education may also be of great importance, as that may foster awareness and enhance effective participation of all stakeholders in decision-making processes.

Finally, the role of *sensitivity analysis* should not be underestimated. Sensitivity and scenario analysis may play an important role in detecting significant distributional consequences. Sensitivity analysis can be performed to identify the impact of changing policy weights. For example, one can change the weights corresponding to a specific stakeholder and observe whether this would have a substantial impact on the final outcome. If there is no such substantial influence, one can conclude that the solution is distributionally neutral. If there is substantial influence, then this issue should be analysed in more depth. Most often, in MCA, substantial sensitivity analyses are performed.

To conclude, the excessive power of some stakeholders may be counterbalanced when each stakeholder effectively participates in the decision-making process; and even if one stakeholder is more powerful than the other, a number of constraints, as described above, will prevent stakeholders from abusing their position. The state acts as a network hub to provide and organize a forum for stakeholder discussion and debate, that is, a forum for balancing stakeholders' power and to ensure that each stakeholder group has equal rights and opportunities to let its views be known. The role of the state as a network hub also consists of further investigating possible distributional consequences of policy measures (for example, through extensive sensitivity analysis in MCA). The neo-institutional approach has the advantage that the conflicting interests among stakeholders become more explicit ('ordered complexity') and that they can, therefore, be better controlled or monitored. As is the case with democracy, the collective benefit of this approach does not result from the individual actions of stakeholders; rather, it is a by-product of a process whereby individual stakeholders (or political parties in the case of democracy) pursue their own, selfish ends. None of these parties or stakeholders pursues the collective benefit, but when taken all together, acting in a pluralistic forum, the collective benefit may eventually arise as a by-product of this process. The output of this process may be viewed as 'agreed upon subjectivity' or 'subjectivity made objective'. A parallel can also be drawn with markets. Individual participants in markets (producers and consumers) pursue their own selfish ends (for example, profits), but when considering all their actions together, an optimum may emerge as a by-product, provided that the price mechanism works efficiently, and that power asymmetries and other market imperfections do not arise.

4. THE ECLECTIC MULTI-CRITERIA ANALYSIS: AN INSTITUTIONALLY DRIVEN EVALUATION TOOL COMBINING MULTI-CRITERIA ANALYSIS AND SOCIAL COST–BENEFIT ANALYSIS

4.1. The Design of the Eclectic Multi-criteria Analysis

In the previous sections, we discussed SCBA and MCA, especially with regard to their institutional foundations. In SCBA, only monetizable effects are taken into account. The outcome of SCBA is one of synthesis, namely net benefits per invested monetary unit are calculated. MCA is sometimes viewed as an imperfect SCBA, since a number of effects have not been monetized. MCA, however, makes it possible to take into account a wide variety of effects, including non-monetizable effects. MCA enables ordering the complexity inherent in most decision-making processes, while SCBA can be seen as providing false simplicity (since the final outcome is synthesized into a single criterion). Stakeholders' interests are properly addressed in MCA. The decision-making process is viewed as a learning process. The final outcome of an MCA may lead to stability (that is, an equilibrium situation) and reduce conflict. From this perspective, SCBA could be considered as an imperfect MCA.

Because both evaluation methods can be viewed as imperfect when applied in isolation, they are often applied in parallel. In practice, several studies are usually conducted for the socio-economic appraisal of large infrastructure projects, namely an SCBA, an environmental impact assessment (EIA), a macro-economic impact study (MEIS) and an MCA. In that case, decision-makers are confronted with a large number of studies, whose results may be conflicting. This, in turn, may paralyse the decision-making process, if no formal procedure was established for integrating these studies. One of the first attempts to integrate the various conflicting evaluation frameworks was made by De Brucker (2000: 245ff), who developed an 'eclectic' evaluation framework called 'eclectic multi-criteria analysis' or 'EMCA'.

The 'EMCA method' is called 'eclectic', since it extracts from specific existing (and sometimes conflicting) evaluation methods those elements most suitable and sufficiently compatible to form the building blocks of a new, integrative evaluation method. An eclectic approach is usually guided by practical motives and adopts what seems most plausible from the various conflicting systems. An eclectic approach does not require logical consistency among the various doctrines/individual evaluation tools with one another. In addition, the EMCA method is also a 'multi-criteria analysis' since MCA serves as the anchoring framework for the integration of the relevant constituent parts. Within this anchoring framework, the method of the analytic hierarchy process (AHP) of Saaty (1977, 1986, 1988 and 1995) plays an important role.

An example of the EMCA method as applied to the Seine-Scheldt link project (see also De Brucker, 2000: 245ff) is described below. In a first stage, all project alternatives are screened in terms of their 'musts' in a so-called 'pre-MCA'. Musts are minimal (or satisficing) levels that must be achieved, as a 'conditio sine qua non', for a project to be considered acceptable to all stakeholders. These musts can be related to parameters such as specific environmental standards (for example, minimization of specific negative external effects such as CO_2 emissions), as well as to the requirement that at least a positive net present value is achieved in the SCBA. As soon as the projects pass the pre-MCA test, an analysis in terms of 'wants'[2] (that is 'aspiration levels' or objectives to be maximized) is applied in the second stage. To this end, a hierarchy is constructed in the EMCA method, as is the case in the AHP method. An example of such a hierarchy as applied to the Seine-Scheldt project is given in Figure 3.3. This hierarchy is constructed using both a bottom-up approach and a top-down approach. In the bottom-up approach, all relevant effects of the infrastructure project are identified and clustered into homogeneous sub-groups and groups, so as to facilitate useful comparisons between these groups in a next stage. In the Seine-Scheldt example described in Figure 3.3, a group of monetized socio- and macro-economic effects are identified, next to a group of non-monetized environmental and safety effects, a group of social effects and finally effects on the internal market and competitive ability (level 2). These groups are split up into sub-groups (at level 3 and 4) that include more specific effects, such as investment and maintenance costs, benefits resulting from economies of scale, benefits related to extra capacity, sustainable value added, effects on landscape, fauna and flora, soil, and so on. On a lower level, these effects are measured using specific criteria (at level 5 or 6).

In the top-down approach, a general objective or focus (shown at level 1) is subdivided into sub-objectives (level 2) and its constituent parts

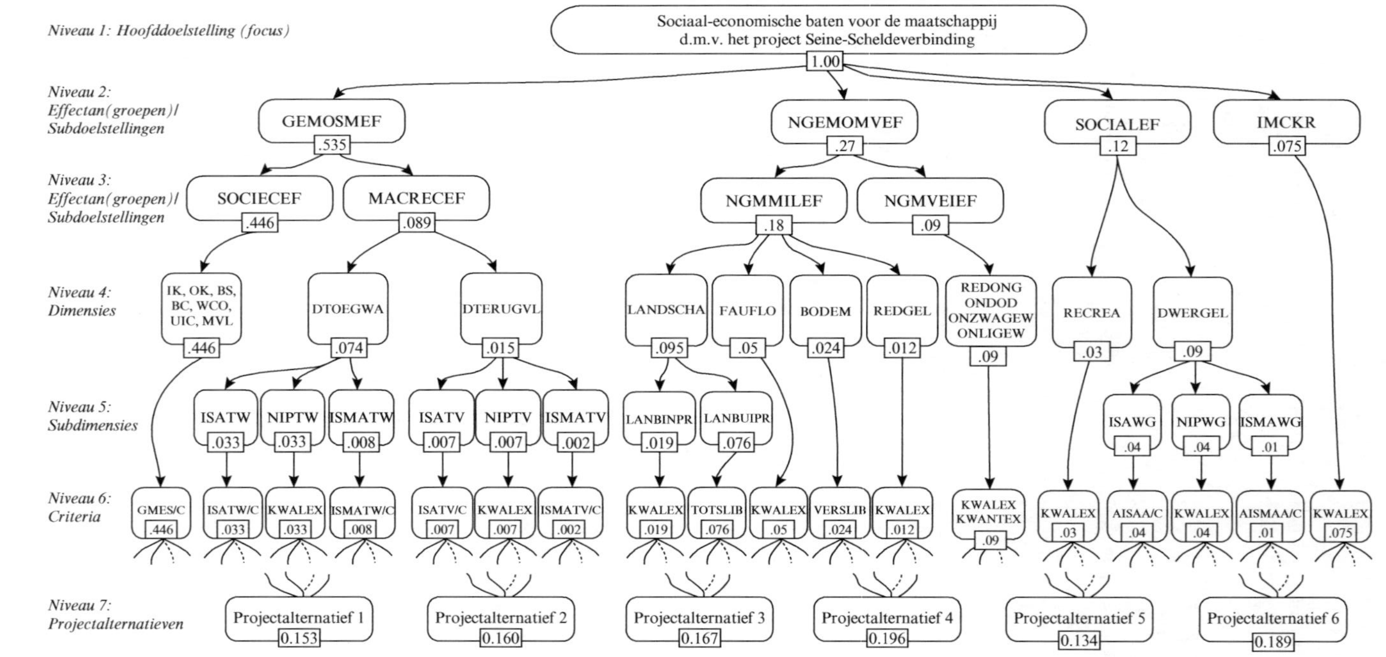

Note: See facing page

Source: De Brucker (2000: 346)

Figure 3.3 Decision hierarchy for the Seine-Scheldt project

EXPLANATION OF THE ELEMENTS INCLUDED IN FIGURE 3.3

Niveau (level) 1:	***Hoofddoelstelling of focus (Main objective or focus) (Creation of socio-economic benefits for society through the Seine-Scheldt project)***
Niveau (level) 2:	***Effecten(groepen)/Subdoelstellingen. (Group of effects/sub-objectives)***
GEMOSMEF :	Gemonetariseerde socio- en macro-economische effecten *(Monetized socio- and macro-economic effects)*
NGEMOMVEF :	Niet-gemonetariseerde milieu- en veiligheidseffecten *(Non-monetized environmental and safety effects)*
SOCIALEF :	Sociale effecten *(Social effects)*
IMCKR :	Gevolgen voor de interne markt en de concurrentiekracht *(Effects on internal market and competitive ability)*
Niveau (level) 3:	***Effecten(groepen)/Sub-doelstellingen – componenten) (Group of effects/subobjectives – components)***
SOCIECEF :	Socio-economische effecten *(Socio-economic effects)*
MACRECEF :	Macro-economische effecten *(Macro-economic effects)*
NGMMILEF :	Niet-gemonetariseerde milieueffecten *(Non-monetized environmental effects)*
NGMVEIEF :	Niet-gemonetariseerde veiligheidseffecten *(Non-monetized safety effects)*
Niveau (level) 4:	***Dimensies (Dimensions)***
IK :	Investeringskost voor de overheid *(Investment cost for government)*
OK :	Onderhoudskost voor de overheid *(Maintenance cost for government)*
BS :	Baat door schaalvergroting *(Benefit resulting from economies of scale)*
BC :	Baat door capaciteitsverhoging *(Benefit related to increased capacity)*
WCO :	Werkgelegenheid bij constructie en onderhoud *(Employment during construction and maintenance)*
UIC :	Uitgestelde internalisering externe kosten v.h. wegvervoer op het vlak van congestie *(Delayed internalization of external costs of road traffic related to congestion)*
MVL :	Milieubaat door vermijding luchtvervuiling *(Environmental benefit resulting from reduced air pollution)*
DTOEGWA :	Duurzame toegevoegde waarde *(Sustainable value added)*
DTERUGVL :	Duurzame terugvloei naar de overheid *(Sustainable backflow to government)*
LANDSCHA :	Visuele landschapsbeïnvloeding *(Visual impact on landscape)*
FAUFLO :	Impact op de fauna en flora *(Impact on fauna and flora)*
BODEM :	Impact op de kwaliteit van de bodem *(Impact on quality of soil)*
REDGEL :	Reductie van het geluidsniveau *(Reduction of noise level)*
REDONG :	Reductie van het aantal ongevallen *(Reduction in number of accidents)*
ONDOD :	Dodelijke ongevallen *(Fatal accidents)*
ONZWAGEW :	Ongevallen met zwaargewonden *(Serious injury accidents)*
ONLIGEW :	Ongevallen met lichtgewonden *(Slight injury accidents)*
RECREA :	Impact op de recreatiemogelijkheden *(Impact on recreation facilities)*
DWERGEL :	Duurzame werkgelegenheid *(Sustainable value added)*
Niveau (level) 5:	***Subdimensies, gesplitst (sub-dimensions, split)***
ISATW :	Isoleerbare structureel aantrekkelijke toegevoegde waarde (*Value added that can be isolated from other value added and that is considered structurally attractive*)
NIPTW :	Niet-isoleerbare potentiële toegevoegde waarde (*Value added that is only potential and which cannot be isolated from the other value added*)

ISMATW : Isoleerbare structureel minder aantrekkelijke toegevoegde waarde *(Value added that can be isolated from the other value added but which is to be considered less attractive from a structural point of view)*

ISATV : Isoleerbare structureel aantrekkelijke terugvloei naar de overheid *(Backflow to government that can be isolated from other backflow and that is considered structurally attractive)*

NIPTV : Niet-isoleerbare potentiële terugvloei naar de overheid *(Backflow to government that is only potential and which cannot be isolated from other backflow)*

ISMATV : Isoleerbare structureel minder aantrekkelijke terugvloei naar de overheid *(Backflow to government that can be isolated from other backflow but which is to be considered less attractive from a structural point of view)*

LANBINPRO : Visuele landschapsbeïnvloeding binnen de projectomgeving *(Visual impact on landscape within the project area)*

LANBUIPRO : Visuele landschapsbeïnvloeding buiten de projectomgeving *(Visual impact on landscape outside the project area)*

ISAWG : Isoleerbare structureel aantrekkelijke werkgelegenheid *(Employment that can be isolated from other employment effects and that is considered structurally attractive)*

NIPWG : Niet-isoleerbare potentiële werkgelegenheid *(Employment that is only potential and which cannot be isolated from other employment effects)*

ISMAWG : Isoleerbare structureel minder aantrekkelijke werkgelegenheid *(Employment that can be isolated from other employment effects but which is to be considered less attractive from a structural point of view)*

Niveau (level) 6 : ***Criteria***

GMESC/C : Gemonetariseerde-effectensynthesecriterium per budgeteenheid (C) (van 1 BEF of 1 EURO) *(Monetized effects synthetic criterion per budgetary unit of 1 BEF or 1 EURO)*

ISATW/C : *ISATW per budgetary unit of 1 BEF or 1 EURO*

KWALEX : Kwalitatieve informatie, die via het oordeel van experten, d.m.v. het paarsgewijze-vergelijkingsmechanisme, in de algemene evaluatie wordt geïntegreerd *(Qualitative information which was integrated into the overall evaluation through expert judgement using the pairwise comparison mechanism)*

ISMATW/C : *ISMATW per budgetary unit of 1 BEF or 1 EURO*

ISATV/C : *ISATV per budgetary unit of 1 BEF or 1 EURO*

ISMATV/C : *ISMATV per budgetary unit of 1 BEF or 1 EURO*

TOTSLIB : Totaal aantal kubieke meter slib (projectgebonden, verontreinigd en niet-verontreinigd samen) dat extern moet worden geborgen *(Total amount of cubic metre silt to be stored [related to the project, polluted and non-polluted together])*

VERSLIB : Aantal kubieke meter verontreinigd slib dat extern moet worden geborgen (projectgebonden) *(Total amount of cubic metre polluted silt to be stored [related to the project])*

KWANTEX Kwantitatieve informatie, die via het oordeel van experten, d.m.v. het paarsgewijze-vergelijkingsmechanisme, in de algemene evaluatie wordt geïntegreerd *(Quantitative information which was integrated into the overall evaluation through expert judgement using the pairwise comparison mechanism)*

AISAA/C : Aantal isoleerbare structureel aantrekkelijke arbeidsplaatsen per budgeteenheid (C) (in manjaar per mioBEF) *(Number of jobs that can be isolated from the other effects on employment and that are*

	considered attractive from a structural point of view, expressed per budgetary unit of 1 BEF or 1 EURO)
AISMAA/C :	Aantal isoleerbare structureel minder aantrekkelijke arbeidsplaatsen per budgeteenheid (C) (in manjaar per mioBEF) *(Number of jobs that can be isolated from the other effects on employment and that are considered less attractive from a structural point of view, expressed per budgetary unit of 1 BEF or 1 EURO)*
Niveau (level) 7 :	***Projectalternatieven (Project alternatives)***
P_1 :	*Lys: two-way traffic. Upper Sea Scheldt: two-way traffic + tide independent*
P_2 :	*Lys: two-way traffic. Upper Sea Scheldt: two-way traffic + tide dependent*
P_3 :	*Lys: one-way traffic. Upper Sea Scheldt: two-way traffic + tide independent*
P_4 :	*Lys: one-way traffic. Upper Sea Scheldt: two-way traffic + tide dependent*
P_5 :	*Lys: two-way traffic. Upper Sea Scheldt: one-way traffic + tide dependent*
P_6 :	*Lys: one-way traffic. Upper Sea Scheldt: one-way traffic + tide dependent*

(levels 3 and following). The final project alternatives are listed at the lowest level (level 7). Relative priorities (and their associated consistency ratios) are derived for each sub-system in the hierarchy using the pairwise comparison mechanism of the AHP method (as described in Tables 3.2 and 3.3). As regards the comparison of the final project alternatives (at level 7) in terms of their contribution to the criteria mentioned at level 6, this pairwise mechanism is applied only for those criteria for which a cardinal value function cannot readily be constructed by the analyst. In that case, the value function is approached indirectly, using qualitative expert judgements which are further processed using the pairwise comparison mechanism of the AHP. Finally, the overall (or global) relative priorities (as well as the associated overall consistency ratio) for the alternatives (listed at level 7) are obtained in the same way as described in section 2.3.B in fine. The various techniques of sensitivity analysis available in standard MCA can also be applied here. This approach can be compared to the Cartesian method (Descartes, [1637] 1987: 21ff), because a decision problem is subdivided into its smallest and most simple elements (*casu quo* the effects of project alternatives) on the basis of which policy objectives are developed. In a subsequent step, the unity of the policy problem is restored, beginning by integrating the simplest elements or the elements one understands best.

It is clear that the EMCA method fits well with a stakeholder orientation. The decision-making process is decomposed into its constituent parts. A decision is then constructed step by step, by making pairwise comparisons. This is done through a learning process whereby the specific interests of stakeholders are integrated. In addition, this approach also allows integrating qualitative and quantitative data. The degree of conflict between objectives or stakeholders can be analysed through extensive sensitivity analysis.

4.2. Some Real-life Applications of the Eclectic Multi-criteria-analysis

This section describes very briefly the application of the theory and methods developed in the former sections of this chapter to two real-life projects, namely a Belgian-French project called the Seine-Scheldt link and a European project called ADVISORS. Other examples are given in further chapters of this book.

A. The Seine-Scheldt link

The EMCA method was first developed by De Brucker (2000: 245ff) and was applied to the Belgian component of the Seine-Scheldt link. This project aims at establishing a better waterway link between the North Sea ports located in the Scheldt basin (Antwerp, Zeebrugge, Ghent and Ostend) on the one hand and the project Seine-Nord on the other hand. This will be achieved by upgrading existing rivers or canals such as the Upper Sea Scheldt (that is, the river Scheldt between Antwerp and Ghent), the river Lys in Belgium and the Canal du Nord or the Canal de Saint-Quentin for the French part of the project (called 'Seine-Nord'). By establishing this link, a substantial modal shift from road traffic to waterborne traffic may be initiated, reducing external effects such as congestion and air pollution. Both projects (the Seine-Scheldt link and the project Seine-Nord) are part of the policy of the European Union regarding Trans-European Networks for Transport (TEN-T). An SCBA, as well as an environmental impact assessment (EIA), were conducted for this project. The EMCA framework was then applied to integrate the results from the SCBA, the EIA and a limited macro-economic impact study (MEIS). In total, six project alternatives were considered. These project alternatives were generated by combining some specific design parameters such as the possibility to navigate tide-independently on the Upper Sea Scheldt, the possible traffic in both directions for ships of 4500 tons on the river Lys and/or on the Upper Sea Scheldt as well. The first project alternative (P_1) had a maximalistic view presenting possible traffic in both directions and tide-independently on all sections. This alternative was associated with the highest investment cost (about €265 000 000 not actualized). The last project alternative (P_6) was the expression of a minimalist view, whereby traffic would only be possible tide-dependently on the Upper Sea Scheldt and in one single direction only, and on the river Lys. This alternative was associated with the lowest investment cost (about €125 000 000 not actualized). The intermittent project alternatives (P_2,...,P_5) were compromise variants between the maximalist and the minimalist project alternatives. In these intermittent alternatives, either traffic for ships up to 4500 tons was restrained to one-way traffic (either on the Lys or on the Upper Sea Scheldt) and/or to tide-dependent traffic on the Upper Sea Scheldt.

For this project, a hierarchy was constructed, showing the causal relationships between the constituent elements (as shown in Figure 3.3). Relative priorities were derived as described in section 2.3.B in fine. Finally a consistency check was also made and a substantial sensitivity and scenario analysis were performed.

Both in the basic scenario and alternative scenarios, the project alternative P_4 obtained the highest relative priority. This alternative was in fact a compromise between the maximalist and the minimalist views (respectively P_1 and P_6) and consisted of one-way traffic on the river Lys and two-way traffic on the Upper Sea Scheldt, but tide-dependent on the latter river. This result is interesting since it shows that a project alternative (in this case P_4), which obtains a relative advantage vis-à-vis the other alternatives on criteria for which the evaluation was performed through expert judgement based on qualitative information (and using pairwise comparisons), is preferred to a project alternative that would have been chosen if only monetized effects were taken into consideration (that is, P_6). In addition, extensive sensitivity analysis and scenario analysis showed that the relative priority of the alternative ranked first (P_4) was stable, both in the basic and in the alternative scenarios. The only difference was that in the basic scenario P_4 was followed by the maximalist or the quasi-maximalist project alternatives (P_1 and P_2 respectively), whereas in the alternative scenarios, P_4 was followed by the minimalist project alternative (P_6). The alternative scenarios studied consisted of, for example, a scenario with emphasis on the Flemish interests (that is the stakeholder corresponding to the ministry of the Flemish region), a network scenario (with emphasis on the creation of the Trans-European network and the interests of the Flemish ports), a scenario with emphasis on inter-regional development (extra emphasis on criteria related to the creation of value added) and a green scenario (with emphasis on environmental effects). The fact that the relative priority of the project alternative P_4 was stable in all scenarios shows that the distributional effects of implementing this project are very small.

B. The ADVISORS project

Another example where the methodology described in this chapter was applied, is the ADVISORS[3] project, an EU-funded project within the Fifth Framework for Research and Development. One work package of this large-scale pan-European study was carried out by De Brucker et al. (2002), even though only a very brief synthesis of the main results of that study is given in this section. The authors' contribution to that research project consisted of evaluating and prioritizing the different technologies called ADAS (advanced driver assistance programmes) from a strategic perspective, taking into account both their technical implementation potential and their value added to the objectives of a wide variety of stakeholders, within the context of various scenarios (possible evolution of relevant parameters in the external environment). A decision hierarchy, representing the various criteria and the stakeholders' interests was constructed as shown in Figure 3.4. Some of the key systems analysed included, *inter alia*, adaptive cruise control (ACC) such as urban stop-and-go, intelligent speed adaptation (ISA), lateral support (LS), driver monitoring systems (DMS), navigation and lane departure warning. The results of this study should be seen as an input for European innovation policy, which aims to stimulate the development of strategic new technologies, and can be usefully informed by the implementation priorities determined in that study.

Within the scope of that research project, a substantial number of stakeholder analyses were conducted, as well as a series of technical performance studies such as driving simulations and field experiments. The sensitivity analysis and the scenario analysis yielded results that were comparable to a large extent, but the stakeholder analysis showed that neither users nor manufacturers are in favour of mandatory ISA systems. Mandatory ISA systems receive, however, a high priority from a societal

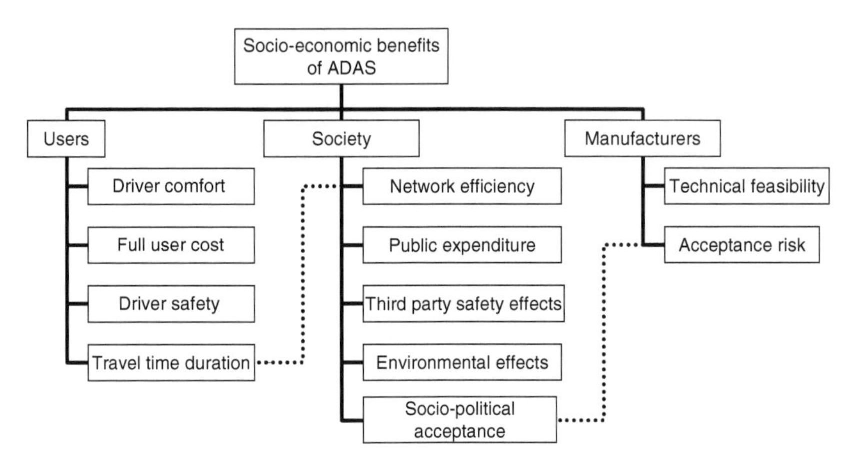

Source: De Brucker et al. (2002: 81)

Figure 3.4 Decision hierarchy for the socio-economic benefits of ADAS

point of view, given the good score on the criterion regarding third party safety effects. It can therefore be concluded that if society would like to propagate the use of mandatory ISA, both substantial incentives and a media campaign may be necessary.

C. The infrastructure and safety (IN-SAFETY) project

The European Commission services recently (2005) commisioned a new pan-European study on road safety. It involves 31 partners (including the authors of this chapter) from 12 different European countries. In this study, priorities will be derived and implementation scenarios established for projects that contribute to making the road environment 'forgiving' (that is, mitigating the effects of actual driver errors) and 'self-explaining' (that is, designing roads that elicit 'correct' expectations from road users). This research project will also identify relevant stakeholder groups and rank the different tools or technologies in terms of their contribution to various stakeholder objectives as measured by specific criteria. The research for this project will be completed in 2008.

5. CONCLUSIONS

In this chapter, we have contrasted two competing economics paradigms, namely the neoclassical paradigm and the neo-institutional paradigm, especially in terms of their implications for the evaluation of investment projects and policy measures. We have also compared two widely used evaluation methods, namely social cost–benefit analysis (SCBA) and multi-criteria analysis (MCA). The former is an evaluation tool, grounded in neoclassical economics, especially neo-Paretian welfare economics, whereas the latter has its roots in a different discipline, namely operations research. We have demonstrated, however, that MCA can be a useful tool in economics-driven project evaluation, especially when a neo-institutional approach to project evaluation is adopted. From this perspective, MCA is closely linked to the (neo-)institutional paradigm in economics. Indeed, the systematic application of MCA can be viewed as an 'institution in action', capable of resolving societal conflicts (that is creating 'institutional equilibria'), by making the distributional challenges more explicit and providing satisfactory responses to the needs and objectives of various stakeholder groups ('ordered complexity'). Important decisions always entail multiple objectives and weighing these objectives through MCA makes it possible to obtain 'agreed upon subjectivity' or 'subjectivity made objective'. However, taking into account stakeholder preferences does not imply anarchy. The formal use of MCA avoids the paralysing

'United Nations' approach to stakeholder management, whereby each stakeholder perspective is given equal weight, and conflicts cannot be resolved due to a lack of selectivity. The United Nations approach may be useful for variety generation but not for selection. Nevertheless, the presence of at least some level of conflict in policy processes may be beneficial, to the extent that such conflict can be managed effectively, for example, through adopting MCA, since this enhances creativity, value-focused thinking and learning.

A variety of strategically positioned stakeholders may attempt to capture a disproportionate distributional advantage through 'rent-seeking behaviour'. Fortunately, the presence of transaction costs, uncertainty, cross-cutting effects, competition and state intervention may, to a certain extent, neutralize such rent-seeking behaviour. Competition among stakeholders may ultimately (and unintentionally) serve the public good or collective benefit, but sometimes, government must act as a network hub for institutional change and thereby provide a countervailing power against the excessive bargaining strength of powerful, strategically positioned stakeholders seeking to obtain a disproportionate distributional advantage. However, state intervention does act as a two-edged sword, constraining and liberating at the same time.

We have also demonstrated in the chapter that neoclassical welfare economics in general and SCBA in particular, are characterized by a number of institutional elements, which, however, remain implicit. With SCBA, policy weights and scores are intertwined and synthesized into one single criterion or score such as the net present value or the profitability index (providing 'false simplicity'). Therefore, it makes sense to complement SCBA with an MCA, or to integrate both approaches into an overall or 'eclectic' approach, in which SCBA and monetized effects constitute a core component. The components included in the MCA may vary in function of the degree of complexity of the relevant effects and the number and the heterogeneity of the stakeholders involved. The EMCA method (eclectic multi-criteria analysis) developed by De Brucker (2000: 245ff) and briefly reported in this chapter permits integrating both approaches. It is especially useful for decision-makers confronted with different studies yielding conflicting results. The EMCA method makes it possible to order the conflicting information and to synthesize it following a structured process ('ordered complexity'). The outcome is 'agreed upon subjectivity' or 'subjectivity made objective'. It is especially useful for the so-called 'swollen middle', that is projects where important non-monetized (or MCA-like) effects need to be included in the analysis, in addition to monetized (or SCBA-like) effects. Depending upon the relative importance of the monetized and non-monetized parameters in this mix, the EMCA could either be reduced to a simple SCBA (whereby only monetized effects are important) or consist of solely non-monetized effects (at least at the benefits side); in practice it will usually remain in the 'swollen middle' between these two extremes.

NOTES

1. The difference between the institutional approach and neoclassical welfare economics is that in the latter approach rent-seeking behaviour is viewed as an exception, occurring only when markets are imperfect (for example, in the case of a monopoly), whereas in the former approach, rent-seeking behaviour and imperfect markets are considered normal phenomena. Perfect markets leading to equilibria are viewed as the exception in the institutional approach.
2. The idea of 'musts' and 'wants' was developed by Kepner and Tregoe (1965: 173ff; 1981: 87–8 and 181) and is similar to the 'elimination-by-aspects method', an MCA method developed by Tversky (1972: 281–99) and Noorderhaven (1995: 32). Forman (1996: 48) and Forman and Selly (2001: 111) also acknowledge the distinction between 'musts' and 'wants'.
3. 'ADVISORS' is the abbreviation of 'Action for advanced Driver assistance and Vehicle control systems Implementation, Standardisation, Optimum use of the Road network and Safety'. This large-scale pan-European research project was co-funded by the European Commission Directorate-General for Transport and Energy, under the Fifth Framework programme for Research and Development (Competitive and Sustainable Growth Programme). The research consortium for this project consisted of 16 partners from 10 different European countries.

REFERENCES

Anderson, L.G. and R.F. Settle (1979), *Benefit–Cost Analysis: A Practical Guide*, Lexington, Toronto: Lexington Books.

Belton, V. and Th. Stewart (2002), *Multiple Criteria Decision Analysis. An Integrated Approach*, Boston and Dordrecht: Kluwer Academic Publishers.

Bergson, A. (1938), 'A reformulation of certain aspects of welfare economics', *Quarterly Journal of Economics*, **52**, 310–34.

Blaug, M. (1992), *The Methodology of Economics. Or how Economists explain*, Cambridge: Cambridge University Press.

Brennan, G. and J. Buchanan (1985), *The Reason of Rule*, Cambridge: Cambridge University Press.

Buchanan, J.M. (1967), *Public Finance in Democratic Process. Fiscal Institutions and Individual Choice*, Chapel Hill: The University of North Carolina Press.

Buchanan, J.M. (1975), *The Limits of Liberty: Between Anarchy and Leviathan*, Chicago and London: University of Chicago Press.

Charness, A. and W.W. Cooper (1961), *Management Models and Industrial Applications of Linear Programming*, New York: Wiley.

Commons, J. [1934](1959), *Institutional Economics, its Place in Political Economy*, Madison: The University of Wisconsin Press.

Condorcet, M.J.A.N. de Caritat (1785), '*Essai sur l'application de l'analyse à la probabilité des décisions rendues à la pluralité de voix*', Paris.

De Brucker, K. (2000), '*Ontwikkeling van een eclectisch evaluatie-instrument voor de sociaal-economische evaluatie van complexe investeringsprojecten, met een toepassing op het project Seine-Scheldeverbinding*', Antwerp: University of Antwerp (RUCA), PhD thesis.

De Brucker, K., A. Verbeke and W. Winkelmans (1998), *Sociaal-economische evaluatie van overheidsinvesteringen in transportinfrastructuur. Kritische analyse van het bestaande instrumentarium. Ontwikkeling van een eclectisch evaluatie-instrument*, Leuven: Garant.

De Brucker, K., C. Macharis, A. Verbeke and E. Bekiaris (2002), '*Integrated multicriteria analysis for advanced driver assistance systems*', Final Deliverable of the research project for the Shared-cost RTD project 'Action for advanced Driver assistance and Vehicle control systems Implementation, Standardisation, Optimum use of the Road network and Safety' (ADVISORS), within the 'Competitive and Sustainable Growth Programme (GROWTH)', contracted with the Commission of the European Union – Department Transport and Energy (DG TREN) in collaboration with the Belgian Institute for Road Safety (Belgisch Instituut voor de Verkeersveiligheid – BIVV), Brussels (also available online: (www.advisors.iao.fhg.de > Reports > Deliverables > D6.1: 'CBA criteria and methodology for ADAS assessment. Potential funding mechanisms and incentives', 140 pp.).

De Jong, M. and H. Geerlings (2003), 'Transport infrastructure. Exposing weaknesses in interactive planning: the remarkable return of comprehensive policy analysis in The Netherlands', *Journal of Impact Assessment and Project Appraisal*, **21**(4), 281–91.

Descartes, R. [1637](1987), *Discours de la méthode plus la dioptrique, les météores et la géometrie,* Corpus des œuvres de philosophie en langue française, Paris: Librairie Arthème Fayard.

Dupuit, J. (1844), 'De la mesure de l'utilité des travaux publics', *Annales des Ponts et Chaussées*, Paris: Ministère des Travaux Publics et des Transports.

Eijgenraam, C.J.J., C.C. Koopmans, P.J.G. Tang and A.C.P. (Nol)Verster (2000), *Evaluatie van infrastructuurprojecten; Leidraad voor kosten-batenanalyse, Onderzoeksprogramma Economische Effecten Infrastructuur, Part 1 (main report) and part 2 (capita selecta)*, The Hague: Ministry of Transport, Public Works and Water Management/Ministry of Economic Affairs.

Forman, E.H. (1996), 'Decision by objectives', working paper at *Sixth International Summer School on Multicriteria Decision Aid (MCDA), Methods, Application and Software (28.08.97–08.08.97)*, Turku (Abo), Finland.

Forman, E.H. and M.A. Selly (2001), *Decision by Objectives. How to Convince Others that you are Right*, New Jersey and London: World Scientific.

Frank, R.H. (1985), 'The demand for unobservable and other nonpositional goods', *American Economic Review*, **75**, 101–16.

Galbraith, J.K. (1958), *The Affluent Society*, Cambridge, MA: The Riverside Press and Boston: Houghton Mifflin Company.

Hayek, F.A. von (1973), *Law, Legislation and Liberty: a new Statement of the Liberal Principles of Justice and Political Economy. Volume 1: Rules and Order*, Chicago: University of Chicago Press.

Hicks, J.R. (1939), 'The foundations of welfare economics', *Economic Journal*, **49**(196), 696–712.

Hodgson, G.M. (1999), *Evolution and Institutions: on Evolutionary Economics and the Evolution of Economics*, Cheltenham, UK and Northampton, MA, USA: Edward Elgar.

Hume, D. [1739](1967), *A Treatise of Human Nature: being an Attempt to Introduce the Experimental Method of Reasoning into Moral Subjects*, Oxford: Clarendon Press.
Johansson-Stenman, O. (1998), 'On the problematic link between fundamental ethics and policy recommendations', *Journal of Economic Methodology*, **5**(2), 263–97.
Kaldor, N. (1939), 'Welfare comparisons of economics and interpersonal comparisons of utility', *Economic Journal*, **49**(195), 549–52.
Keeney, R. (1996), *Value-Focused Thinking. A Path to Creative Decisionmaking*, Cambridge, MA: Harvard University Press.
Keeney, R. and H. Raiffa (1993), *Decisions with Multiple Objectives. Preferences and Value Tradeoffs*, Cambridge: Cambridge University Press.
Kepner, C.H. and B.B. Tregoe (1965), *The Rational Manager: a Systematic Approach to Problem Solving and Decision Making*, New York: McGraw-Hill.
Kepner, C.H. and B.B. Tregoe (1981), *The New Rational Manager*, London: John Martin Publishing.
Klein, P. (1984), 'Institutionalist reflexions on the role of the public sector', *Journal of Economic Issues*, **18**(1), 45–68.
Knight, J. (1998), *Institutions and Social Conflict*, Cambridge: Cambridge University Press.
Mankiw, N.G. (2004), *Principles of Economics*, Mason: Thomson–South-Western.
Marshall, A. [1890](1922), *Principles of Economics*, London: Macmillan.
Menger C. [1883](1985), *Investigations into the Method of Social Sciences with Special Reference to Economics*, New York: New York University Press.
Mitchell W.C. (1969), *Types of Economic Theory: from Mercantilism to Institutionalism*, New York: Augustus M. Kelley Publishers.
Mullins, L.J. (2005), *Management and Organisational Behaviour*, Harlow: Prentice Hall, Pearson Education.
Myrdal, G. [1932](1963), *Das Politische Element in der Nationalökonomischen Doktrinbildung*, Hannover: Verlag für Literatur und Zeitgeschehen.
Niskanen, W.A. (1971), *Bureaucracy and Representative Government*, Chicago: Aldine-Atherton.
Niskanen, W.A. (1975), 'Bureaucrats and politicians', *Journal of Law and Economics*, **18**(3), pp. 617–43.
Niskanen, W.A. (1994), *Bureaucracy and Public Economics*, Aldershot, UK and Brookfield US: Edward Elgar.
Noorderhaven, N.G. (1995), *Strategic Decision Making*, Wokingham: Addison and Wesley.
North, D. (1990), *Institutions, Institutional Change and Economic History*, New York: Norton.
Pareto, V. (1927), *Manuel d'Economie Politique*, translation of the Italian 1906 edition by A. Bonet, review by the anthor, Paris: Giard.
Posner, R.A. (1987), 'The law and economics movement', *American Economic Review*, (77), 1–13.
Rawls J.A. (1971), *A Theory of Justice*, Cambridge: Harvard University Press.
Robbins, L. (1932), *An Essay on the Nature and the Significance of Economic Science*, London: MacMillan & Co.
Roy, B. (1968), 'Classement et choix en présence de points de vue multiples (la méthode Electre)', *Revue française d'Informatique et de Recherche Opérationnelle*, (8), 57–75.
Roy, B. (1985), *Méthodologie Multicritère d'Aide à la Décision*, Paris: Economica.

Roy, B. and D. Bouyssou (1993), *Aide Multicritère à la Décision: Méthodes et Cas*, Paris: Economica.
Saaty, T.L. (1977), 'A scaling method for priorities in hierarchical structures', *Journal of Mathematics and Psychology*, **15**, 234–81.
Saaty, T.L. (1986), 'Axiomatic foundation of the analytic hierarchy process', *Management Science*, **32**(7), 841–55.
Saaty, T.L. (1988), *The Analytic Hierarchy Process*, New York: McGraw-Hill.
Saaty, T.L. (1995), *Decision Making for Leaders. The Analytic Hierarchy Process for Decisions in a Complex World*, Pittsburgh: RWS Publications.
Samuelson, P.A. (1947), *Foundations of Economic Analysis*, Cambridge: Harvard University Press.
Schärlig, A. (1985), *Décider sur Plusieurs Critères*, Lausanne: Presses Polytechniques Romandes.
Schotter, A. (1981), *The Economic Theory of Social Institutions*, Cambridge: Cambridge University Press.
Self, P. (1975), *Econocrats and the Policy Process: the Politics and Philosophy of Cost–Benefit analysis*, London: The Macmillan Press.
Sen, A.K. (1987), *On Ethics and Economics*, Oxford and New York: Blackwell.
Steunenberg, B. (2001), *Institutionele Verandering*, Bussum: Coutinho.
Thaler, R.H. (1980), 'Toward a positive theory of consumer choice', *Journal of Economic Behavior and Organization*, (1), 39–60.
Tversky, A. (1972), 'Elimination by aspects', *Psychological Review*, **79**, 281–99.
Van Delft, A. and P. Nijkamp (1977), *Multi-criteria Analysis and Regional Decision-making*, Leiden: Martinus Nijhoff Social Sciences Division.
Van Hees, M. (2000), *Legal Reductionism and Freedom*, Dordrecht: Kluwer.
Veblen, T.B. (1899), *The Theory of the Leisure Class*, New York: MacMillan (re-edited by The Viking Press, 1965).
Veblen, T.B. (1919), *The Place of Science in Modern Civilisation and Other Essays*, New Brunswick and London: Transaction Publishers.
Vincke, Ph. (1989), *L'Aide Multicritère à la Décision*, Brussels: Editions de l'Université Libre de Bruxelles.

4. Socio-economic impact of transport policies: an institutional approach

Enrico Musso, Simona Sanguineti and Cécile Sillig

1. INTRODUCTION

The socio-economic impact of transport policies is becoming a key issue in transport economics. Major transport projects – namely in the infrastructure domain – cause substantial consequences and changes not only in the transport system, but in the economy, in the social context, as well as in the environment. Apart from the latter impact, whose assessment routines appear relatively easy to set up, both the economic and social impact are subject to assessment procedures which are often obscure to most stakeholders and even to decision-makers. The reliability and trustworthiness of these practices is often questioned, due to some well-known technical and methodological problems. Moreover, they seem to forget the institutional context in which the transport policy is expected to take place. Indeed, the close link between the institutional context and the transport system is often underestimated or just ignored. As a result, transport planning and policies happen to face a lack of consensus largely depending on the 'distance' between the technical routines for the socio-economic impact assessment on one side, and the community with its values, rules and institutions on the other side.

In this chapter we intend to focus on institutional aspects which should be considered in the techniques employed for assessing the socio-economic impact of transport projects and policies. Section 2 provides the key definitions and techniques in the assessment of socio-economic impact. Section 3 outlines the key concepts of institutionalism and its main achievements in the progress of economics. Section 4 highlights which issues in transport economics and policy appear to be closely related to the institutional context, with a special focus on new institutional issues in European transport governance, also related to the transition to post-industrial economy. Section 5 discusses some of the institutional and socio-economic limits of most common evaluation tools, such as cost–benefit analysis and multi-criteria analysis, and focuses on the negative consequences of the fact that these techniques fail to consider institutional aspects properly. Finally, section 6 provides some indications on innovative tools aiming at improving current techniques through forms of citizens' and stakeholders' participation in policy planning, and some suggestions for future research. It is our belief that a careful and suitable consideration of institutional features would allow a substantial improvement in the effectiveness of impact assessment and consequently of transport policies.

2. SOCIO-ECONOMIC IMPACT ASSESSMENT

The term 'impact' is intended as the scenario expected once a proposed project or intervention has been implemented. Therefore, the impact assessment aims at comparing (at least) two different situations, for example the one expected to occur once the project has been implemented and the option of no intervention (the so-called 'do-nothing' solution), in order to estimate the positive or negative effects of the project.

A number of different impacts can be considered, for example: fiscal, economic, demographic, social, transport, environmental impacts. Nevertheless, they are usually grouped into three main categories: economic, social and environmental impacts. Assessment will then assume a different name depending on the impact being evaluated: social impact assessment, economic impact assessment, environmental impact assessment, integrated impact assessment, and so on.

The purpose of this chapter is to focus on the socio-economic impact. It depends on the fusion of two out of the three main impact categories mentioned above. The scientific literature does not agree on an unambiguous definition for such impact assessment.[1]

According to the most established definition (Canter et al., 1985), socio-economic impact assessment aims at estimating those effects which characterize and influence the community's social and economic well-being, and may be grouped in the following categories: economic–demographic impacts; public service impacts; social impacts; fiscal impacts; quality of life. The authors deliberately exclude environmental impacts, although they also influence human environment, since they are more properly evaluated through specific analytical tools (which normally form specific impact assessment methodologies, such as EIA – Environmental Impact Assessment).

According to this definition, economic–demographic impacts mainly concern changes in the economic system (growth or decline of cities and regions, location patterns of firms, prices of goods and services, level of income), in employment (labour market structure, employment and unemployment rates), in demography (variables such as age, gender, death rate, rates of school attendance and education, migrations)[2]. Public service impact involves: services in education, health care, security and defence, waste disposal, water, energy, and so on. Social impact concerns land use patterns (households, firms, public services such as hospitals, schools, public parks), property, transportation. Fiscal impact includes variations in tax yield due to economic changes. It is, however, difficult to define the last impact category, the so-called 'quality of life', which should include impacts on 'social well-being' (sometimes referred to just as 'other social effects'), in our opinion closely related to the four categories previously mentioned. Examples of some possible indicators include: security with regard to theft and crime; suicide and alcoholism rates; equality and equity; employment and family stability. This category also includes the so-called 'cultural impact', involving not only the arts, but mainly changes in customs and folkways, general beliefs and institutions.

Another classification, contained in the *Guidelines and Principles For Social Impact Assessment* (Interorganizational Committee for Social Impact Assessment, 1994), describes social impact under a more institutional key line.[3] The social impact is defined as:

> the consequences to human population of any public or private actions that alter the ways in which people live, work, play, relate to one another, organise to meet their needs and generally cope as members of society. The term also includes cultural impacts involving changes to the norms, values and beliefs that guide and rationalise their cognition of themselves and their society.

The variables to consider are clustered into five groups:

1. Population's characteristics: ethnic and racial differences, inhabitant typology, seasonal and leisure changes, and so on.
2. Institutional and community structures: size, structure and organization of local governments, including the links with the general political system; but also industrial and employment diversification, differentiation in voluntary service, religious organizations, interest groups, and the way these institutions are linked.
3. Political and social resources: distribution of power authority, interested and affected public, leadership capability and capacity within the community or region.
4. Individual and familiar changes: all factors involving daily life of families and people, including the perception of risk, health and security.
5. Community resources: natural resources and land use, residence availability, services such as health care, security, transports, and so on. This definition highlights that historical and cultural resources are the keys for continuity and survival of community.

This second classification is, in our opinion, most useful to our purposes, since in the first definition all these effects were included synthetically (and quite vaguely) in the 'quality of life' sub-category. It concerns a branch that should necessarily be considered, even if it is difficult to study and evaluate (and for this reason often just ignored).

In the most frequently employed assessment methodologies, such as cost–benefit analysis (CBA) and multi-criteria analysis (MCA), socio-economic impacts are often not correctly evaluated, namely social issues.

Moreover, institutional aspects – which will be defined in the next sections – are often neglected, while they should be considered from the beginning of the analysis in order to determine the relative weight of different impacts. Cost–benefit analysis is intrinsically unable to take these aspects into account: the main deficiency of this methodology is that a monetary value is assigned to each element to be evaluated, which will necessarily mirror, at best, the current social and institutional framework, and changes occurring in it cannot be considered. Multi-criteria analysis can consider these aspects instead, since it does not assign a monetary value to each impact. However, so far, the construction of weights (decision on which criteria are a priority) is done by the analyst and do not proceed – through direct surveys and other participative techniques – from the real community needs and wishes.

3. KEY CONCEPTS IN INSTITUTIONAL ECONOMICS[4]

When we refer to 'institutions', there is a wide array of interpretations. In this text, following the definition usually adopted in institutional economics, we will assume the broadest vision in which they are seen as 'the durable relations embedded in collectivities of norms, mores, folkways, organisations, and effective laws which fundamentally condition and act as means toward social practices' (O'Hara, 2000). Therefore, institutions encompass all the constitutive rules of a society, and not solely those that are formalized by specific organizations such as the government, the labour unions or the Stock Exchange.[5]

Institutional economics differs from neoclassical economics (and from other schools) mainly in its definition of the critical issues of economical science. While neoclassicals focus on allocation efficiency and (therefore) on the market structure, institutional economists place the crucial issue of economical analysis upstream: to them, the market structure is only one component of the economy. It is not the market that allocates the resources, rather it carries out a resource allocation determined by the institutional context. The concept of 'optimum' is therefore not so important to them, since it results from a given resource allocation depending on a specific institutional structure.

For institutional economists, the economy has therefore to be studied in a dynamic (or evolutionary) perspective. Unlike the mainstream approach, economic fundamentals such as preferences and technology are no longer considered exogenous, but key economic issues, since they are constitutive elements of institutions. Their interaction and evolution has then to be analysed. Since the interdependencies between different components of the economy are considered particularly important, institutionalists prefer a holistic approach rather than a reductionist one. Also, the importance of group behaviour is emphasized instead of individual behaviour.

Institutional economists are broadly divided into two main schools of thought, partly conflictual.[6] One, influenced by Veblen and then by Ayres, considers itself as being antithetical to neoclassical thought, while the other one, influenced by Commons, considers that issues addressed by institutional economics are complementary to neoclassical ones.[7] These two schools adopt very different positions with regard to institutions. The school of Commons considers institutions as a critical explanatory variable governing the economy. The school of Veblen and Ayres introduces a distinction between technology (in its broadest meaning, that is all the tools used for production) and institutions: the former is seen as the key factor of economic progress while institutions are a restraining force.

The institutional structure and its evolution are analysed under three main features: power, knowledge and psychology.

As for the first feature – the most emphasized – the issue of organization and control of the economy is traced back to the distribution of power, rights and wealth in society. Issues such as pollution, underdevelopment or unemployment are seen as contradictory relations between different socio-economic processes and different species, nations, institutional players (for example: state vs. market or public vs. private sector), and so on. These conflicts are seen as the main reasons for the problems and evolution of the economy.

With regard to the second feature, obviously no perfect knowledge is assumed, rather focus is directed on the uncertainty and the role of institutions in controlling and canalizing information. Information coming from market signals is considered as insufficient to understand and manage the economy properly. There is a lack of information, and its control by a few players creates problems such as the principal–agent one, or environmental externalities. Therefore, high levels of instruction and information – extended to all the members of society – are considered crucial issues for a fair working of the economy.

Furthermore, the significance of information is considered 'filtered' by the cultural context. For this reason, rather than knowledge per se, values and opinions are emphasized as causes of choice and economic action. This is the key issue in the 'psychological' feature, which contemplates the existence of variable psychological states, as well as traditions, customs and social imitation roles.

The issues dealing with knowledge have been developed, among other things, in the Instrumental and Ceremonial Function of Institutions (ICFI) theory. In its holistic version, the instrumental function of institutions is represented by the progressive force of the participative action of the members of a democratic and highly integrated community, where a high degree of widespread 'warranted' knowledge leads to the creation and change of rules, laws and customs.[8] This instrumental function is contrasted by the ceremonial (or invidious) function, whose purpose is the preservation – through the control of information and power – of some existing powers and economical privileges by the ruling class. The well-being of an economical system is then defined by the supremacy of instrumental function in relationships internal to each institutional sphere (state, market, and so on) as well as between different spheres.[9]

Besides the study of institutions, institutionalist analysis includes two other levels: institutional spheres and the social structure of accumulation.

With regard to the first one, five main institutional spheres are contemplated: 'production', 'finance', 'the state', 'the family' and the 'world economy'. These spheres are interrelated, but they remain quite autonomous while they hold different functions. The most analysed sphere is the state, namely its economic role.[10] The state and its legal structure are critical determinants for production and performance of the economy. Consequently, the 'laissez-faire' approach is considered to be meaningless. Moreover, while the economic system is influenced by the state and legal system, the other economic players (or lobbies) will try to influence the government too in order to maintain or change the existing structure of rights and power. In the context of the post-world war industrial society, institutionalists have largely backed the welfare state and democratic processes of planning and coordination, taking the side against the excessive power of some business and financial players.[11]

The study of the capitalist system and industrial society in its different stages is another of the institutionalist's favourite themes. The aggregation of the five main institutional spheres gives rise to the social structure of accumulation (SSA). During the evolution of industrial society, with a strong acceleration in the second part of the twentieth century, the five spheres became more and more interrelated. The weight of institutions in modern capitalism (understood as a social macrosystem) has therefore become dominant.[12]

4. INSTITUTIONAL ISSUES IN TRANSPORT ECONOMICS AND POLICY

The transport system is based on a set of institutions. At a given time societies have rules (formal/statutory and informal) that define accepted behaviour and action patterns for institutions such as property rights, provision of infrastructure (private or public), management practices, governance, and the role of markets (Stough and Rietvield, 1997). The design of the above-mentioned aspects depends on the definition of macro-economic objectives in transport policy. This section aims at analysing the present institutional context for the transport system, following the current deep socio-economic changes, with a special focus on governance and planning.

During the last two centuries, the production of transport changed from being mainly oriented to efficiency (at the time of the industrialization of transport), to prevailing equity concerns (at the time of public involvement in transport provision) and finally to a growing concern for environment and sustainability issues.

The slowness in the change of these macro-objectives depends on the fact that cultural determinants are relatively stable over time. Sometimes, however, sudden technological and/or economic changes give rise to fast and impressive transformations of the overall institutional context. Telematic revolution and the transition to post-industrial society seem to be one of these periods of rapid evolution of the institutional context.[13]

In the era of Fordism, the rigid organization of manufacturing processes gave rise to a quite clear differentiation in the roles of institutional actors. If some major lobbies did influence governance, this happened mainly through pressure on national governments, since the role of administration was mainly concentrated at the national level. Nowadays the industrial production process is more flexible and also administration is more decentralized. This means that the number of relevant actors involved in the production process increases, and so do the number of stakeholders involved in transport, due to the emergence of new socio-economic issues that are more and more interrelated (equity, development, sustainability, and so on).

As a consequence, the governance of the transport system must be not only more flexible (that is capable of quickly adapting itself to changes in the socio-economic context and in demand), but also decentralized, in order to match different needs in different local contexts, oriented to a higher integration of transport modes, and able to encompass and conciliate an enlarged base of interests. In other words, there is a need for a more flexible governance of the transport system, in order to face a more complex society.

In European Union countries, a profound institutional change is caused by the relevant powers and competencies shifting from member states to the Union, or, on the other side, to regional governments. The enlargement of powers of regional bodies allows a higher adhesion of policies and actions to local needs. On the other side, some new problems arise: the decision process at the national or international level becomes more complex due to the increase in the number of actors. Moreover, there is a risk of spatial externalities or spillover, since extra-regional effects of local policies are not contemplated.

At the European Union level, the most interesting issues are the harmonization of transportation policies and standards, and the planning and financing of major transnational infrastructures. If the process of European integration has always been oriented to the achievement of common goals, the European construction itself – and nowadays the European Constitution – also should imply the acceptance of a common cultural base (in other words, the Constitution would give assertion to the as yet informal institutional framework). This seems to justify the 'institutional activism' that the EU shows, when it supports the assertion of some values, such as environmental sustainability, through incentive policies.[14]

The common market and the international transport industry are nonetheless facing some major institutional constraints. Problems of interoperability and international integrations mainly depend on the adaptation to different regulations and standards frameworks. These differences result in transaction costs, representing a disincentive to international trades, so that the need for harmonization in transportation policies is self-evident. Some neo-institutionalists do underline the fact that the role of institutions is fundamental to achieving economic success through the reduction of transaction costs.[15] But harmonization is not simple and does not depend solely on economic interests (for example, speed limits or alcohol-consumption standards). Since different cultures coexist inside the EU, these non-economic factors must be properly considered in order to define an effective European transport policy.[16]

The planning of an international transport infrastructure must also take into account additional problems resulting from different planning procedures. The complexity of planning routines and implementation means longer times for planning and construction, which affects all countries involved in the international network. The comparison of different routines and procedures should give scope for their improvement, leading to an acceleration in the whole process.

At least two other institutional changes of the post-industrial era seem to be relevant here. First, the renaissance of the role of the private sector in transport, which on the one hand has positive consequences in terms of flexibility of supply, and on the other hand might jeopardize the achievement of sustainability goals. Second, the acceleration in technological innovation, which could reduce the need for new infrastructure through a more efficient use of those already in existence. Substantial institutional and sometimes legislative changes are needed in order to make these tools accepted by the community and its representatives.

5. SOCIO-ECONOMIC IMPACT AND INSTITUTIONAL ASPECTS

The institutional aspects listed in the previous section normally influence the transport system, as well as influencing major transport projects and policies. A proper assessment of the impact of these projects or policies is therefore necessary to take this influence and its changes over time into account. Indeed, an underestimation of these aspects leads to a misleading impact assessment, with the possible consequence of a biased decision-making process.

Nevertheless, the most widespread impact assessment techniques – namely the cost–benefit analysis (CBA) and the multi-criteria analysis (MCA) – largely fail to consider these aspects.

The conceptual and methodological framework of cost–benefit analysis (CBA) is conceived to take into account all real costs and benefits of a project, regardless of their monetary or non-monetary nature and regardless of the actor on whom they have an effect. However, this technique ultimately aims at assigning a monetary value to any cost or benefit considered, even to intangible effects, so that the criteria applied are often neither reliable nor realistic.[17] Other major problems of CBA, as the literature points out,[18] are the choice of the discounting rate and – quite obviously – the difficulty in being able to foresee all effects, above all indirect, resulting from the project.

The relevance of these problems leads to the introduction of new assessment techniques, the most commonly used being the multi-criteria analysis (MCA). MCA[19] does not aim to turn all costs and benefits into monetary values. Each impact is considered separately, by using the most appropriate techniques, indicators and values for each of them, and keeping their own units of measurement.

However, the most important limitation of this technique, in the institutional context, is that the weight factors used to weigh impacts are actually arbitrarily chosen by the evaluator, therefore remaining largely independent from the cultural values of the stakeholders.

Clearly, if the evaluation also aims to give consideration to the institutional framework in which the project is to be implemented and where its impact is expected, then the technique employed should provide for a preliminary definition of what the relevant impacts for the community are, and consequently of the weight that has to be associated to each impact.

Therefore, the weight should be defined by the stakeholders themselves and not 'a priori' and arbitrarily by the evaluators, on the basis of what they, or 'literature experts', consider relevant, or on the basis of guidelines given by a political decision-maker. It might be argued that politicians, as representatives of the community, can be accepted, to some extent, as representatives of stakeholders. But the stakeholders do not normally coincide with voters, and moreover the impact assessment approach is conceived precisely to avoid a discretionary evaluation of these representatives on what is actually the best for the community they represent, so as to reduce or avoid the bias often occurring between the interests and goals of representatives and those of represented people.

Unfortunately, socio-economic impact assessment often suffers from the same lack of representativeness of the community's and stakeholders' dynamical preferences. Therefore socio-economic impact assessment also has to improve to better include their perception and their system of values. This issue will be addressed in the next section, while here we investigate problems arising when institutional aspects are overlooked or wrongly interpreted in impact analysis.

In section 4, we have considered how the transport system is deeply influenced by (and in turn influences) some institutional or social characteristics, such as territorial governance, population income level, culture, customs, and so on. In addition, values such as quality of life, the research of beauty, the respect for nature and the environment, ethics and equity in the distribution of wealth, and so on, are becoming more and more important for many people in the community. And most of these elements are totally neglected in current assessment techniques.

If we try to include institutional aspects and their changes over time, impact assessment certainly becomes more complicated and time consuming, yet it leads to results which are possibly more reliable and definitely closer to the interests of the community.

For example, let us assume that a policy of lowering road speed limits is planned. Expected benefits will range from reduction of casualties, savings in health care, lower emissions and lower fuel consumption; while higher travel times and the cost of enforcement will be the expected costs. The impact assessment of this policy requires that these expected effects are evaluated, either in monetary units (in a CBA framework) or not (MCA). Values must be assumed for variables such as human life, health, air quality, time. The techniques actually used attempt to estimate these values as objectively as possible, but the existence and importance of these values are taken as a fact (not questionable). Therefore the analyst concentrates only on measuring the entity of the impacts and not on the importance that the community gives to those kind of impacts. It is clear, instead, that the importance assigned to these elements will be different in different institutional contexts, according to values, culture, and so on. Indeed, even the fiscal cost of implementing the policy, though it is already expressed in monetary terms (and therefore is normally not subject to any 'weighing' procedure), should be evaluated according to the political importance of budget surplus or deficit in the specific context, which obviously changes over time according to the state of public finance, the political commitments of the government, and so on.

The failure in considering the institutional aspects is evident if we assume, in our example, that the policy is preceded and prepared by an educational and/or advertising campaign enhancing the value of the environment, safety, and so on. After the campaign (that is, within a new institutional context), the value of the above-mentioned benefits would certainly increase, and the result of the assessment would be different. It is therefore clear that current techniques fail to consider that the result of their evaluation is related to a specific context, which can be changed by a proper policy, or can just change over time for other reasons.

In our example, the speed limits can then be enforced not merely with sanctions, but with education in road safety issues, introduced from the primary school stage. This means 'going to the source of the problem', involving changes in the community's uses and values. Apparently, the first strategy is more effective and allows additional revenues for the public authority (fines paid by the sanctioned drivers). Yet, comparatively higher costs of enforcement should be considered; also, police control will be effective only until it goes on (that is, the lower police control, the lower road safety). In the latter case, road civic education requires a change in teaching programmes which probably does not involve additional costs since it does not require more teaching hours.

Acting at the institutional level – such as in the case of focused primary school education – needs a (much) longer period to be effective, but it is much more effective and lasting once the sphere of community values changes. Also, the acceptation level from the citizens is higher, since it does not imply sudden and coercive changes in their habits. Furthermore, the expected behaviour will be based on values such as: the importance of health, human life, wholesome air, sustainability (as a consequence of a reduction in fuel consumption), and so on. These are actually key elements in the purpose of an efficient, effective and sustainable mobility; all of them belong to the cultural and institutional sphere, and traditional techniques of impact assessment fail to consider and evaluate them properly. Therefore the expected information concerning which solution has to be adopted or which project has to be implemented is no longer reliable, since it does not match these fundamental issues.

Also transport sustainability is highly affected by institutional factors; however some of them influence sustainability positively, and some negatively, as shown by the following two examples:[20]

- The development of an urban underground railway is a technological change which would lead to benefits in sustainability due to the employment of a zero-(local) emissions transport mode; yet it can be hampered at the institutional level (for example, if property rights on the subsoil are established);
- sometimes constraints on mobility (traffic or parking limitations, road or park pricing, and so on) are needed to reduce congestion, and to improve living conditions in inner cities or specific zones; which can cause great discontent among some citizens and city-users that have to change their habits (prohibition to use a private car, lack of parking places). So, what do we mean by 'mobility right', or 'right to have a less congested city'? Clearly, the definition depends upon a particular context and is likely to vary over time.

Since the consensus of the community is needed, and in the meantime the community understanding of specific policy importance is required, it is therefore necessary to consider the opinions of all subjects affected by any specific project, which is clearly a difficult task. It often happens that the formulation of a policy measure, such as road-pricing implementation, is not accepted by the community, thus implying potential political cost for the decision-maker who has suggested or implemented the measure. This is an additional reason to innovate traditional impact assessment techniques, in order to consider institutional aspects properly.

It is then clear that using the wrong institutional issues or omitting those issues from impact assessment techniques generates misleading results, a wrong evaluation of costs and benefits and a possible deficit creation. The suggested policy can then fail to be effective because of its irrelevance to the institutional context in which it is applied, leading to lack of concern and/or opposition of communities and stakeholders.

6. INSTITUTIONAL CONTEXT AND NEW PARTICIPATION TECHNIQUES

It seems then that assessment techniques developed so far and currently employed fail to properly consider the effects related to institutional aspects of the society or community where the project under evaluation is expected to be implemented. These aspects are possibly the most closely related to the culture and values of citizens and stakeholders in general; therefore their underestimation has serious consequences for the degree of consensus and the overall effectiveness of the impact assessment.

Even in more sophisticated techniques, such as the multi-criteria analysis, the weights of different impacts considered are indeed determined by either:

- analysts, who will use their own view on values rather than those of the community involved;
- politicians, who are also likely to use inappropriate weighting since their goals are basically different from those of the community they represent.

Some survey techniques, such as Delphi techniques, do attempt to better understand stakeholders' orientation, yet they are once again performed by analysts and based upon the evaluation of a small number of experts or opinion leaders. Indeed, they are still highly discretionary and are prone to a high degree of error.

Do better alternatives exist? Within an MCA framework, which seems much more suitable than CBA for our purpose of including the changing institutional context in the impact assessment, we normally work with a routine where weights for variables including institutional issues are given, as shown in Figure 4.1. What is needed is a weighing process derived from citizens and stakeholders, as shown in Figure 4.2.

Possible ways of including institutional issues in assessment techniques are related to citizens' and stakeholders' participation. In some countries some effective techniques have already been developed and are currently used (albeit not properly linked with the impact assessment procedure), while further improvements can be expected due to the progress in telecommunication technologies.

On the first point, a few examples of participation procedures could be quoted. One which seems quite effective is the 'public debate' ('*débat public*')[21]

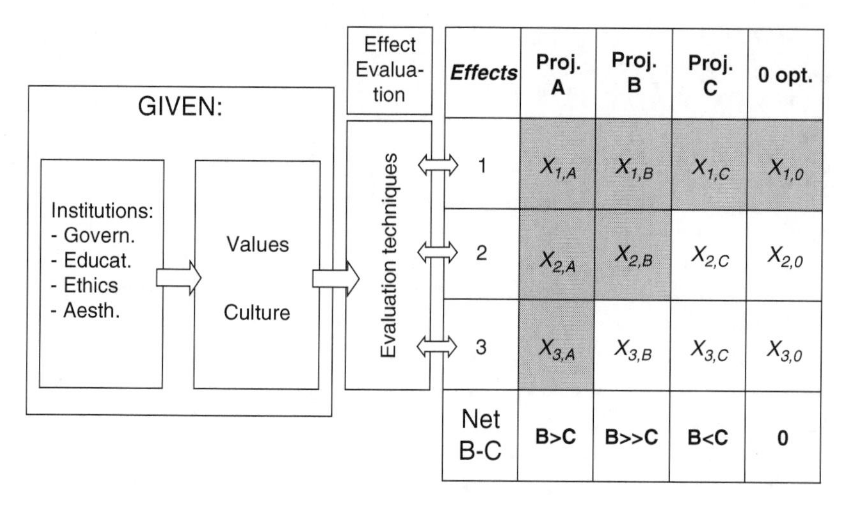

Source: Authors

Figure 4.1 Traditional multi-criteria analysis

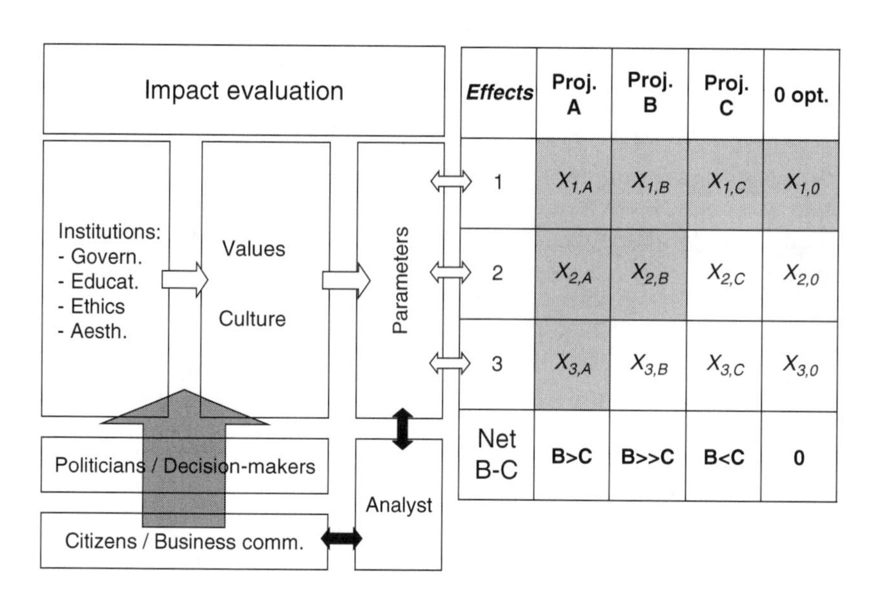

Source: Authors

Figure 4.2 Participative multi-criteria analysis

set up and currently employed in France for major infrastructure projects with substantial environmental impact and/or high social and financial costs.[22]

The procedure starts after the assessment (with current techniques) of the main possible socio-economic impacts of the project, as well as of its financial and social costs. On the basis of this first assessment a national independent administrative body (the '*Comité National du Débat Public*') decides whether the *débat public* is necessary.

If the debate is to start, the first step involves giving widespread information to the communities of the involved territories, through media, conferences, flyers, normal and electronic mail, relevant review publications, contacts with environmentalist and consumers' organizations, and so on.

Then the debate starts up, based on (i) the institution of a specific Project Committee (*Comission Particulière du Débat Public*); (ii) the collection of reactions and suggestions by the citizens and stakeholders (through dedicated websites, free phone numbers, and so on); (iii) the organization of public conferences, workshops and other forms of direct debate; (iv) the publication and examination of citizens' suggestions and proposals. The results of the debate must be taken into consideration in the following planning phases. Apart from ensuring the stakeholders' participation, the *débat public* also has the merit of being a time-scheduled debate, which avoids an excessively long and uncertain project appraisal phase.

As mentioned above, the progress in telecommunication technologies might ensure in the near future a further, substantial improvement in citizens' and stakeholders' participation, namely in the collection of opinions and suggestions and in gaining consensus on a project. The word '*e*-democracy' is often used for describing a number of procedures partially overlapping each other, such as *e*-voting, *e*-conferences, *e*-governance.[23] The European Scientific Foundation programme 'Towards E-democracy' (TED) suggests that: 'the WWW and other communications infrastructure provide a mechanism for involving stakeholders much earlier in the process'. Consequently *e*-democracy is defined as follows:

> The envisaged methodology is based on a common WWW tool-set to provide decision support and a communication infrastructure to support stakeholder interactions. It recognises that citizens not only wish to be informed about major issues, but wish also to articulate their opinions in a way that can affect the decision making process. The tools will both help all parties understand issues and also build a shared understanding between the stakeholders.[24]

While the *e*-democracy toolbox can be used for different purposes, the most relevant here is the opportunity to employ Information and Communication Technologies for including citizens' and stakeholders' opinions in the multi-criteria analysis framework, namely as a tool for determining the weight of different effects.[25] The key purpose is not so much 'democracy' (which should be ensured by the political representation), rather the link of public choice to the culture and knowledge[26] of the community. The participation process should then ensure (Winkler, 2003) that deliberation (i) creates new legitimation and a basis for decision-making; (ii) enforces the trust of citizens into institutions (less scepticism of citizens towards institutions); (iii) improves the informational basis of citizens; (iv) is community-building; (v) can create a public opinion that may be defined as 'common' public opinion.

E-democracy could then be used in an MCA framework in order to reflect the dynamic character of stakeholders' preferences, which have numerous facets and change over time and space. The literature has recently started to address the technical issues for inserting *e*-democracy into the MCA framework.[27]

7. CONCLUSION

It seems that, so far, the most used and widespread impact assessment techniques largely fail to consider the interaction between the project and policies which are being evaluated and the institutional context in which they are expected to be implemented.

This failure is possibly one of the major reasons for the gap frequently occurring between the evaluation of transport projects and policies and the degree of consensus coming from citizens and stakeholders.

Actually, current assessment procedures and impact evaluation parameters do not match the institutional changes nor do they account for them, for a number of reasons: (i) most 'institutional-related' impacts are difficult to detect and to estimate (for example the 'intangibles'), (ii) time for these changes to occur is normally very long, (iii) even monetary impacts should be estimated according to the 'weight' of (namely public) money in a given political context.

The elements illustrated above seem to be too complex to be modelled in a CBA framework which did not possess the methodological elements necessary to match institutional issues, while the MCA framework might be more suitable. Nevertheless, the weight of different impacts is still considered as given, and therefore they are evaluated directly by the analyst (even if sometimes with the help of experts or of politicians).

This obviously does not allow institutional aspects to be included in the impact assessment. What should be done – instead of using techniques which aim at precisely measuring the effects but start from 'given' values or weights – is rather to include, in the evaluation process, changes occurring over time in the institutional sphere. A possible way to do this is to include stakeholders in the weighting process (for example, through *e*-democracy techniques).

Clearly, we do not assert that the entire decision process should be assigned to citizens and stakeholders. Yet some degree of participation should be introduced in order to be aware of the cultural and institutional context in which the project is to be implemented, and to relate its evaluation to that context as much as possible, so that the final project, if implemented, can match the real needs and will of the people for whom it has been planned. This can be made possible only if all stakeholders take part in the process. It is therefore necessary to educate citizens to participate on specific issues, while the current planning and assessment procedures have frequently obtained the opposite result, that is to turn them away and estrange them from the decision-making process, and to lose their confidence in the planners.

NOTES

1. Literature seems quite confused even about the definition of 'assessment'. With regards to socio-economic impact, it frequently refers to Social Impact Assessment (SIA), which officially dates back to the 1969 National Environmental Policy Act (NEPA). Burdge and Vanclay (1996, p. 62) affirm: 'New studies elaborated by SIA arise from the need to apply knowledge on sociology and other social sciences to prefigure social effects of environmental changes, linked to development process, subject to NEPA jurisdiction in USA'. However, many variations appear in the scientific literature (see Wolf, 1983; Finsterbush, 1983; Canter et al., 1985; Erickson, 1994; Interorganizational Committee for Social Impact Assessment, 1994; Canter, 1996); some texts only refer to social evaluations, others to both social and economic evaluations, others also include environmental impacts and/or socio-economic impacts in this analysis, as a first step of environmental analysis.
2. These aspects should be more properly included within the social impact.
3. It is important to make clear that the 'core' of the two mentioned sources is not identical; the first one includes a detailed review of models and methods to estimate the impact; the second one refers to the phases of performing an evaluation and includes no models or indicators.
4. With regards to the taxonomy of economic schools of thought, a distinction between old and new institutionalism is often applied. Old institutionalism is more heterodox, holistic and descriptive while new (or neo-) institutionalism generally insists on individualism, rationalism and use of mathematical language. In this chapter we don't apply the distinction between the two tendencies, which remain closely linked; anyway the approach illustrated in this paragraph can be considered closer to the old institutionalist school. For a comparative study of old and new institutionalism, see M. Rutherford (1994).
5. Institutions and organizations should never be confused: while 'governance' is an institution, 'government' is an organization (that is the institutional subject) defining its contents. Education is an institution, school is an organization, and so on (Stough and Rietvield, 2003).

6. For the first school, see, among others, Veblen (1904), Ayres (1978) and Galbraith (1972); for the second one, see mainly Commons (1924) and Witte (1954).
7. In the sense that institutional economics studies how the structure of power ultimately governs resource allocation, while neoclassical economics is interested in the working out of optimal, gain-trade maximizing results within the existing power structure (Samuels, 1988a: 3).
8. For the holistic version of ICFI see for example Bush (1987). In the ICFI technological version, institutions are ceremonial while technology is instrumental. See for example Ayres (1978).
9. The ICWP (Index of Community, Warranted knowledge, and Participation) macroeconomic performance index has been built on these criteria: see O'Hara (1997).
10. Although we would not subscribe to this point of view, institutional economists generally refute the distinction between public and private or between 'legal' and 'economic', because of the magnitude and complexity of the social process in which both are involved. Furthermore, they recognize that the definition of roles for the different institutional players cannot avoid subjective assumptions: in the real world as in the economic analysis conceptualization. The conceptualization itself can be an opinion, more than a body of knowledge (Samuels, 1988b: 3). On this last point, and on the methodological and epistemological aspects of institutional economics, see Neale (1982) and W. G. Samuels (1988b).
11. Institutionalists have proposed different socialist models, usually more pragmatic than the Marxian one. See for example Galbraith (1972) and Myrdal (1960). For a discussion of the role of the state and on institutionalists' activism see Gruchy (1974).
12. With regard to weight and structure of the institutional spheres during the last decades, a regress deterioration in the welfare state in numerous industrialized countries can be identified, as well as the development of international institutions, the deregulation of the financial system and a more and more flexible production system (O'Hara, 2000).
13. Institutionalists would define this period as the appearance of a new SSA.
14. The role of the EU in promoting sustainable mobility policies also depends on the subsidiary principle and on distribution of powers in this field. On this subject see Commission of the European Union (2001). In our opinion, since it is a 'top-down' activism, measures based on incentives have to be considered better than those based on restraints.
15. These reductions mainly concern property rights and contractual procedures: on this point see North (1990).
16. The 'informal' institutional components should also be evaluated in projects for major infrastructures. Rietveld (1994) argues that, because of formal and informal institutional factors, when transport crosses a border, this often results in a substantial reduction in transport flow. For this reason, besides the reduction in transaction costs expected from the harmonization, major transnational infrastructure projects should also ensure that a conspicuous demand really exists for trans-border flows (Stough and Rietvield, 1997).
17. The total economic value of any good includes exchange value, option value and existence value. All techniques conceived to evaluate the monetary value of parts not reflected in the price (option and existence value and sometimes a part of the value of use) appear imperfect and/or subjective, especially for intangible goods, and when the existence value is not related to direct utility (for example: altruism). Even the concept of 'real value' remains quite ambiguous.
18. Key references on cost–benefit analysis are Mishan (1967, 1988), Button (1993) and Berechman (1995).
19. For the multi-criteria analysis technique see for example Roy and Bouyssou (1993).
20. See: Deliverable 16, STELLA Project (2004).
21. With law 276/2002.
22. See: www.debatpublic.fr.
23. In the literature there are different definitions for the word *e*-democracy, sometimes just referring to *e*-voting, *e*-conference or to a mix of different tools. For a definition of them, see Moreno-Jimenez and Polasek (2003).

24. Quoted in Bollinger and Pictet (2003: 67).
25. On this topic see Moreno-Jimenez and Polasek (2003) and Bollinger and Pictet (2003).
26. 'Knowledge' intended here, in the 'institutional' way, as the interpretation of available information.
27. On this topic see Moreno-Jimenez and Polasek (2003), TED (2003) and Bollinger and Pictet (2003).

REFERENCES

Ayres, Clarence (1978), *The Theory of Economic Progress: A study of the Fundamentals of Economic Development and Cultural Change*, 3rd edn, Kalamazoo, MI: New Issues Press.

Berechman, J. (1995), 'Transport infrastructure investment and economic development', in D. Banister (ed.) *Transport and Urban Development*, London: E & FN Spon.

Bollinger, Dominique and Jacques Pictet (2003), 'Potential use of *e*-democracy in MCDA processes. Analysis on the basis of a Swiss case', *Journal of Multi-Criteria Decision Analysis*, **12**, 65–76.

Burdge, R.J. and F. Vanclay (1996), 'Social impact assessment: a contribution to the state of the art series', *Impact Assessment*, **14**, March.

Bush, Paul D. (1987), 'Theory of institutional change', *Journal of Economic Issues*, **21**(3), September, 1075–116.

Button, K.J. (1993), *Transport Economics*, 2nd edn, Aldershot, UK and Brookfield, US: Edward Elgar.

Canter, L.W. (1996), *Environmental Impact Assessment*, 2nd edn, New York: McGraw-Hill.

Canter, L.W., S.F. Atkinson and L.F. Leistritz (1985), *Impact of Growth: a Guide for Socioeconomic Impact Assessment and Planning*, Chelsea, Michigan: Lewis Publishers.

Commission of the European Communities (2001), white paper, *European transport policy for 2010: time to decide*, Brussels: COM (2001) 370 final.

Commons, John R. (1924), *The Legal Foundation of Capitalism*, New York: MacMillan.

Eatwell, John, Murray Milgate and Peter Newman (eds) (1987), *The New Palgrave: a Dictionary of Economics*, London: MacMillan.

Erickson, P. (1994), *A Practical Guide to Environmental Impact Assessment*, San Diego: Academic Press.

Finsterbush, K. and C.P. Wolf (1981), *Methodology of Social Impact Assessment*, 2nd edn, Stroundsburg, Pennsylvania: Hutchinson Ross Publishing Company.

Galbraith, John K. (1972), *Economics and the Public Purpose*, Boston: Houghton Mifflin.

Gruchy, Allan G. (1974), 'Government intervention and the social control of business; the neoinstitutionalist position', *Journal of Economic Issues*, **8**(2), June, 235–49.

Interorganizational Committee on Guidelines and Principles for Social Impact Assessment (1994), *Guidelines and Principles for Social Impact Assessment*, US.

Layard, R. and S. Glaister (1994), *Cost–Benefit Analysis*, Cambridge: Cambridge University Press.

Mishan, E.J. (1967), 'Interpretation of the benefits of private transport', *Journal of Transport Economics and Policy*, **1**, 184–9.

Mishan, E.J. (1988), *Cost–benefit Analysis*, London: Allen & Unwin.
Moreno-Jimenez, José M. and Wolfgang Polasek (2003), '*e*-democracy and knowledge. A multicriteria framework for the new democratic era', *Journal of Multi-Criteria Decision Analysis*, **12**, 163–76.
Musso, Enrico and Claudia Burlando (1999), *Economia della Mobilità Urbana*, Turin: Utet.
Myrdal, Gunnar (1960), *Beyond the Welfare State*, New Haven: Yale University Press.
Neale, Walter C. (1982), 'Language and economics', *Journal of Economic Issues*, **16**(2), June, 355–69.
North, Douglas C. (1990), *Institutions, Institutional Change and Economic Performance*, Cambridge: Cambridge University Press.
O'Hara, Philip A. (1997), 'A new measure of macroeconomic performance and institutional change: the index of community, warranted knowledge, and participation', *Journal of Economic Issues*, **31**(1), March, 103–28.
O'Hara, Phillip A. (2000), *Marx, Veblen, and Contemporary Institutional Political Economy*, Cheltenham, UK and Northampton, MA, USA: Edward Elgar.
Rietveld, Piet (1994), 'International transportation and communication networks in Europe the role of barrier effects', *Transportation Planning and Technology*, no. 17, 311–17.
Roy, B. and D. Bouyssou (1993), *Aide Multicritère à la Décision: Méthodes et Cas*, Paris: Economica.
Rutherford, M. (1994), *Institutions in Economics: the Old and the New Institutionalism*, Cambridge: Cambridge University Press.
Samuels, Warren J. (eds) (1988a), *Institutional Economics, I*, Aldershot, UK and Brookfield, US: Edward Elgar.
Samuels, Warren J. (eds) (1988b), *Institutional Economics, II*, Aldershot, UK and Brookfield, US: Edward Elgar.
Samuels, Warren J. (eds) (1988c), *Institutional Economics, III*, Aldershot, UK and Brookfield, US: Edward Elgar.
STELLA project (2004), 'A policy research document with an agenda proposing desirable research on the theme institutions, regulations and markets in transportation', Position paper STELLA Focus Group 5, Deliverable 16, August 2004.
Stough, Roger R. and Piet Rietvield (1997), 'Institutional issues in transport systems', *Journal of Transport Geography*, **5**(3), 207–14.
Stough, Roger R. and Piet Rietvield (2003), 'Institutions, regulations and markets', Position paper STELLA Focus Group 5, Draft, September.
TED (2003), *Toward Electronic Democracy: Internet-based Complex Decision Support*, Strasbourg: European Scientific Foundation.
Veblen, Thorstein (1904), *The Theory of Business Enterprise*, New York, Charles Scribner's Sons.
Winkler, R. (2003), 'E-democracy: potentials and constraints of online participation in the political public sphere', in A. Prosser and R. Krimmer, *E-Democracy: Technologie, Recht und Politik*, Vienna: OCG, pp. 5–15.
Witte, Edwin E. (1954), 'Institutional economics as seen by an institutional economist', *Southern Economic Journal*, **21**, October, 131–40.
Wolf, C.P. (1974), *Social Impact Assessment*, Milwaukee, Environmental Design Research Association.

5. Multi-criteria analysis as a tool to include stakeholders in project evaluation: the MAMCA method

Cathy Macharis

1. INTRODUCTION

For the evaluation of transport projects several aspects have to be taken into account. Not only are pure economical effects important, but also ecological, spatial and social aspects are increasingly gaining importance. The consequences of the projects are usually far-reaching and the different policy alternatives are numerous and difficult to predict. Several pressure or action groups have also emerged causing an even more complex decision-making process. In the UK there has recently been a shift towards a New Approach to Appraisal (NATA) for infrastructure projects, including several new criteria which were not included in the standard cost–benefit analysis. A multi-criteria approach is now followed in order to include the different aspects. In France there has been a move away from multi-criteria analysis (after extensive use of it in the 1980s) as there was no satisfying and transparent way the weights were given (Sayers et al., 2003). We come back to the weighting problem in section 4.

At the same time, the importance of stakeholders within this evaluation process is being recognized. Research on transport projects is generally carried out to provide information to policy makers who have to operate within restrictive parameters (political, economical, social, and so on). Researchers should therefore take greater account of the different priorities of stakeholders such as policy makers, private enterprises and households (Van Ham and Van Wee, 2003). These stakeholders should be incorporated explicitly in the evaluation process.

In this chapter we propose a multi-actor, multi-criteria approach or short MAMCA methodology for the evaluation of transport projects. With transport projects, we mean the whole spectrum ranging from large infrastructure projects, policy measurements and transport technologies.

In the next section the concept of stakeholders is explored. In section 3 the possible introduction of the concept of stakeholders in the existing evaluation tools for transport projects will be discussed. In section 4 the introduction of the stakeholder concept in a multi-criteria analysis framework is described. In section 5 the MAMCA methodology is presented. Section 6 illustrates this methodology by applying it to some case studies.

2. THE CONCEPT OF STAKEHOLDERS

The concept of stakeholders was first introduced in the management literature, where stakeholders have to be taken into account once a company or organization has adopted the idea of corporate social responsibility (Donaldson and Preston, 1995; Buysse and Verbeke, 2003). The broadest definition of the concept is found in the work of Freeman (1984) where a 'stakeholder is by definition any individual or group of individuals that can influence or are influenced by the achievement of the organisation's objectives'. Each stakeholder has views on strategic positions (aims, performance and outcomes) and if set in a group stakeholders identify with each other as part of a strategic stakeholder group (Hensher and Brewer, 2001). Each stakeholder has a set of norms or standards established to govern situations and outcomes. In the context of the transport sector these stakeholder groups can be the users, the investors/operator, the society as a whole and the government.

Depending on the situation, a more participatory process can be followed where the stakeholders can participate in the policy process (as proposed by Rotmans and Van Asselt, 2000). The level of participation will depend on the resources and time devoted to the project, as it takes time and money to involve the stakeholders in the process. There are some disadvantages to complete participatory process. Not all stakeholders will be able or ready to participate in the policy analysis process but they should not be ignored by the scientific team. If the participation is organized in focus groups, the powerful stakeholders will influence the others and a focus group is never meant to be representative. So the input of such a participatory process should be done critically and compared to other sources of knowledge. Another problem with the use of focus groups for the participation of stakeholders is that only organized groups are seen as stakeholders (Munda, 2004).

The participation of stakeholders is, however, necessary if the quality of the decision can not be guaranteed by the analyst alone (because he or she does not have the necessary information or if the problem is ill-structured). Consultation of the stakeholders or participation is then necessary. Another category of necessary stakeholder participation occurs when the decision is highly controversial and the acceptance rate low (Vroom, 1974). By creating a participatory process, the acceptability of the projects or policy measures can be increased.

In conclusion, the most important thing is to identify the stakeholders and to be aware of their stake and objectives. If the interests of the stakeholders are not taken into account the study or analysis will be ignored by policy makers or be attacked by the stakeholders (Walker, 2000). The methodology we propose in this chapter makes these stakeholders explicit and allows for the participation of the stakeholders in the evaluation process. According to the situation, this participation can be very active or more passive.

3. METHODS USED FOR THE EVALUATION OF TRANSPORT PROJECTS

Several evaluation methods can be employed for the evaluation of transport-related projects. In this section an overview of these methods will be given, and the adaptability of them to include the necessary multi-criteria, multi-stakeholder approach (as argued above) will be discussed. Five commonly used evaluation methods can be identified, namely the private investment analysis (PIA), the cost-effectiveness analysis (CEA), economic-effects analysis (EEA), the social cost–benefit analysis (SCBA) and the multi-criteria decision analysis (MCDA).

The private investment analysis (PIA) or private cost–benefit analysis, the cost-effectiveness analysis (CEA) and economic-effects analysis (EEA) are applied in specific cases. These three methods are, however, not of great interest if we want to include stakeholders in the analysis. The private cost–benefit analysis takes into account the pure financial costs and benefits of the project. It is being executed from the point of view of the private or public investor and does not take broader objectives into account.

The cost-effectiveness analysis (CEA) looks at the effectiveness of the measure in terms of the investment costs of the government. The CEA has thus a uni-criterion, uni-actor perspective. It looks at the effectivity with regard to one specific goal. The economic-effect analysis (EEA) or regional economic impact study (REIS) looks at the project's impact on added value, employment and fiscal revenue. Input–output tables are used and indirect effects are captured through the use of multiplicators. The EEA is specifically designed for the government perspective and takes into account only three criteria of this stakeholder.

The social cost–benefit analysis (SCBA) is grounded in welfare theory. It takes a wider societal perspective and in this sense it can also include the external costs of transport. It is usually used when there are only a few possible alternatives to be examined. A discount rate is used to calculate the net present value and the internal rate of return of the project. The monetarization of all the effects, however, still remains a problem. Some of the external effects of transport are difficult to assess and translate in monetary terms (Button, 1993; Kreutzberger et al., 2006).

Another problem with an SCBA is that it is based on the compensation criterion. It is not clear who the losers and winners are in the transport project. The introduction of a stakeholder analysis in an SCBA is in principle possible if the costs and benefits are structured according to the stakeholders. So for each stakeholder the costs and benefits would be listed and calculated. However, at the end of the process the costs of one stakeholder can be compensated by the benefits of another. The redistribution effects are not clearly shown with such an analysis. This problem can be avoided by creating an end table per stakeholder (containing all the costs and benefits of that stakeholder) so as to get a cost–benefit analysis of the project per stakeholder. The problem of monetarization will, however, exclude many more subjective or qualitative costs or benefits from the analysis. An SCBA or CBA can, however, be part of the multi-criteria analysis.

4. MULTI-CRITERIA ANALYSIS FOR THE EVALUATION OF TRANSPORT PROJECTS

Multi-criteria decision analysis (MCDA) provides a framework to evaluate different transport options with several criteria.[1] Information necessary to perform a multi-criteria analysis are:

- The options, alternatives, scenarios, policy measures or strategies that have to be compared to each other;
- The evaluation criteria that will be used to assess these options;
- The importance of these criteria (that is the weights)
- The evaluation of the options on the different criteria. These evaluations can be given on a numerical or ordinal scale.

Some methods also require preferences of the decision-maker, such as the preference functions used in the PROMETHEE method.

The first generation of MCDA models concerned decisions that encompassed several options or alternatives, which had to be evaluated using several criteria for a single decision-maker. For the evaluation of transport projects, the eclectic multi-criteria analysis method developed by De Brucker (2000), for example, enables the integration of different types of analysis tools used in transport project evaluation, such as the environmental effect analysis, safety effects, economic impact analysis, and so on.

The group decision support methods (GDSM) can be called a second generation of MCDAs. These GDSMs are of particular interest for this chapter, as they allow the concept of stakeholders to be introduced in multi-criteria analysis. In Springael and De Keyser (2005) several types of GDSM are identified. In the first type the group of decision-makers decide upon the criteria, the options and the evaluation of these options with the criteria. The aim here is to come to a consensus on the input data, and by this process to a consensus on the final ranking. The multi-criteria analysis models of the first generation can be used here. The second type differs in that each participant can fill in his or her own preferences (that is weights and preference degrees), but the criteria, evaluations and options are the same. The *n* multi-criteria analyses are aggregated in a second phase. The result of this final aggregating MCDA is considered as a group ranking. In the third category, the ranking and preferential structure are taken along in the second phase. Most of the GDSMs related to the most popular multi-criteria analysis tools, such as AHP (Saaty, 1989) and PROMETHEE (Macharis et al., 1998), can be classified in this category. It is this last category which is the most interesting for the introduction of stakeholders, as it makes it possible for each stakeholder group to leave them the freedom of having their own criteria, weights and preference structure.

The idea of incorporating several decision-makers in a multi-criteria decision analysis is thus not new. Many methods have extended their approach and software for group decision support methods (GDSM). The PROMETHEE method for example has been extended in Macharis et al. (1998); the analytical hierarchy process (AHP) method in Saaty (1989); and ELECTRE in Leyva-López and Fernández-González (2003). However, the concept of stakeholders was not clearly defined in these extensions. The decision-makers were referred to as players, parties or participants. The concept of stakeholders was first introduced in MCDA by Banville et al. (1998). As denoted by Banville et al. (1998) multi-criteria analysis is useful for the introduction of the stakeholder concept. In their paper, a first framework for the introduction of the concept of stakeholders is introduced. They argue that in the first three stages of a multi-criteria analysis the concept of stakeholders can certainly enrich the analysis, but they do not include the stakeholders in the methodology further on. In this chapter a multi-stakeholder, multi-criteria analysis is proposed. It has been successfully applied in several projects for the evaluation of transport-related strategic decisions.

5. THE MULTI-STAKEHOLDER, MULTI-CRITERIA ANALYSIS EVALUATION FRAMEWORK

The methodology consists of seven steps (see Figure 5.1). The first step is the definition of the problem and the identification of the alternatives (step 1). The various relevant stakeholders are then identified as well as their key objectives (step 2). Next, these objectives are translated into criteria and then given a relative importance (weights) (step 3). For each criterion, one or more indicators are constructed (for example, direct quantitative indicators such as money spent, number of lives saved, reductions in CO_2 emissions achieved, or scores on an ordinal indicator such as high/medium/low for criteria with values that are difficult to express in quantitative terms) (step 4). The measurement method for each indicator is also made explicit (for example willingness to pay, quantitative scores based on macroscopic computer simulation, and so on). This permits the measurement of each alternative performance in terms of its contribution to the objectives of specific stakeholder groups. Steps 1 to 4 can be considered as mainly analytical, and they precede the 'overall analysis', which takes into account the objectives of all stakeholder groups simultaneously and is more 'synthetic' in nature. Here, an evaluation matrix is constructed aggregating each alternative contribution to the objectives of all stakeholders (step 5). The MCDA yields a ranking of the various alternatives and gives the strong and weak points of the proposed alternatives (step 6). The stability of this ranking can be assessed through a sensitivity analysis. The last stage of the methodology (step 7) includes the actual implementation. The various phases are discussed in more detail below.

Step 1: Define Alternatives

The first stage of the methodology consists of identifying and classifying the possible alternatives submitted for evaluation. These alternatives can take different forms according to the problem. They can be different technological solutions, possible future scenarios together with a base scenario, different policy measures, long-term strategic options, and so on. There should be a minimum of two alternatives to be compared. If not, a social cost–benefit analysis might prove to be a better method for the problem. In section 4 different examples are given.

Step 2: Stakeholder Analysis

In the stakeholder analysis the stakeholders are identified. Stakeholders are people who have an interest, financial or otherwise, in the consequences of

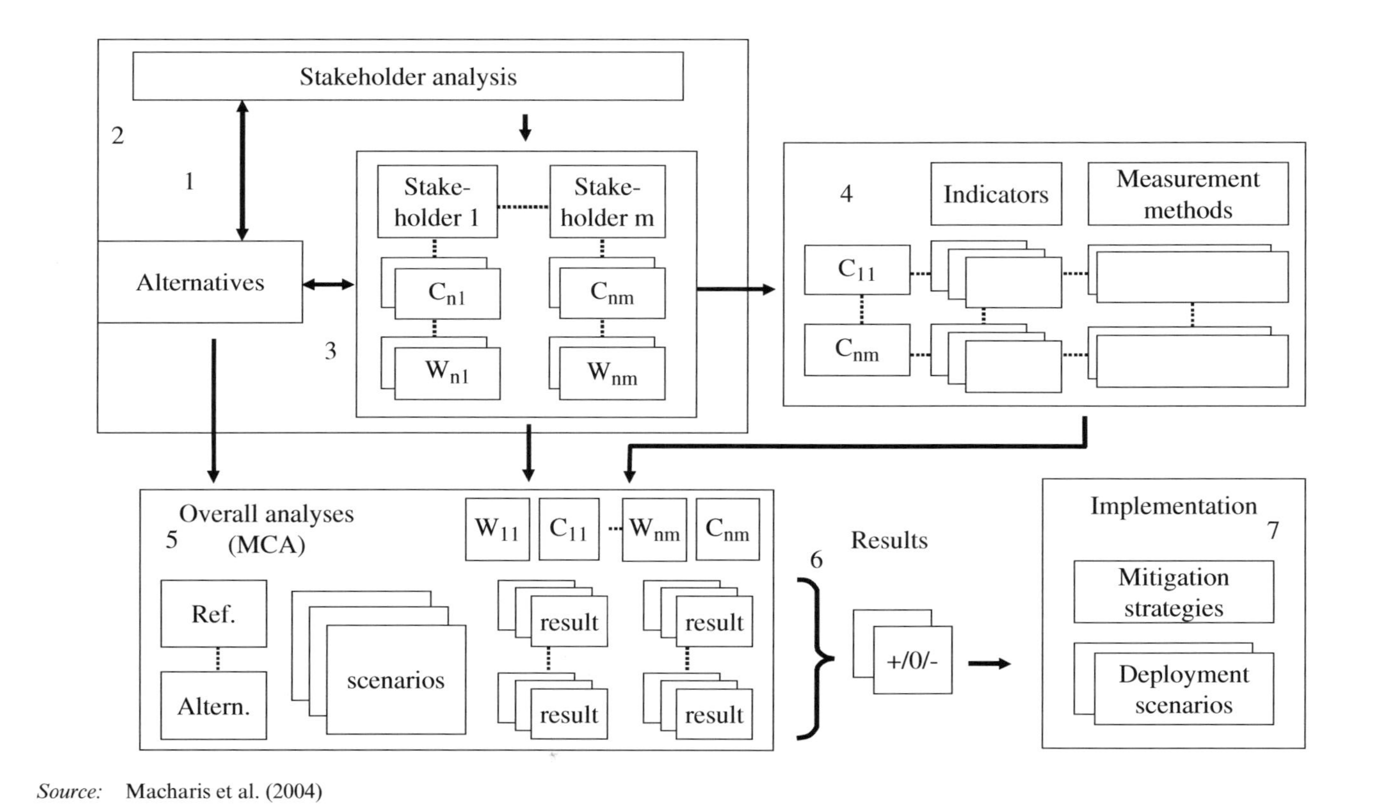

Source: Macharis et al. (2004)

Figure 5.1 Methodology for a multi-stakeholder, multi-criteria analysis (MAMCA)

any decisions taken. An in-depth understanding of each stakeholder group's objectives is critical in order to assess the different alternatives appropriately. Stakeholder analysis should be viewed as an aid to properly identify the range of stakeholders to be consulted, whose views should be taken into account in the evaluation process. Once identified they might also give new ideas on the alternatives that have to be taken into account. However, this does not mean that a pure participatory study line should be followed, as argued in the introduction.

Step 3: Define Criteria and Weights

The choice and definition of evaluation criteria are based primarily on the identified stakeholder objectives and the purposes of the alternatives considered. A hierarchical decision tree can be set up (see section 6 for examples).

Several methods for determining the weights have been developed. The weights of each criterion represent the importance that the stakeholder allocates to the considered criterion. A description of these methods is given in Nijkamp et al. (1990) and Eckenrode (1965). In practice the pairwise comparison procedure proves to be very interesting for this purpose. The relative priorities of each element in the hierarchy are determined by comparing all the elements of the lower level in pairs against the criteria with which a causal relationship exists. This pairwise comparison is done on a scale of 1 to 9.

In Table 5.1 several criteria (g_j) are compared to each other in terms of their importance to the overall goal or focus F. $P_F(g_j,g_j')$ represents the preference intensity for a specific pair of criteria (g_j, g_j') in terms of the higher level element (*casu quo*, the focus F). This preference intensity is measured on a scale of 1 to 9 as illustrated in Table 5.2.

The applied multi-criteria analysis method and software (see step 6) allow an interactive process with the stakeholders in order to perform

Table 5.1 Pairwise comparison matrix in the AHP

F	g_1	. . .	. . .	g_j'	. . .	g_n
g_1	1					
. . .		[1]				
g_j			[1]	$P_F(g_j,g_j')$		
. . .				[1]		
. . .					[1]	
g_m						1

Source: Saaty (1988)

Table 5.2 Pairwise comparison scale in the AHP

Intensity of importance $Pg_j(a_i,a_i,')$ Definition	Explanation
1 Both elements have equal importance	Both elements contribute equally to the criterion considered
3 Moderately higher importance of row elem. (RE) as compared to column elem. (CE)	Experience and judgement reveal a slight preference of RE over CE
5 Higher importance of RE as compared to CE	Experience and judgement reveal a strong preference of RE over CE
7 Much higher importance of RE as compared to CE	RE is very strongly favoured over CE, and its dominance has been demonstrated in practice
9 Complete dominance in terms of importance of RE over CE	The evidence favouring RE over CE is of the highest possible order of affirmation
2, 4, 6, 8 (Intermediate values)	An intermediate position between two assessments
1/2, 1/3, 1/4, . . . 1/9 (reciprocals)	When CE is compared with RE, it receives the reciprocal value of the RE/CE comp.
Rationals Ratios arising from the scale	If consistency were to be forced by obtaining *n* numerical values to span the matrix
1.1–1.9 For tied activities	RE and CE are nearly indistinguishable; moderate is 1.3 and extreme is 1.9

Source: Saaty (1988)

sensitivity analysis. The weights of the stakeholders themselves are usually set equal (Munda, 2004). These equal weights show that the point of view of each stakeholder is being given equal consideration. However a sensitivity analysis can also be executed here. The main advantage of a multi-actor, multi-criteria analysis is that the discussion about the weights is done within the stakeholder group. As inherent in the concepts of stakeholders (see introduction), stakeholders have a common view on how important the criteria are. The discussion on the weights is less important than in the previous single multi-criteria analysis.

Step 4: Criteria, Indicators and Measurement Methods

In this stage, the previously identified stakeholder criteria are 'operationalized' by constructing indicators (also called metrics or variables) that can be used to measure whether, or to what extent, an alternative contributes to each individual criterion. Indicators provide a 'scale' against which a project's contribution to the criteria can be judged. Indicators are usually, but not always, quantitative in nature. More than one indicator may be required to measure a project's contribution to a criterion and indicators themselves may measure contributions to multiple criteria.

Step 5: Overall Analysis and Ranking

The MCDA method used to assess the different strategic alternatives can be any MCDA method. Most of the cases discussed below are analysed using the analytical hierarchical process (AHP). This method, described by Saaty (1982, 1988), involves building a hierarchical tree and working with pairwise comparisons. The consistency of the different pairwise comparisons as well as the overall consistency of the whole decision procedure can easily be tested in the AHP, which can handle both quantitative and qualitative data, the latter being very important for transport evaluations. Certain criteria in transport concern the ecological impact or road safety issues. These criteria are difficult to quantify. Moreover, the method is relatively simple and transparent to decision-makers and to the public. The method does not act like a black box since the decision-makers and the stakeholders can easily trace the way in which a synthesis was achieved. The AHP is supported by a user-friendly software package (EXPERT CHOICE), which makes it possible to determine not only the overall priorities of the alternatives studied but also to investigate the sensitivity of the final ranking.

It is also possible to work via profile charts if the pairwise comparison proves too difficult to manage (see Dooms and Macharis, 2003).

Step 6: Results

The multi-criteria analysis developed in the previous step eventually leads to a classification of the proposed alternatives. A sensitivity analysis is performed in this stage in order to see if the result changes when the weights are changed. More important than the ranking, the multi-criteria analysis reveals the critical stakeholders and their criteria. The multi-actor, multi-criteria analysis provides a comparison of different strategic alternatives, and supports the decision-maker in making his or her final decision by pointing out for each stakeholder which elements have a clearly positive or a clearly negative impact on the sustainability of the considered alternatives.

Step 7: Implementation

When the decision is taken, steps have to be taken to implement the chosen alternative by creating deployment schemes. This implementation process can be complemented by cost–benefit analysis for well-defined projects.

6. CASE STUDIES

The methodology can be applied in a very broad range of applications. In the area of transport it can be used for the evaluation of transport policy measures (such as the evaluation of mobility rights, Crals et al., 2004), infrastructure projects or the evaluation of transport technologies (such as the evaluation of advanced driver assistance systems, see Macharis et al., 2004); or the determining of sustainable traction battery technologies (see Macharis et al., 2005). In this section, several recent applications of the methodology will be discussed in the area of transport.

The methodology was first applied to evaluate the location of intermodal terminals (Macharis, 2000; 2004). The so-called LAMBIT model (Location Analysis Model for Belgian Intermodal Terminals) provided the framework for the decision-making process on the location of new intermodal terminals. In a preliminary phase the traffic potential of the terminal projects was determined. In order to have a sustainable terminal, the traffic potential in the surrounding area of the terminal must be large enough to support it. Furthermore, the impact of the new projects on the market area of the existing terminals must be analysed. A network model determined the traffic potential and the impact on the existing terminals. In the risk analysis, the proposed locations were screened according to predetermined standards (large enough for an intermodal terminal, grants by the local district, ability to get permissions, and so on). In the next phase a more comprehensive evaluation of a discrete set of terminal projects was applied. The criteria used in this evaluation represented the aims of the parties involved, namely the users of the terminal, the operators/investors and the community as a whole. The results of the analysis of the affected parties were brought together in order to get a global ranking of the projects. A sensitivity analysis closes the procedure.

In Figure 5.2 the decision tree is given. This tree shows the three stakeholders with their respective criteria and sub-criteria. For every criterion

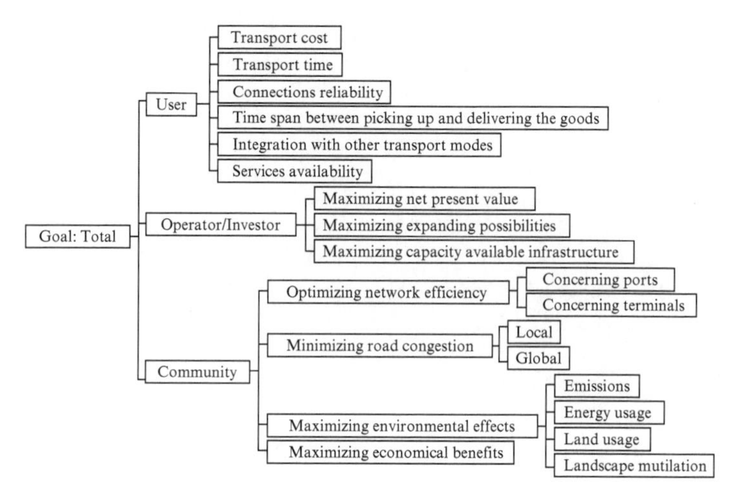

Source: Author's set-up

Figure 5.2 Decision tree in the LAMBIT model

and sub-criterion used in the model, indicators have to be chosen, which makes it possible to evaluate the alternatives with these criteria.

For the criteria of the operator/investor and more in particular the maximization of the net present value, a cost–benefit analysis was used. The possible combination of multi-criteria with a cost–benefit analysis is very useful and expands the analysis. This combination of multi-criteria analysis was also performed in the BRUGARWAT case study (Brussels Garbage by water), where the possible modal shift of waste transport in the Brussels region was analysed (Macharis and Boel, 2004). A social cost–benefit analysis was done in iteration with a multi-criteria analysis.

The social cost–benefit analysis made it possible to get an idea of the social desirability of the project, while the multi-criteria analysis was used for the choice between the several possible types of package units that can be used. The alternatives were the ISO 20′, 30′ and 40′ containers that compact the waste, ISO 40′ open top containers and MSTS containers (multi-service transport system) or bulk transport. For the garbage operator (Net Brussel) the operational results (containers, ships, terminals, savings compared to road transport) are important issues. For the local community the effects on visual intrusion, noise, smell and congestion are important. For the community as a whole the impact of the modal shift on accidents, global congestion, global noise, pollution and climate change were taken into account.

In the framework of the Masterplan of the Port of Brussels (Dooms et al., 2004) the methodology was used in two types of applications. The first type of application was for a location analysis and planning for a separate port site (that is the site of Carcoke and Béco). In the Minimasterplan Carcoke, for example, the possible destinations of the site were compared. The strategic alternatives were here a European distribution centre (EDC), value added logistics (VAL) or recycling.

The second type of application was for the long-term strategic planning for the whole port area. For each port area the possible strategic development options were compared. This consisted of a proactive and a status quo scenario. Depending on the area, different stakeholders were included in the analysis. Four main stakeholders are important in the context of port planning: government, local community, port authority and potential port users. A main stakeholder can be unbundled into several sub-categories with their own specific criteria (for example local community can be unbundled into tourists, residents, adjacent non-port firms and organizations) if the characteristics of a zone necessitate this approach. The definition of criteria for each stakeholder follows the approach followed for the definition of stakeholders: the criteria depend on the purpose, that is on the characteristics of each zone. This is very relevant for stakeholders, such as government and the local community, as their objectives often change throughout the port area. For example, in some port zones government objectives will be oriented towards economic development, whereas other port zones will be considered suitable for housing development and recreation. The objectives of the port authority and the port companies are much more stable, although there can be variations depending on port zone, but not as intense as for government or local community stakeholders. Another reason for this difference is that the port authority can be considered as 'identical' or 'univocal' over the whole port area, whereas the identity of local community stakeholders and sometimes even government (for example municipalities) can change depending on the considered port zone. The last step of the methodology consisted here in checking if the different strategic options proposed in each port zone were consistent with each other.

In Figure 5.3 the hierarchical decision tree is provided. The introduction of a new HST terminal in Brussels (Meeus et al., 2004) was analysed according to the same methodology. Seven possible alternatives were proposed and compared. The stakeholders here were the railway operator NMBS, the government, the local community and the users. In Figure 5.4 the criteria for these stakeholders are given.

A last and very interesting case was the evaluation of the possible extension of DHL at Zaventem International Airport. This case will be explored in depth by Dooms, Macharis and Verbeke in Chapter 9 of this book.

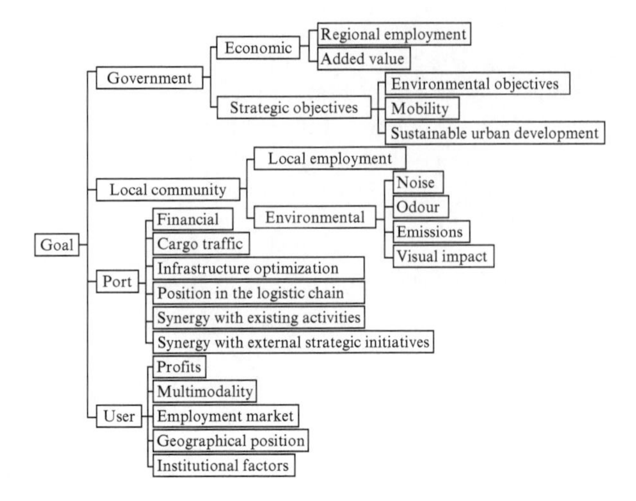

Source: Dooms et al. (2004)

Figure 5.3 Hierarchical tree for the Masterplan of Brussels (Béco dock)

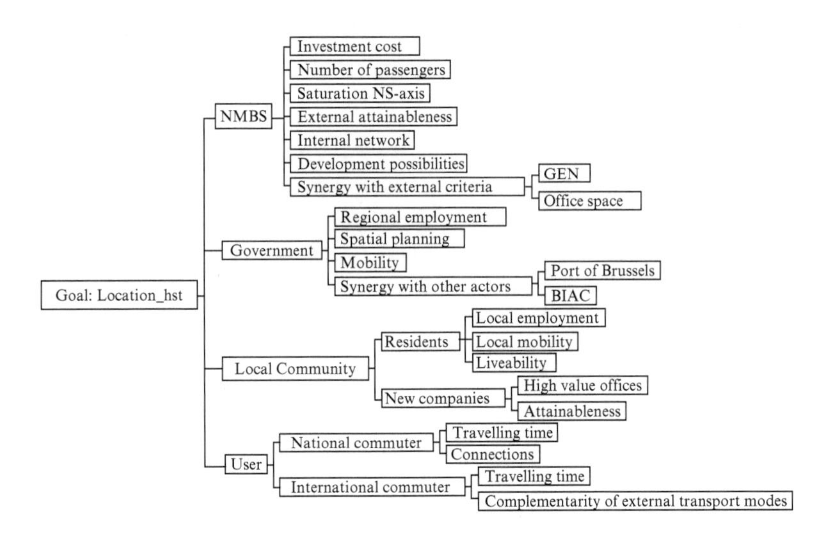

Source: Meeus et al. (2004)

Figure 5.4 Hierarchical decision tree for the evaluation of a new HST terminal

5. CONCLUSION

For the evaluation of transport projects several stakeholders are involved and several criteria have to be included. The proposed methodology allows these points of view and several criteria to be incorporated in the analysis. The methodology has been applied in a variety of projects, ranging from the evaluation of infrastructure projects to the evaluation of new technologies. Including stakeholders in the analysis takes more time in the beginning, but improves the likelihood of acceptance of the proposed solution in the end.

NOTE

1. Some hundred methods exist for aggregation of the evaluation (see Vincke, 1992 for an overview).

REFERENCES

Banville, C., M. Landry, J-M. Martel and C. Boulaire (1998), 'A stakeholder approach to MCDA', *System Research*, **15**, 15–32.

Button, K. (1993), *Transport Economics*, Aldershot, UK and Brookfield, USA: Edward Elgar.

Buysse, K. and A. Verbeke (2003), 'Proactive environmental strategies: a stakeholder management perspective', *Strategic Management Journal*, **24**, 453–70.

Crals, E., M. Keppens, C. Macharis, R. Ramboer, L. Vereeck and I. Vleugels (2004), 'Nog te veel vragen en te weinig mogelijkheden. Resultaten onderzoek naar verhandelbare mobiliteitsrechten', *De Verkeersspecialist*, **110**, 15–18.

De Brucker, K. (2000), 'Ontwikkeling van een eclectisch evaluatie-instrument voor de sociaal-economische evaluatie van complexe investerrings projecten, met een toepassing op het project Seine-Scheldeverbinding', Ph.D. thesis, UA-RUCA, Antwerpen.

De Brucker, K., A. Verbeke and W. Winkelmans (1998), *Sociaal-economische evaluatie van overheidsinvesteringen in transportinfrastructuur*, Leuven: Garant.

Donaldson, T.J. and L.E. Preston (1995), 'The stakeholder theory of the corporation: concept, evidence and implications', *Academy of Management Review*, **20**(1), 65–91.

Dooms, M. and C. Macharis (2003), 'A framework for sustainable port planning in inland ports: a multistakeholder approach', Proceedings of the 43rd European Congress of the Regional Science Association (ERSA), Young Scientist Sessions, University of Jyvaskyla, 27–30 August, 2003.

Dooms, M., C. Macharis and A. Verbeke, in cooperation with Ecorys, BGDA and COOPARCH-RU (2004), *Masterplan van de Haven van Brussel: Interimrapport 5*, Haven van Brussel, Brussel.

Dooms, M., A. Verbeke, C. Macharis and R. S'Jegers (2006), *De zaak DHL. Het regionale hub project van DHL in Brussel-National: een Socio-economische en maatschappelijke evaluatie*, Antwerpen: Garant.

Eckenrode, R. (1965), 'Weighting multiple criteria', *Management Science*, **12**(3), 180–92.

Freeman, R.E. (1984), *Strategic Management: A Stakeholder Approach*, Boston: Pitman.

Hensher, D.A. and A.M. Brew (2001), 'Developing a freight strategy: the use of a collaborative learning process to secure stakeholder input', *Transport Policy*, **8**, 1–10.

Kreutzberger, E., C. Macharis and J. Woxenius (2006), 'Intermodal versus unimodal road freight transport – a review of comparisons of the external costs', in B. Jourquin, P. Rietveld and K. Westin (eds), *Transportation Economics – Towards Better Performance Systems*, New York: Routledge.

Leyva-López, J. and E. Fernández-González (2003), 'A new method for group decision support based on ELECTRE III methodology', *European Journal of Operational Research*, **148**, 14–27.

Macharis, C. (2000), 'Strategische modellering voor intermodale terminals. Socio-economische evaluatie van de locatie van binnenvaart/weg terminals in Vlaanderen', Ph.D. thesis, Brussels, Vrije Universiteit Brussel.

Macharis, C. (2004), 'The optimal location of an intermodal bargeterminal', in M. Beuthe, V. Himanen, A. Reggiani and L. Zamparini (eds), *Transport Developments and Innovations in an Evolving World*, Berlin: Springer, Part C, pp. 211–32.

Macharis, C. and B. Boel (2004), 'BRUGARWAT: Brussels Garbage by water', Vervoerslogistieke werkdagen, 4–5 November, Hoeven, Nederland, in C. Ruijgrok and R. Rodenburg (eds), *Bijdragen Vervoerslogistieke Werkdagen*, Delft: Connekt, pp. 229–42.

Macharis, C., J. Brans and B. Mareschal (1998), 'The GDSS Promethee procedure', *Journal of Decision Systems*, **7**, 283–307.

Macharis, C., A. Verbeke and K. De Brucker (2004), 'The strategic evaluation of new technologies through multi-criteria analysis: the advisors case', in E. Bekiaris and Y. Nakanishi (eds), *Economic Impacts of Intelligent Transportation Systems. Innovations and case studies*, Amsterdam: Elsevier.

Macharis, C., J. Van Mierlo, W. Van Autenboer, J.-M. Timmermans, J. Matheys and P. Van den Bossche (2005), 'Multi-criteria analysis dedicated to the determining of sustainable traction battery technologies', submitted for publication in *Transportation Research, part D*.

Meadows, D., www.sustainer.org/, accessed 10 March 2005.

Meeus, T., C. Macharis and M. Dooms (2004), 'Inplanting van tweede HST-terminal te Brussel: scenario Brussel-Nationaal moet verder worden onderzocht', *De Lloyd*, Universiteit en Transport.

Munda, G. (2004), 'Social multi-criteria evaluation: methodological foundations and operational consequences', *European Journal of Operational Research*, **158**, 662–77.

Nijkamp, P., P. Rietveld and H. Voogd (1990), *Multicriteria Evaluation in Physical Planning*, Amsterdam: Elsevier Science Publishers.

Rotmans, J. and M.B.A. Van Asselt (2000), 'Towards an integrated approach for sustainable city planning', *Journal of Multi-criteria Decision Analysis*, **9**, 110–24.

Saaty, T. (1982), *Decision Making for Leaders*, Lifetime Learning Publications, Belmont, CA: Wadsworth.
Saaty, T. (1988), *The Analytic Hierarchy Process*, New York: McGraw Hill.
Saaty, T. (1989), 'Group decision making and AHP', in B. Golden, E. Wasil and P. Harker (eds), *The Analytic Hierarchy Process: Applications and Studies*, New York: Springer-Verlag.
Sayers, T.H., A.T. Jessop and P.J. Hills (2003), 'Multi criteria evaluation of transport options-flexible, transparent and user-friendly?', *Transport Policy*, **10**, 95–105.
Springael, J. and W. de Keyser (2005), 'A branch and bound algorithm to construct a consensus ranking based on Kendall's t', Research Paper/UA, Faculty of Applied Economics, 2005: 30.
Van Ham, H. and B. Van Wee (2003), 'The changing role of research in the policymaking process', in W. Dullaert, B. Jourquin and J. Polak (eds), *Across the border*, Antwerp: De Boeck.
Verbeke, A., C. Macharis, M. Dooms and R. S'Jegers (2004), *Economische impact-studie van de uitbreiding van de hubactiviteiten van het koeriersbedrijf DHL op de luchthaven van Zaventem (Brussel Nationaal; Brussels Airport). EINDRAPPORT*, studie in opdracht van de provincie Vlaams Brabant, Antwerpen: Garant.
Vincke, Ph. (1992), *Multicriteria Decision-Aid*, New York: John Wiley & Sons.
Vroom, V. (1974), 'A new look at managerial decisionmaking', in D. Kolb (ed.), *Organisational Psychology: A book of Readings*, Englewood Cliffs, NJ: Prentice-Hall.
Walker, W.E. (2000), 'Policy analysis: a systematic approach to supporting policy-making in the public sector', *Journal of Multi-criteria Decision Analysis*, **9**, 11–27.

6. Ad hoc project procedures for the development of transport infrastructures

Eric Van Hooydonk

1. INTRODUCTION

Investments in new transport infrastructures such as roads, railways, seaports and airports must conform to ever more complicated procedural rules on public decision-making, planning and zoning, environmental impact assessments, public participation, public procurement and so on. The purpose of this chapter is to assess the (in)efficiency of regular project procedures and to discuss the merits of ad hoc procedures for individual projects of special or strategic interest. The emergence of specific procedures for individual projects based on exceptional legal rules is a recent and much criticized phenomenon. After a brief analysis of typical cases mainly derived from Belgian and Dutch practice relating to seaport development, we shall first attempt to demonstrate that, with regard to ad hoc procedures and their political evaluation, a fundamental distinction should be made between 'orderly' and 'emergency' ad hoc procedures. Secondly, we shall argue that the increasing recourse to ad hoc procedures is probably not problematic in itself, but rather the consequence of the inefficiency of regular procedures.

2. DEFINITION OF PROJECT PROCEDURES

There exists no generally accepted definition of a project procedure. Project procedures may be understood to include several elements, such as the initial administrative decision to start a project, subsequent zoning and planning decisions, procedures for the compulsory acquisition of land or buildings (including court proceedings), all kinds of administrative authorizations (for example building permits), advice to be sought compulsorily from various higher or subordinate authorities or advisory bodies, oral public participation sessions, written public consultation rounds, cost–benefit analyses and other economic assessments, decisions on the provision of public funding, environmental impact assessments, procedures to be followed under public procurement rules (or, as the case may be, under specific rules on public–private partnerships), administrative and/or judicial appeal and review procedures, and so on. In brief, a project procedure covers all the administrative decisions, formalities and assessments that are prescribed by mandatory legal rules, including subsequent appeal procedures. In other words, it encompasses all the preparatory bureaucracy that the initiator of any investment project has to comply with, including litigation.

3. THE INTERNATIONAL AND EU LEGAL FRAMEWORK

Project procedures are increasingly governed by or harmonized through international and European legal rules. Public participation and access to courts are guaranteed by the Aarhus Convention.[1] International environmental impact assessments must conform to the Espoo Convention.[2] Together with the protection of private property and the non-discrimination principle, the fundamental principle of access to courts is also safeguarded by the European Convention on Human Rights.[3] EU environmental legislation including the Birds and Habitats Directives,[4] the Environmental Impact Assessment Directives[5] and the Water Framework Directive[6] regulates the designation of nature protection areas, conservation measures, public participation, the appropriate assessment of the implications of plans and projects for protected sites and so on. These and other international and European rules are implemented, elaborated or supplemented by national, regional and local laws.

Besides this constantly growing body of rules and standards on the protection of the environment and of citizens' rights, public authorities and investors – including environmental enforcement authorities and courts – should also take into account international and EU rules ensuring the proper management and use of transport infrastructures or promoting their further development. A case in point are the nineteenth century treaties determining the status of international rivers, which oblige riparian states to maintain and improve the fairways.[7] Similarly, the development of roads, railways, ports and other infrastructures may constitute an obligation on EU Member States under competition law[8] and the TEN Guidelines.[9] EU funding programmes such as Marco Polo[10] and Motorways of the Sea[11] contain further incentives to make available efficient transportation facilities to users. Within the framework of its state aid policy, the European Commission approves the public funding of new seaport, inland navigation and multi-modal terminals which contribute to the modal shift.[12] The so-called Strawberry Regulation obliges Member States to take action in the case of interruptions of the free movement of goods through blockades of ports, waterways and roads.[13]

To say the least, these two bodies of legal provisions – environmental rules and citizens' rights on the one hand, transport policy-related rules on the other hand – are insufficiently co-ordinated and integrated. In a number of cases, environmental protection measures have simply overridden existing zoning schemes intended for future transport infrastructure development. While it is outside the scope of the present chapter to elaborate on this fundamental policy and legal problem, it should be clear that it further complicates project procedures which are often already intricate enough in themselves. For a detailed discussion of the interrelation between international and EU rules on environmental protection and port and waterway development, we refer to a study carried out in 2006 on behalf of the European Commission.[14]

4. INEFFICIENCY OF REGULAR PROCEDURES

4.1. Definition of Regular Procedures

In normal circumstances, the development of transport infrastructure projects must follow the procedural rules applicable to any other infrastructure or building project. By a 'regular' procedure, we understand a procedure governed by a national legal framework which is generally applicable to an unlimited number of undefined projects or to certain broadly defined categories of projects. In most cases, its scope is not limited to transport infrastructure projects.

4.2. A Selection of Cases[15]

4.2.1. The reactivation of the Iron Rhine railway (Netherlands)[16]

The Iron Rhine is a railway link between the port of Antwerp in Belgium and the German industrial heartland of the Ruhr area. Over a distance of 48 kilometres, it crosses Dutch territory. Built in the 1870s on the basis of the Belgo-Dutch Separation Treaty of 1839,[17] it was one of the first cross-border European railways. In the 1980s, the line partly fell into disuse and traffic was redirected over the more southerly Montzen route, but soon afterwards Antwerp interests demanded a reactivation of the Iron Rhine. Since the 1990s, the Belgian and Dutch governments have been negotiating over the reopening and modernization of the line. Complications have arisen from the unilateral designation by the Dutch government of nature conservation areas on top of two short stretches of the railway. In the view of local opponents, reusing the Iron Rhine would be incompatible with the newly created environmental protection status of these areas. The regular administrative procedure leading to the reactivation (the so-called Line Infrastructure Procedure),[18] which was initiated by the Dutch government in 1999, was unilaterally stopped a few years later, given disagreement with the Belgian government over environmental measures and their financing. As a consequence, the two governments brought their dispute before international arbitrators under the auspices of the Permanent Court of Arbitration at The Hague. Their judgment, which was rendered mid-2005,[19] established that Belgium and the Netherlands must share the cost of reactivation and provided the parties with cost allocation criteria for each of the sub-stretches of the line. On condition that a final agreement on the investments be reached, the Dutch project procedure might be resumed. At present, however, it is still unclear whether and, if so, when the reactivation will take place.

4.2.2. The third deepening of the River Scheldt (Netherlands)[20]

The Scheldt river is the maritime access route to the Belgian port of Antwerp, the second largest seaport of Europe. Its mouth lies on Dutch territory. In order to be able to receive the ever larger container ships, the channel needs to be deepened through dredging works on both the Belgian and Dutch stretches of the river. Notwithstanding its existing treaty status, which is based on the aforementioned Separation Treaty of 1839[21] and which guarantees Belgium a right to have the deepening works carried out, the two governments have in 1996 entered into negotiations which have led to a common strategic EIA, a cost–benefit analysis, and a final memorandum of understanding signed in 2005. Pursuant to this memorandum, the programme and the financing of the deepening works were laid down in a bilateral treaty signed in December 2005, which was awaiting ratification at the time of going to press. The project procedures will, however, be organized on the basis of regular national legislation applicable in both countries. Although the recent treaty holds out the political and legal commitment of the deepening works starting in 2007 and being terminated by 31 December 2009 at the latest, earlier studies have pointed out that the option to follow regular procedures entails numerous uncertainties and could lead to delays which may in the worst case postpone the improvement of the fairway to 2017.

4.2.3. The Deurganckdok in the port of Antwerp (Belgium)[22]

The Deurganckdok is a gigantic tidal container dock dug in the left bank area of the port of Antwerp. A preliminary study was prepared by the Flemish Ministry in 1995; the decision to construct the new facility was taken by the Flemish government early in 1998. As a result of local opposition from inhabitants and some environmental splinter groups, who successfully challenged the project procedures before the Supreme Administrative Court of Belgium,[23] the construction works were unexpectedly interrupted for more than one year. In order to remedy this situation and to restart the works within a reasonable time span, the Flemish legislator enacted several emergency decrees which declared the project of general interest and strategic importance.[24] Consequently, the construction works were resumed and could be pursued without further interruptions. A first berth at the Deurganckdok opened mid-2005.

4.2.4. The Western Scheldt Container Terminal at Flushing (Netherlands)

The Western Scheldt Container Terminal project entails the construction of a 2.65 kilometre tidal quay for the handling of containers at the mouth of the river Scheldt in the port area of Flushing in the Netherlands. The provincial authorities of Zeeland are the driving force behind this project, which was launched in 1997. As the project would inevitably result in the loss of the protected area of the Kaloot beach, a place where from time to time rare fossils are found, local opponents went to the Dutch Supreme Administrative Court.[25] There they obtained the reversal of the provincial authorities' decision on the basis, among other things, of the absence of a sufficient investigation into possible alternatives and of a proper demonstration of the overriding public interest of the project which is, under the EU Habitats Directive, a precondition for any measure affecting nature conservation areas.[26] As a consequence, the project procedure was interrupted. At the time of going to press, the provincial authorities had not reached a final decision on whether or not to take the project further. If the project is brought back to life, the quay wall is likely to be considerably shortened and the project will encounter a delay of at least three years.

4.2.5. The Second Maasvlakte at Rotterdam (Netherlands)[27]

A similar doomsday scenario unfolded for the Second Maasvlakte project at the port of Rotterdam, the largest seaport in Europe. The Second Maasvlakte is a large-scale extension of the outer port of Rotterdam and will consist of the reclamation of additional port areas in the Dutch territorial sea and the construction of several tidal docks for the largest container vessels and oil tankers, with a total quay length of 12 kilometres. Preparatory studies started in 1997. In 2002, the formal project procedure was started with a basic zoning decision[28] taken by the Dutch government and assented to by the Dutch parliament. Notwithstanding a favourable opinion of the European Commission on the compliance with the EU Habitats Directive, this project was interrupted as well by the Dutch Supreme Administrative Court. The Court found that the effects of the construction of the new port area on the transport of fish larvae and silt along the coast – which in turn may have a significant impact on the more northerly Waddenzee, a protected area within the meaning of the Wild Birds Directive – had been insufficiently assessed.[29] Moreover, the Court found that the Dutch government had provided insufficient guarantees that the planned compensation measures for the loss of other nature conservation areas would effectively be implemented. As a result of this judgment, the Dutch government unveiled a reparation plan which would limit the delay to the project to 1.5 years. As a consequence, the construction of the new port facilities would commence in 2008 instead of 2006, and it is envisaged that in 2012–2014 the first containers will be handled.

4.2.6. The Dibden Bay container terminal at Southampton (United Kingdom)[30]

The Dibden Bay container terminal project was a major port extension project in the South of England. It was initiated by Associated British Ports (ABP) in the 1990s and would have consisted of the construction of a large container handling facility with a 1.85km-long quay wall in the ecologically sensitive area of Dibden Bay near the port of Southampton. After massive protests from ecological interest groups and public bodies, who referred to obligations under the EU Birds and Habitats Directives, the UK Transport Minister on 20 April 2004 accepted the recommendation of the Dibden Bay Inquiry Inspector to turn down ABP's proposal. As a consequence, the plans for the construction of the new container terminal facilities were definitively cancelled. This decision was reached after a 13-month public inquiry. It did not give rise to further litigation before the courts.

4.2.7. Conclusions

From the brief overview of cases above, it may be concluded that regular procedures for transport infrastructure projects often take five, ten or more years. Whilst we would wish to question neither the outcome of the procedures in any individual case nor even the objections raised against certain plans, it can hardly be denied that the regular procedures have appeared rather cumbersome and protracted. Moreover, they are essentially unstable due to political uncertainties, the complexity and vagueness of the legal framework, local opposition – including the NIMBY (Not In My Back Yard) syndrome – and the sheer unpredictability of court judgments, especially in environmental matters. To sum it up, current procedural legislation may be held to lack efficiency and to cause severe legal uncertainty to the detriment of public authorities, investors and third parties alike. As a consequence, regular procedures increasingly discourage investments. As they may cause or prolong congestion of transportation facilities, delays resulting from the interruption of project procedures and construction works may sometimes bring about additional environmental damage in themselves.

5. AD HOC PROCEDURES

5.1. Definition of ad hoc Procedure

An 'ad hoc' project procedure may be defined as a specific project procedure governed by a legislative framework established with a view to one or more individual projects. In current legislative practice in Belgium and the Netherlands various denominations are used, such as 'specific', 'ad hoc', 'interim', 'experimental', 'exceptional', 'temporary', 'emergency', 'incidental', 'speed' or simply 'project' procedures or laws. Sometimes the more general term *lex specialis* is used. It should be noted that legislators also have recourse to *leges speciales* in other sectors than transport infrastructure development. As a legislative and political phenomenon, the adoption of ad hoc laws is in other words not exclusive to transport policy. The present chapter, however, focuses on the latter domain.

5.2. A Selection of Cases

5.2.1. Deepening of Scheldt Authorisation Act (Netherlands)

In 1996, a previous deepening programme for the river Scheldt was interrupted as a result of a decision of the Dutch Supreme Administrative Court establishing that, contrary to environmental law prescriptions, one of the required administrative permits had not been delivered. Since the Dutch government had committed itself to authorize deepening works in a bilateral international treaty with the Flemish government in Belgium and since it attached great importance to the principle of good neighbourliness, it proposed a special Scheldt Authorisation Act which was subsequently adopted by parliament and which contained all the necessary administrative permits for the deepening of the river itself, thereby bypassing the regular legal procedures.[31]

5.2.2. 5th Runway at Schiphol Airport Act (Netherlands)

In 1998, the Dutch legislator adopted a specific Act in order to speed up the project procedure for the construction of an additional runway at the national airport of Schiphol.[32]

5.2.3. Broadening of Motorways Speed Act (Netherlands)

In 2003, a similar bill was enacted for the purpose of the broadening of Dutch motorways. In order to combat traffic congestion, the Act provided for a specific and accelerated project procedure in order to turn hard shoulders into additional traffic lanes.[33]

5.2.4. Deurganckdok Emergency Decrees (Flanders)

As we have explained above,[34] the administrative decisions relating to the construction of the Deurganckdok in the port of Antwerp were suspended by various judgments of the Belgian Supreme Administrative Court. In order to create a new legal basis for the project, the Flemish legislator enacted several emergency bills declaring the project of general and strategic interest for the Flemish economy.

5.2.5. Lex Airbus (Germany)

The specific Airbus Act adopted by the Free and Hanseatic City of Hamburg in 2002 is a similar case. The Airbus airplane factory is located at Finkenwerder close to the port of Hamburg and is the largest employer in the city. Its state-of-the-art premises were partly built in the Mühlenwerder Loch, a wetland in the Elbe river which had to be filled in. Ecologist interest groups and inhabitants successfully challenged the decision before a local law court, but upon appeal this judgment was reversed. In order to emphasize the general interest and the strategic economic importance of the investment project and to ensure the full co-operation of the City State, the regional parliament of Hamburg enacted an ad hoc bill which is nicknamed the Lex Airbus.[35] This did not prevent the courts from suspending the works for the extension of the factory's runway in 2004. The compulsory acquisition of land with a view to this extension has remained a contentious issue ever since.

5.3. A Further Classification of ad hoc Procedures

Partly on the basis of the above presentation of examples of ad hoc procedures, we would like to propose a further distinction between emergency ad hoc procedures, orderly ad hoc procedures (or project procedures in the strict sense), and improved regular procedures.

Emergency ad hoc procedures find their origin and *raison d'être* in the threat of legal proceedings or in actual interruptions of a regular procedure imposed by courts or other authorities, and always occur *after* a regular procedure has been started and has subsequently failed or threatened to fail. Such was the case with the Deurganckdok Emergency Decrees, the Deepening of the Scheldt Authorisation Act and the Lex Airbus.

Orderly ad hoc procedures (or project procedures in the strict sense) are more efficient and stable specific procedures which are organized *before* the project starts in order to accelerate the process and/or to avoid the risk of interruptions and delays; in other words *in order to avoid the need for emergency procedures*. As a matter of fact, specific procedures appear to be, to a certain extent, exactly the opposite of emergency procedures. Typical examples include the Dutch 5th Runway at Schiphol Airport and Broadening of Motorways Speed Acts.

A third and closely related category of specific procedures, which we have not discussed above, includes *improved regular procedures* which are enacted in order to accelerate the project procedures for large-scale projects of major interest. The scope of such 'specific regular' procedures is not limited to one or more individually designated projects. Such procedures fall somewhere in between ad hoc procedures and regular procedures. Recent examples taken from Dutch legislative practice are the State Projects Procedure Act[36] and the Shortened Line Infrastructure Procedure Act[37] which allow a rapid and co-ordinated approach of large projects of national interest. Another measure of a general nature which has attracted large attention in the Netherlands is the interweaving of the procedures for administrative authorizations, environmental impact assessments and public procurement.[38] Finally, the Dutch Parliament advocates the introduction of specific rules for political control and monitoring of large-scale infrastructure projects, which take into account the social and technical complexity of such projects as well as the financial uncertainties which are characteristic of their execution.[39]

Similarly, the German Parliament adopted in 2006 new[40] legislative measures to render the existing zoning procedures for the construction of transportation infrastructures more smooth, rapid and efficient.[41] These measures include the introduction of time bars for complaints by private associations and, for exceptionally important projects such as the improvement of the sea and hinterland connections of German seaports, the limitation of the judicial process to one instance, thereby abolishing the right to appeal. The projects which come under the scope of these new rules are exhaustively mentioned in a list and include works in the rivers Elbe and Weser. It is expected that the new rules will on average lead to a gain of time amounting to two years. The new regime has found political support with the City State of Hamburg, which has a special interest in some important, mainly port-related projects including the deepening of the river Elbe (planned since 2002), the construction of a partly privately financed motorway through the port area (planned since 1969) and the electrification of a railway link to the port of Lübeck (planned since 1992).

5.4. Objections against ad hoc Procedures

The increased use of ad hoc project procedures is abundantly criticized in Dutch legal literature.[42] In a remarkable Belgian analysis of 'incident legislation' it was even assumed that such legislation is generally characterized by a lack of transparency in the motives because it is in most cases masked as if it were made for a generality of cases, not for one particular case.[43] Objections are often heard in political circles as well. As a matter of fact, there appears to exist a standard or even classical set of objections against ad hoc procedures.

Upon closer scrutiny, some of these objections turn out to be based on mere prejudices which all too often overlook the basic distinction between orderly ad hoc procedures and emergency ad hoc procedures explained above.

A first complaint which is often heard is that ad hoc procedures lead to an unjustifiable discrimination: public authorities stretch and twist the ordinary legal framework in order to conform it to their own needs, while citizens must abide by the regular procedures. In this respect reference may be made to the German Constitution which expressly prohibits limitations of fundamental rights through laws which only apply to one particular case.[44]

Secondly, ad hoc procedures are said to interfere with normal legal proceedings and are considered to be contrary to the fundamental if not constitutionally embedded principle of the separation of powers (aka the Montesquieu doctrine). Moreover, an ad hoc project procedure laid down in an inviolable parliamentary bill may totally cut off access to courts for citizens and therefore entail a violation of human rights. Also, it is said that the legislator changes the rules of the game during the game.

Thirdly, ad hoc procedures, which are suspected of rushing through projects regardless of public opinion, are believed to reduce or annihilate public participation and to be contrary to present day democratic achievements.

Fourthly, ad hoc procedures are said to run counter to international and EU environmental obligations. They all too often do away with sound procedural requirements laid down with a view to the protection of scarce nature areas from uncontrolled and in any event irrevocable infrastructure developments.

Fifthly, and seen from a political rather than a legal point of view, ad hoc legislation or procedures are allegedly not based upon a balancing of interests from a general perspective, which should mark the work of the legislator as compared with that of the administration and the judiciary.

5.5. Good Reasons for Adopting ad hoc Procedures

Notwithstanding the canon of standard objections set out above, there exist, in our view, several good reasons for adopting project procedures in certain circumstances.

Firstly, *nulla regula sine exceptione*: project procedures should be geared to the specific if not totally exceptional characteristics of large-scale infrastructure projects,[45] such as their political priority, their strategic economic and social importance as well as their social and technical complexity. More particularly, the procedures should take into account the need to make use of innovative construction techniques and of specific or alternative financial sources, as well as the exceptional burden which their preparation and execution place upon the competent public authorities. In short, large infrastructure projects go beyond daily administrative routine and can even become a once-in-a-lifetime experience for the responsible civil servants and politicians; therefore the rigid application of regular project procedures is often simply unrealistic.

Secondly, ad hoc procedures prevent often unacceptable delays of strategic priority projects and avoid the typical problems arising from a legal complexity that public authorities are often not able correctly to cope with themselves. Governments become increasingly aware that regular procedures are often unrealistically long-lasting and cumbersome. When the law, for example, offers the opportunity for the general public to participate in the decision-making process at three consecutive stages – which can take months or years – or even to lodge formal complaints at each of these stages – which may lead to repeated interruptions of the project – one can wonder whether the protection of citizens' rights is not disproportional to the importance of the project.

Thirdly, ad hoc procedures often allow a circumvention of completely superfluous legal prescriptions and administrative bureaucracy.

Fourthly, an ad hoc project procedure is in many cases the only way to ensure legal certainty for public authorities and private investors.

As we have explained above, the administrative preparation of decisions takes a considerable amount of time and all too often, carefully prepared decisions – like the Dutch one on the construction of the Second Maasvlakte – surprisingly turn out not to withstand the test of scrutiny by law courts. When the chance of violating the relevant regular legislation becomes greater than the chance of correctly implementing it, the question arises whether such legislation is not unlawful in itself and whether the State should not be held liable for the consequences. Given the general trend towards the acceptance of the liability of the State for wrongful legislative acts,[46] such considerations will only gain importance. One can only wait for the first frustrated investor to put the ball back into the court of the State by accusing it of having adopted impracticable legislation, introduced unstable administrative procedures and organized unpredictable legal proceedings, which does not offer basic legal certainty for investors in projects which the same State has declared to be of strategic importance.

Fifth, far from being incompatible with environmental law, the adoption of project procedures finds an express legal basis in EU environmental legislation itself. Indeed, the EU EIA Directive contains an explicit provision allowing Member States to adopt projects through specific legal provisions.[47] Similarly, the adoption of ad hoc procedures which override regular requirements is only a logical consequence of the provision of the EU Habitats Directive exceptionally allowing important projects to affect nature conservation sites for 'imperative reasons of overriding public interest':[48] the same overriding interest should also be recognized when it comes to the organization of the preparatory administrative procedure.

Sixth, it should be remembered that the European Commission has called upon the Member States to co-ordinate project procedures in order to streamline regular procedures for important cross-border projects forming part of the Trans-European Network.[49] This exhortation can be reasonably understood as an invitation of national governments to adopt ad hoc procedures for certain trans-boundary projects of European interest.

Seventh, the above considerations gain importance as the European Commission is pressing Member States' governments to have recourse to private funding of investments in new transport infrastructure.[50] A shift towards public–private partnerships and private financing schemes seems hardly realistic as long as the legal framework does not ensure minimum economic stability and legal security, which regular procedures are often unable to offer.

To conclude, ad hoc procedures will remain a vital necessity as long as the regular procedures are deficient. In this respect, orderly ad hoc procedures are much to be preferred to emergency procedures. That is not to say that orderly ad hoc procedures are an ideal: the optimal solution would be to improve regular procedures for large-scale projects of strategic interest. Hopefully, the recent initiatives taken to that effect by the Dutch and German governments will become trend-setting.

5.6. Preconditions for good ad hoc Procedures

Whilst there exist, in certain circumstances, perfectly valid reasons for the adoption of ad hoc project procedures, such procedures should in any case conform to a number of basic standards.

First and foremost, they must conform to the international and EU legal framework. More in particular, they should respect minimum standards relating to environmental protection and public participation. Also, they should guarantee minimum access to courts as guaranteed under the European Human Rights Convention which, according to case law of the ECHR, does, however, allow certain limitations of access to courts in the general interest.[51]

On the other hand, national rules and measures pertaining to environmental protection, public participation and access to courts, which would go beyond and gold-plate minimum international and EU standards, should be carefully assessed before their introduction. Their added value in terms of improved protection of the environment and citizens' rights should be balanced against their impact on the efficiency of the procedure and the smooth execution of the project.

Finally, ad hoc procedures should be based on thorough, detailed and transparent grounds setting out the compelling reasons for the adoption of specific rules for the case in point and which objectively balance all the interests at stake.

6. CONCLUSIONS

In recent legislative practice in Belgium and Holland, there is a general tendency to bypass regular project procedures for infrastructure and especially seaport development through the adoption of ad hoc procedures. As it is considered to entail a circumvention of sound environmental standards and of fundamental rules on the protection of citizens' rights, this new phenomenon is much criticized. In our view, these specific procedures are only the symptom of the real disease which is the sheer inefficiency of regular procedures. Ad hoc procedures would simply not be needed if the regular procedures were well organized. In order to avoid a further spread of ad hoc procedures, an overhaul of existing regular procedures seems highly recommendable. Some governments have already taken initiatives to create specific improved procedures for broadly defined categories of large-scale projects of strategic interest.

Next, we have pointed out that a basic distinction should be made between well-considered 'orderly' ad hoc project procedures in the strict sense, which are deliberately organized before a procedure starts, and 'emergency' project procedures, which are rendered necessary by – all too frequent – interruptions of the regular procedures after they were started, or by acute threats of such interruptions. Emergency procedures tend to interfere with normal legal proceedings and should only be applied in extreme cases. Orderly ad hoc procedures, on the other hand, will remain unavoidable as long as regular procedures remain time-inefficient and do not offer sufficient legal certainty to public authorities and investors. In certain circumstances and on condition that a number of preconditions are met with, there may exist perfectly valid reasons for adopting such ad hoc procedures.

Finally, the above considerations gain importance as the European Commission is requesting Member States' governments to have recourse to private financing for infrastructure development. A shift towards public–private partnerships seems hardly realistic as long as the legal framework does not ensure minimum economic stability and legal certainty.[52]

NOTES

1. Convention on Access to Information, Public Participation in Decision-making and Access to Justice in Environmental Matters, Aarhus, 25 June 1998.
2. Convention on Environmental Impact Assessment in a Transboundary Context, Espoo, 25 February 1991.
3. Convention for the Protection of Human Rights and Fundamental Freedoms, Rome, 4 November 1950.
4. Directive No 79/409/EEC of the Council of 2 April 1979 on the conservation of wild birds (OJ 1979 L 103/1); Directive No 92/43/EEC of the Council of 21 May 1992 on the conservation of natural habitats and of wild fauna and flora (OJ 1992 L 206/7).
5. Directive No 85/337/EEC of the Council of 27 June 1985 on the assessment of the effects of certain public and private projects on the environment (OJ 1985 L 175/40); Directive No 2001/42/EC of the European Parliament and of the Council of 27 June 2001 on the assessment of the effects of certain plans and programmes on the environment (OJ 2001 L 197/30).
6. Directive No 2000/60/EC of the European Parliament and of the Council of 23 October 2000 establishing a framework for the Community action in the field of water policy (OJ 2000 L 327/1).
7. See for example Art. 113 of the Vienna Final Act (1815), Art. 9 of the Treaty on the Separation of Belgium and the Netherlands, signed in London on 19 April 1839 and Art. 28 of the Revised Rhine Act, signed in Mannheim on 17 October 1868.
8. See especially Art. 82 of the EC Treaty and the related essential facilities doctrine.
9. Decision No 1692/96/EC of the European Parliament and of the Council of 23 July 1996 on Community guidelines for the development of the trans-European transport network (OJ 1996 L 228/1).
10. Regulation (EC) No 1382/2003 of the European Parliament and of the Council of 22 July 2003 on the granting of Community financial assistance to improve the environmental performance of the freight transport system (Marco Polo Programme) (OJ 2003 L 196/1).
11. Art. 12a Decision No 884/2004/EC of the European Parliament and of the Council of 29 April 2004 amending Decision No 1692/96/EC on Community guidelines for the development of the trans-European transport network (OJ 2004 L 167/1).
12. Compare, for example, the Commission's decisions in state aid cases SG(2000) D/107700 – N 577/1999 (RSC Rotterdam and RSC Maasvlakte), SG(2000) D/100617 – N 293/99, Vlaamse Intermodale Kring, C(2001)3944fin – N 550/2001, PPS laad-en losinstallaties and C(2001)4512fin – N 649/2001, Freight Facilities Grant (FFG).

13. Council Regulation (EC) No 2679/98 of 7 December 1998 on the functioning of the internal market in relation to the free movement of goods among the Member States (OJ 1998 L 337/8).
14. See E. Van Hooydonk, *The Impact of EU Environmental Law on Ports and Waterways, including a Proposal for the Creation of* Portus 2010, *a Coherent EU Network of Strategic Port Development Areas*, Antwerp/Apeldoorn, 2006, p. 317.
15. Most of the cases referred to below are discussed in greater detail in our study on the impact of EU environmental law on ports and waterways cited above.
16. Compare E. Van Hooydonk, 'Het internationaal statuut van de IJzeren Rijn: van het Scheidingsverdrag tot de Trans-Europese Netwerken', in F. Witlox (ed.), *De IJzeren Rijn en de Betuweroute. Het debat op de juiste sporen?*, Leuven-Apeldoorn: Garant, 2000, pp. 21–74; E. Van Hooydonk, 'Het juridisch statuut van de Belgisch-Nederlandse verkeersverbindingen in actueel en Europees perspectief', in E. Van Hooydonk (ed.), *De Belgisch-Nederlandse verkeersverbindingen. De Schelde in de XXIste eeuw*, Antwerpen/Apeldoorn, Maklu, 2002, pp. 91–368, especially 223 et seq.; see also www.projectijzerenrijn.nl (consulted on 4 December 2006).
17. Art. 12 of the London Treaty cited above, note 7.
18. In Dutch *Tracéwetprocedure*.
19. See www.pca-cpa.org/ENGLISH/RPC/#Belgium/Netherlands (consulted on 4 December 2006).
20. See E. Van Hooydonk, 'Het juridisch statuut', op. cit, p. 165 et seq.; www.proses.be (consulted on 20 September 2005).
21. See note 7 *supra*.
22. See the Report of the Belgian State Auditor's Office of the construction of the Deurganckdok (*Rekenhof / Cour des Comptes*) of 14 June 2005 in the Acts of the Flemish Parliament, 2004–2005, no. 37-F/1; www.deurganckdok.be (consulted on 20 September 2005).
23. In Dutch *Raad van State*.
24. Flemish Decrees of 14 December 2001, 29 March 2002, 27 June 2003, 13 February 2004, 7 May 2004 and 17 December 2004 relating to building permits of compelling major general interest.
25. In Dutch *Raad van State*.
26. Dutch Council of State, judgment of 16 July 2003, Case 200205582/1.
27. See www.maasvlakte2.com (consulted on 20 September 2005).
28. In Dutch, *planologische kernbeslissing*.
29. Dutch Council of State, judgment of 26 January 2005, Case 200307350/1.
30. UK Department for Transport, *Dibden Bay Decision letter*, www.dft.gov.uk/stellent/groups/dft_shipping/documents/pdf/dft_shipping_pdf_028330.pdf, consulted 19 September 2005.
31. Act of 18 June 1997.
32. Act of 24 December 1998.
33. Act of 2 June 2003.
34. See *supra*, para 4.2.3.
35. Act of 18 June 2002.
36. Act of 20 November 2003.
37. Act of 20 October 2005. It should be added that the initial Line Infrastructure Act was already an attempt at introducing shorter and simpler procedures for the development of infrastructures of national interest.
38. See the *Werkwijzer vervlechting tracé/m.e.r.- en aanbestedingsprocedure bij infrastructurele projecten*, issued by the Dutch Ministry of *Verkeer en Waterstaat* in February 2005.
39. See especially the Duivesteijn report in the Acts of the *Tweede Kamer*, 2004–2005, no. 29 283–6.
40. Germany already adopted specific zoning rules for road construction back in the 1990s (See the *Verkehrswegeplanungsbeschleunigungsgesetz* of 16 December 1991 and the *Planungsvereinfachungsgesetz* of 17 December 1993).

41. *Gesetz zur Beschleunigung von Planungsverfahren für Infrastrukturvorhaben*, adopted by the Bundesrat on 24 November 2006.
42. See especially Th.G. Drupsteen, 'Kroniek van het milieurecht', *Nederlands Juristenblad*, 1997, (1490), pp. 1491–92; Ph. Eijlander, 'Gelegenheidswetgeving. Een rechtsstaat onwaardig?', *Ars Aequi*, 2004, pp. 484–91; A.Q.C. Tak, 'Misbruik van wetgeving', *Openbaar Bestuur*, 1997, 12, 7–9; P.J.J. Van Buuren, 'Vergunningwet Westerschelde niet voor herhaling vatbaar', *Milieu & Recht*, 1997, pp. 122–4; J.M. Verschuuren, 'De formele wetgever als uitvoerder: de Vergunningwet Westerschelde en het streven naar een integrale afweging', *Bouwrecht*, 1998, pp. 361–7; J.M. Verschuuren, 'Schiphol en wéér een vlucht in projectwetgeving', *Nederlands Juristenblad*, 1998, pp. 357–8.
43. R. Van Gestel, 'Incident- of gelegenheidswetgeving: balanceren op het smalle koord van de trias politica', *Tijdschrift voor Privaatrecht*, 2004, pp. 1667–720.
44. Art. 19 (1) of the German *Grundgesetz* reads: 'Soweit nach diesem Grundgesetz ein Grundrecht durch Gesetz oder auf Grund eines Gesetzes eingeschränkt werden kann, muß das Gesetz allgemein und nicht nur für den Einzelfall gelten. Außerdem muß das Gesetz das Grundrecht unter Angabe des Artikels nennen'.
45. The specific nature of large projects is acknowledged in the Dutch Duivesteijn Report cited *supra* at note 39.
46. See for Belgium P. Popelier, 'De rechtspraak van het Arbitragehof over lacunes in de wetgeving', *Tijdschrift voor Bestuurswetenschappen en Publiekrecht*, 2005, Vol. 4 and 5 (p. 284), p. 295, no. 47–48.
47. Art. 1 (5) of Directive 85/337/EEC.
48. Art. 6 (4) of Directive 92/43/EEC.
49. See recital (20) and Art. 1 10) and 13) of Decision No 884/2004/EC of 29 April 2004 amending the aforementioned Decision 1692/96/EC (OJ 2004 L167/1).
50. White Paper 'European transport policy for 2010: time to decide', COM/2001/0370 final, 59–60; see also Green Paper on public–private partnerships and Community law on public contracts and concessions, COM/2004/0327 final; Art. 29 Directive 2004/18/EC of the European Parliament and of the Council of 31 March 2004 on the co-ordination of procedures for the award of public works contracts, public supply contracts and public service contracts (OJ 2004 L 134/114).
51. See, inter alia, ECHR 24 June 1986, *Lithgow*, http://hudoc.echr.coe.int/Hudoc2doc/HEJUD/sift/111.txt, at para 195; ECHR 23 October 1997, *National & Provincial Building Society*, http://hudoc.echr.coe.int/Hudoc2doc/HEJUD/ sift/81.txt, at para 105; ECHR 28 October 1999, *Zielinski*, at para 57. Compare, for example, on the incompatibility with a Belgian constitutional standstill rule on environmental protection, the EU EIA Directive and the Aarhus Convention of a Decree of the Walloon Region in Belgium on a simplification of zoning formalities for certain industrial investments, judgment no. 137/2006 of the Belgian Cour d'Arbitrage of 14 September 2006.
52. In May 2007, the UK Government published a White Paper entitled *Planning for a Sustainable Future* which contains proposals for more efficient planning procedures, including for key national infrastructure projects (see www.communities.gov.uk).

PART II

Empirical studies and applications of economic transport project evaluation in a complex European environment

7. A new guideline for 'ex ante' evaluation of large infrastructure projects in the Netherlands

Martin de Jong and Bert Van Wee

INTRODUCTION

In the Netherlands, the past decade and a half, roughly speaking, has seen both increased congestion levels and a dramatic increase in the attention paid to investing in transport infrastructures. Since people experience the consequences of limitations in their mobility directly and personally, the failure and success of policies regarding transport are hotly debated in policy arenas, research and in 'normal life'. A new railway line or motorway, the introduction of road pricing, tolls or another system of having vehicle drivers pay for the use of infrastructure, levies on fuels, and public transport subsidies, are all subjects discussed with fervour. Large transport infrastructure projects have offered opportunities to combat traffic congestion or increase travel speed for people and goods, but they are also quite expensive and have a non-negligible impact on other aspects related to the quality of life. In order to make sure the public's money is spent wisely, the subject of conducting a systematic analysis of such large transport infrastructure projects has come much more to the fore.

Because of their impacts on society and the costs of infrastructure it is no surprise that researchers have developed frameworks to make *ex ante* evaluations of infrastructure projects. In addition, policy makers and politicians need *ex ante* evaluations for policy making to back up their political decisions. In a special issue of *Transport Policy*, an overview of methods used in several countries is presented. In that special issue Hayashi and Moritsugi (2000) give a comprehensive account of the practices in the selected countries, concluding that nowadays cost–benefit analysis (CBA) is a widely-used method to evaluate the impacts of transport infrastructure. The Netherlands is no exception to this rule: it has a guideline for CBA application which has been made obligatory for large projects (Eijgenraam et al., 1999). This guideline was sent to parliament in early 2000. It was decided that it should be applied to all official proposals for major transport infrastructure plans, not only major roads and rail projects but also other projects such as harbour and airport expansions, and canals. Since then it has been applied to all official proposals for major national transport infrastructure projects.

This chapter aims to describe the problematical situation in the Netherlands before the introduction of the guidelines, leading to the conclusion that a guideline had to be developed. The third section presents the main features of the guideline, while the fourth section deals with the experience policy makers and analysts have had with its application thus far. In the fifth section, the future prospects of *ex ante* evaluation of transport infrastructure projects in general, and, more specifically, the Dutch version of CBA, are explored. The final section presents the main conclusions.

THE ROAD TO THE DUTCH GUIDELINE FOR CBA OF TRANSPORT INFRASTRUCTURE

As is the case in many other Western countries, the Dutch government has invested lots of money in its infrastructure. This has been mostly in roads, but some new railway lines have been constructed as well. After the reduction in infrastructure expenditure in the 1970s and 1980s many people felt things had to change. New infrastructure had to be built to boost the economy. For example, the rail connection between Rotterdam Harbour and its so-called hinterland (mainly the Ruhr area in Germany) was quite poor. On the other hand Germany had better rail connections from the Northern harbours to the Ruhr area and ambitious plans for further investments. To improve the competitive position of the Port of Rotterdam and to boost the economy a new dedicated rail-freight line was proposed, the so-called Betuwe Line. This line would not only have a positive impact on macro-economic development, but also on the levels of emissions from freight transport due to a modal shift from road to rail, and on the congestion levels the motorways increasingly have to cope with. A very effective lobby favouring the Port of Rotterdam (consisting amongst others of representatives from the Port Authority itself, the Dutch National Railway Company and the Ministry of Transport) succeeded in establishing a positive climate for the project among politicians. The approval from the Dutch government and both Chambers of Parliament was rapidly secured.

In the 1990s more and more information became available showing that it was far from certain whether the benefits of the project would indeed exceed the costs. The first official plan announcing the Betuwe Line, the

Second Transport Structure Plan (Ministerie van Verkeer en Waterstaat, 1990), assumed costs would amount to approximately 2.3 billion Dutch guilders, just over 1 billion euros. In 2005, the costs of the railway line, which is currently under construction, are estimated at 4.8 billion euros. An important factor explaining the difference is the addition of many infrastructure elements to reduce local impacts: to gain support (or, better, to reduce resistance) of local and regional authorities and the public, many amendments were made to the line. The economic benefits were based on forecasts that were not 'neutral' forecasts, but rather 'wishful thinking' scenarios (Janse et al., 2000). The environmental legitimacy was based on a very simple line of thought: rail-freight transport produces less emission per tonne kilometre compared to road-freight transport. Therefore construction, maintenance and operation of the line would benefit the environment. However, calculations made in 1994 showed that the reduction of emissions of CO_2 and NO_x by freight transport that would occur in the Netherlands would certainly not be more than 0–2.5 per cent, if these reductions occurred at all. This paradoxical conclusion could be drawn from the scenarios for the transport impacts of the line, which were used as a basis for the economic calculations. It was assumed that additional rail-freight transport in the Netherlands due to the Betuwe Line would otherwise be transported via other countries (50 per cent), via barge (40 per cent) or via road (10 per cent) (Van Wee et al., 1994). This distribution was chosen because it was assumed that the added value of transporting goods via rail is bigger in comparison to barge, but smaller when compared to road transport. The scenario was therefore biased in favour of higher economic impacts for the new rail line. However, this assumption was in contradiction with the simple line of reasoning for the environment. In fact, more generally, assumptions used for the economic calculations seemed inconsistent with those used to support the environmental legitimacy. Despite, or possibly because of, more than 2 metres of reports, there was no clear or useful overview of pros and cons or costs and benefits of the project, making it very doubtful on what grounds the decision-making was based. To summarize, the experience with the *ex ante* evaluation of the Betuwe Line was less than positive, to put it mildly. In fact, it was an incarnation of just about everything that could go wrong: a huge underestimation of the costs, inconsistent use of scenarios, transport volume forecasts that proved to be wishful thinking, a lack of overview for decision-makers, and finally a railway link that nearly all consider as a bad project.

The sobering experience with the Betuwe Line is the most extreme example of the major debates on several infrastructure projects, other examples being the high speed rail link from Amsterdam to Brussels, the expansion of Schiphol Airport and the second seaport expansion of

Rotterdam Harbour. The debates on these projects had a large part to play in the decision of Dutch policy makers that a guideline had to be developed showing how *ex ante* evaluations of infrastructure projects had to be carried out. Two ministries, the Ministry of Transport and Public Works, and the Ministry of Economic Affairs, financed a research project in which almost all Dutch institutes and researchers involved in transport economics participated and developed methods. The approach aimed to reach consensus between involved actors on how to evaluate transport projects. Among the various research institutes, the Central Planning Bureau (CPB) and the Netherlands Economic Institute (NEI) played key roles, since these institutes developed the guideline based on the many background documents produced by the wider group of institutes. In general the guideline is supported by the main researchers and policy makers in this area. In the following section, this guideline will be described.

MAIN CHARACTERISTICS OF THE CBA GUIDELINE FOR TRANSPORT INFRASTRUCTURE PROJECTS

In this section we focus on the main aspects of the guideline (Eijgenraam et al., 1999). For a full overview we refer to the English language version of the manual (Ministry of Transport, Public Works and Water Management and Ministry of Economic Affairs, 2000).[1] The guideline is largely in line with the British SACTRA report (Standing Advisory Committee on Trunk Road Assessment) (SACTRA, 1999) (and the guidelines for several types of projects based on the SACTRA project as can be found on the website of the UK Ministry). Both SACTRA and the Dutch guideline recommend CBA. Both studies stress the importance of wider economic impacts and distribution effects. The Dutch study is somewhat more applied and uses many examples to illustrate the dos and don'ts.

Preliminary CBAs and Comprehensive CBAs

As mentioned before, the guideline for the *ex ante* evaluation of large infrastructure projects (Eijgenraam et al., 1999) concludes that CBA is the preferred method, not multi-criteria analysis or scorecards, mainly because of the possibilities to manipulate outcomes by changing the weights for evaluations criteria. It distinguishes between two categories of CBAs, preliminary CBAs and comprehensive CBAs. The first type is to be used for decision-making at an early stage, that is to find out whether project alternatives or the base case alternative are preferred, and which alternatives might be interesting and deserve more attention. Comprehensive CBAs can then focus more on the most promising alternatives and evaluate them in more detail, implying the use of more indicators and more advanced methods to evaluate the value of the indicators for the alternatives.

Obligatory for Large Infrastructure Projects

All large infrastructure projects have to be evaluated *ex ante* following the guideline. For other ones, including local and regional projects, its application is strongly recommended. For such projects a simplified version of the guideline was written. There is not a sharp definition on what a 'large project' is, but in practice there is not much discussion about this. Note that infrastructure projects not only include roads, railways and waterways, but also port and airport extensions. In fact, the guideline has been applied to plans for extensions of both the Port of Rotterdam and Schiphol Airport.

A guideline, not a blueprint

As the name suggests, the document is a guideline, and not a blueprint. It leaves possibilities for interpretation and other degrees of freedom. However, some aspects are prescriptions: the CBA approach, the definitions of effect categories, the discount rate and the value of time are obligatory. For models and methods the guideline gives the pros and cons of several options. In fact, even though analysts now agree on the general principles, some still disagree on the ways in which these should be fleshed out in practical circumstances.

The base case

Very important is the role of the base case (also called reference alternative). In many countries and for many types of evaluations, such as CBA, multi-criteria analyses (MCA) and Environmental Impact Assessment (EIA) the base case is often described as business as usual (BAU), do nothing, or 'current policy'. The Dutch guide, however, states that the base case should be the best alternative available for the project. This may be 'do nothing', 'current policies', but it might also be an alternative for the plan under consideration. Compare a person putting his money in an old sock. A bank might say: we give you 2 per cent interest, so this is to be preferred. But if another bank gives an interest rate of 4 per cent, this is a better option. The same is true for infrastructure projects. If the project alternative is to build a new motorway to stimulate economic growth in a region, the base case might be business as usual, but it might also be building a rail line, building another major road but not a motorway, costing less money, or to stimulate economic growth in that region by fiscal measures making it more attractive for firms to locate to that region.

Indirect Effects

Policy makers often legitimize infrastructure projects claiming significant 'strategic' or indirect effects. Indirect effects can be added to the direct transport benefits. The guideline states that indirect effects may exist, and can be both positive and negative. However, effects claimed to be indirect are often direct effects passed through to other actors. An example is a transport company saving money because of shorter travel times due to faster roads. If the company then reduces the tariffs for the shipper, the benefits for the shipper are not additional, but only direct benefits passed on to the shipper. The CBA guide states that most of the wider economic effects are due to a redistribution of the original direct effect through the markets. According to the guide, additional benefits can only be realized if markets do not function optimally and if the project influences the size of these imperfections or, alternatively, results in international displacement of production or consumption. Indirect effects have played an important role in many discussions related to the guideline (see next section).

Disaggregations

CBAs have often been criticized for focusing only at the national level, ignoring the fact that there are actors winning and other actors losing (see next section). The guideline states explicitly that in some cases it might be beneficial to disaggregate, examples being income classes, regions or interest groups (such as transport companies).

The Treatment of Risk

People are risk-averse. Therefore, the guideline concludes that additional risks of a project will represent negative effects on welfare. The guide stresses the theoretical advantages of risk evaluation but does not advise on a practical method to do this.

EXPERIENCES WITH THE GUIDELINE THUS FAR

The guideline has been applied to some 15 transport infrastructure projects to date. The authors have found four different evaluations, some of which were conducted by consultants, others by academics. The official evaluation commissioned by the Ministry of Transport and Public Works was drafted by Buck Consultants International (2002) on behalf of the Ministry of Transport and Public Works. The other three were conducted by the

Central Planning Bureau (CPB, 2003), the Research Institute for Public Health and the Environment (RIVM) and the Foundation for Social and Economic Research (SEO) (Annema et al., 2002) and two scholars from Delft University of Technology and Erasmus University Rotterdam respectively (de Jong and Geerlings, 2003). These evaluations have been taken quite seriously by the Ministry of Transport and Public Works and were translated into new insights for a new, adjusted CBA practice and incorporated into a set of additions to the guideline which was issued at the end of 2004. By doing this, the authors believe a major step was taken towards the further improvement of the quality and usefulness of *ex ante* evaluations for decision-making purposes. This section will present the main points of criticism which were raised in the various evaluations (without claiming comprehensiveness), whereas the following section will show the action undertaken by the Ministry to remedy these weaknesses. Because we focus on the criticism, the positive experiences may easily be overlooked. Therefore we would first like to state that in our opinion the introduction of the guideline significantly improved the quality of research related to decision-making with respect to large infrastructure projects. Besides, such research had its impact on the project proposals, leading to improvements of the original proposals. For example, due to the CBA of the Rotterdam Harbour extensions it was concluded that a phasing of these extensions should be considered (Annema et al., forthcoming).

General criticism of CBA echoed in some of the evaluations

To some degree, criticisms voiced against the Dutch edition of CBA mirror international and general points raised about the methodology behind cost–benefit analysis itself. Annema et al. (forthcoming) summarize these critics, and base their conclusions on authors such as Kelman (1981), Heinzerling and Ackerman (2002), Sen (2000), Kopp et al. (1997), and Posner (2000). The methodological dispute concerning CBA can be summarized in five main points of criticism.

First, some scientists argue that, fundamentally, CBA represents a flawed appraisal method, based as it is on utilitarianism, which they consider an unsatisfactory moral system. One of the basic principles of CBA is that all the impacts of a project on individuals are valued on the basis of the impact issue: that is does it or does it not satisfy individual preferences? This concept of 'utilitarianism' as the base for decision-making has been widely attacked (the authors suppose this is the core of the dissension); 'satisfaction of people's "manifest" preferences is not an adequate index of well-being because there are conceivable circumstances in which these preferences might be satisfied, even though the individuals' true interests were far from being served' (Scanlon, 1991). This seems to suggest that people cannot always be relied on to understand and seek their self-interest, because they delude themselves or are deluded by biased information. In such cases, an independent analyst must estimate and value certain goods and services that otherwise would be overlooked. For example, some independent study should be done concerning nature/endangered species when building a new – economically highly attractive – port in a wildlife area, since one cannot rely on CBA to include such irreplaceable (ecocentric as opposed to anthropocentric) values.

The second criticism of CBA is that the market analogy valuation methods for non-priced goods, required in most CBAs for infrastructure projects, are inherently flawed. In mainstream cost–benefit analysis, non-priced impacts are valued using 'willingness to pay' (WTP). According to this strand of criticism, not all non-priced impacts such as nature, landscapes or a clean environment can be valued with a price tag (see for example, Heinzerling and Ackerman, 2002; Niemeijer and Spash, 2001).

A third criticism of CBA is that it ignores distribution effects and equity issues related to these effects. Some claim that decision-making based solely on CBAs threatens to reinforce existing patterns of economic and social inequality. It will, by means of example, strengthen the position of already economically central or privileged regions based in developed industrial areas with higher congestion levels by focusing infrastructure construction there.

A fourth point in the debate is the concern that CBAs can easily provide incomplete or incorrect information for the decision-makers. Mackie and Preston (1998) emphasize that impacts that are difficult to value in monetary terms tend to be excluded in CBAs. Next best to exclusion seems to be the inclusion of these impacts in a qualitative form, or listed as physical units. But whether they will attract the same level of attention when it comes to final valuation and calculation remains to be seen.

Finally, CBA is severely attacked because, in the words of Heinzerling and Ackerman (2002), 'it fails to produce the greater objectivity and transparency promised by its proponents'. The authors find that the highly complex, resource-intensive and expert-driven nature of the CBA appraisal method makes it extremely difficult for the public to understand and participate in the process. This last observation is probably also valid for most of the population – advisers, civil servants, politicians – directly involved in the decision-making process. De Jong (1999a) compared several countries with respect to policy decisions and related research on infrastructure evaluation. His comparison shows that for only two of the seven countries compared, did a standardized appraisal method seem 'relatively effective'. One explanation given by him for this fairly poor result is the seeming complexity of the evaluation methods. Because of this complexity, politicians may find it hard to interpret the results or they may doubt the results because of their incomprehensibility. Another explanation de Jong gives for the relatively ineffective standardized appraisal methods is that they are developed or applied without support from relevant policy actors. This is an invitation to actual or potential enemies rapidly to invent alternative methodologies. De Jong (1999a) observes the danger in many countries that elaborate and carefully balanced appraisals are used selectively as political toys or that the evaluation results lead silent lives in the bosom of the national ministries.

Objections raised against the Dutch edition of CBA

The overview above illustrates that the discussion on CBA is to a large extent an international discussion. The discussions in the Netherlands are partly connected to this international debate, but also show some national characteristics related to the position of CBA within the institutional structure and administrative process. Among decision-makers and pressure groups there is a relatively strong agreement that cost–benefit analysis is the best way to go, and has certainly been a major improvement when compared to the practice before its adoption, with its lack of systematic evaluation. This implies that the first and second general methodological points mentioned previously go relatively unnoticed in pragmatic Dutch decision-making practice. It is perhaps remarkable that environmental groups have mostly gone along with this too, but that can be explained by the fact that some unpopular transport infrastructure projects, which were expected to have a negative impact on the environment, have been brought into disrepute or even cancelled as a result of CBA reports. The third, fourth and fifth points (distribution effects, incomplete or incorrect information and lack of transparency, respectively) did evoke quite a lot of attention, as we will see below.

Annema et al. (forthcoming) evaluated the experiences with the guidelines so far by studying the CBA reports, using benchmarks for both the quality of the CBAs as well as for the process (that is the policy impacts). Their overall conclusion is that the Dutch CBA as carried out since 2000 has had mostly positive effects on the quality and thoroughness of project evaluation, despite the limitations mentioned in the literature. We may therefore safely conclude that, with the benefit of hindsight, the introduction of CBA for infrastructure project evaluation in the Netherlands has been a good idea. Constructive critics, however, have still brought up a number of issues that needed to be resolved.

Complications in the way Dutch CBA Studies were Operationalized

First, the Dutch edition of CBA comprises the comparison of the intended project with a theoretical base case. In practice there is a lot of discussion about the base case: it is complicated to conclude what the best alternative is. In practice the alternatives considered in the reference scenario are transport infrastructure or at least transport systems alternatives, and alternatives outside the transport system, such as in the example given of fiscal measures to make the region more attractive for firms, are not included.

Secondly, it appears that in spite of the fact that preliminary CBAs should remain exactly what their name says they are, being preliminary and generic, analysts often cannot resist the temptation to include more indicators than intended and to use more or less the same methods as for comprehensive CBAs. As a consequence, the distinction between preliminary and comprehensive studies often tends to be blurred.

Thirdly, many decision-makers and observers have noted that non-priced effects have not played an important role in the political discussion so far. This is claimed to be a result of their being included in summarizing CBA tables as just PM (Pro Memoria), while in practice in the accompanying texts they are hardly referred to. Whether the policy analysts like this or not, there is a strong urge among those politically involved to move towards clear figures, and PM posts can never be included in the calculations.

Fourth, and relatedly, the name of the method led to quite some misunderstanding. The (Dutch) original abbreviation of the guideline was OEEI, which stands for Research Program on Economic Effects of Infrastructure. The inclusion of the word 'economic' was the big culprit here: many people thought that only economic effects were incorporated in the reports and nothing else. The results were consequently seen as biased and largely incomplete. Some even did not realize that non-monetary benefits such as travel time savings were included, even though some of them have no impact on GDP. In a letter to the Second Chamber of Parliament, the Minister of Transport and Public Works therefore suggested to drop the word 'economic' and re-baptise OEEI to OEI, meaning Overview of Effects of Infrastructures, implying that other than economic impacts were also a part of the evaluation.

Complications in the way Dutch CBA was positioned in the decision-making process

Since almost exclusively economists were involved in the initial development of Dutch CBA, sensitivity to political, institutional and administrative issues was comparatively low and the position it would acquire amidst the decision-making process remained unclear. Many people assumed that cost–benefit studies were to be conducted before the political decision-making process could begin. Besides, the guideline assumed that policy analysts would remain neutral analysts and stay aloof from political and value debates. In practice, it appeared that CBAs are an integral part of the decision-making process itself and analysts often operate on behalf of political masters who commission and pay for their work. They are bound to use assumptions, which inherently are never value-free. In addition, they usually express preferences on the desirability of projects as a result of their studies and often become embroiled in political debates once the results of their reports are debated in public. In addition, politicians and senior officials often pay more heed to 'executive summaries' than to the details of reports, both because of time constraints and because the intricacies of the studies escape them. Finally, the relation of CBAs to Environmental Impact Assessments (EIAs) and the formal-legal procedures for spatial planning and development, of which transport infrastructure evaluation and planning are clearly an important component, remained unclear.

It can be concluded from the previous argument that the specific place that CBAs, preliminary as well as comprehensive, occupy in the decision-making process was unclear, and the moments at which it was decided to conduct them were mostly ad hoc and/or propitious to the actor(s) commissioning the study.

ADJUSTMENTS MADE IN THE REVISED 2004 GUIDELINE

Largely based on the experiences with the guideline so far, the Dutch Ministries of Transport and Public Works and Economic Affairs launched a new document in addition to the guideline which includes all the additions and changes based on the previously mentioned evaluations. This was published at the end of 2004 (Ministerie van Verkeer en Waterstaat, 2004). Most of the alterations answered methodological and operational issues, but the institutional ones also received some attention.

Changes Concerning Method and Operationalization

First, suggestions were made to improve the manner in which research results in the CBA report are presented. Improvements include, amongst other things, the transparency of the methods as they are shown to the reader and the way in which non-monetized effects are presented in the final tables of the report. Using handsome summarizing tables with effects that include monetary, other quantitative and qualitative results in a standardized form makes the results much more accessible to the non-initiated. The importance of a clear summary is stressed, including the way in which the main results should be presented on one page, including a summarizing table that should also include physical effects, and not only effects in monetary terms.

Second, additional guidelines with respect to direct effects are given. A very important category of benefits of transport projects is travel time savings. The additions state that the best estimation of the real increase in the value of time over time, for business travel as well as for non-business travel, is half the increase in real wages. However, it is also concluded that additional research is needed into the subject to reach firmer conclusions.

Third, the definition of indirect effects is sharpened. A demarcation of different types of indirect effects is presented, as well as conditions that can result in welfare effects due to indirect effects. Also an overview of research methods for the estimation of indirect effects is presented, and advice is given for the presentation of indirect effects. The additions conclude that a model approach is important for the consistency of many interrelated effects. Besides, a distinction between (1) direct effects (project and network related), (2) additional indirect economic and network effects, and (3) direct and indirect external effects is recommended by the authors of the additions to the guideline.

Fourth, the additions pay attention to the effects on nature. These effects are very difficult to monetize because no markets exist for them. Nevertheless, it is advisable to translate the physical effects of infrastructure on nature, water and soil into welfare effects. The additions show how these effects may be quantified and monetized, using economic methods.

Fifth, the importance of distribution effects is stressed. The additions conclude that the original guidelines should be made more specific and operational and that it is not only the contents that matter, but also the process leading to the estimation and presentation of distribution effects. This opens the way to a more interactive and participatory evaluation process without stating this explicitly.

Finally, the additions pay attention to risk evaluation and distinguish between categories of uncertainties and risks, including uncertainties with respect to the political decision itself, exceptional events (risks in their pure form), risks that are not related to macro-economic trends (so that their positive and negative impacts on different projects compensate each other) and macro-economic risks. Decision-related risks should not be monetized but should be included in the scenarios. Some other risks can be monetized and expressed in constant prices using a discount rate. Because of the high level of uncertainty with respect to risk and risk evaluation it was decided to apply the recommendations for two years and then to evaluate them.

Changes Concerning the Position in the Decision-making Process

The Ministries of Transport and Public Works and Economic Affairs have also realized that the place and function of the preliminary and comprehensive CBAs within the total institutional framework on spatial, environmental and infrastructure development needed to be clarified. Improvements here refer to the relationship with other important policy documents such as the Environmental Impact Assessment (EIA), both with respect to the contents and to the process. This includes the timing of publication of the reports and the domain of application of the guidelines. It was decided not to incorporate the CBAs into the legal procedures in the same way as had been done with EIAs, because that would make its timing and performance subject to the 'institutional rigidities' noted in the implementation of the EIAs. However, co-ordination between the two instruments where necessary and desirable is, of course, to be applauded. Moreover, CBAs and other related documents should always focus on the same project alternatives, use the same time horizons and make use of the same scenarios and the same reference alternative.

To conclude, the recent additions can be seen as important improvements of the 'old' guideline, which are in line with the findings of the evaluations of the application of the old guide, and also respond to the points of contention raised against cost–benefit analysis in the international arena. Note that less than five years have passed since the application of the guideline began, that since it was embraced it has been applied to some 15 projects, that one official and a few independent evaluations of these applications have been made and that already now an extensive adjustment of the original guideline has taken place. The authors consider this a relatively short time span which is indicative of an open-minded attitude on the part of the CBA-champions. CBA for the assessment of transport infrastructure projects, at least in the Netherlands, has overall been quite successful and is there to stay.

FUTURE PROSPECTS

We think that some major future prospects include (1) the further improvement of the quality of the CBAs and (2) the position of CBAs in the decision-making process. We will start with the further improvements of the quality of CBAs. A ground-breaking recent publication on mega-projects by Flyvbjerg et al. (2003) claims, based on research regarding a large number of infrastructure projects around the world, that the underestimation of project costs and the overestimation of project benefits are largely due to the way in which responsibilities and risks are allocated to actors. Therefore we consider that better estimations of both costs and benefits are of major importance to the usefulness of CBA for decision-making. Actors that benefit from a 'positive' decision, that is the decision to construct an infrastructure project, should not be able to influence CBA and underlying studies. Unfortunately this will not always be possible. For example, in the case of a maglev railway line the availability of some information might be limited to possible constructors only. In such cases introducing or organizing counter-forces (making use of independent experts) is a crucial aspect in compensating for this bias.

The second challenge is related to the position of CBA in the political decision-making process. We will illustrate this challenge by highlighting recent events in the Netherlands. The second half of the year 2004 and the first half of 2005 in the Netherlands have seen a renewed political and public debate on investments in transport infrastructure. A Temporary Parliamentary Investigation Committee on Infrastructure, going by the name of the Duijvestein-Commission, made an elaborate study into the decision-making processes regarding the Betuwe Line and the Dutch section of the High Speed Railway Link from Paris to Amsterdam (Tweede Kamer, 2004a; 2004b; 2004c; 2004e; 2004f). Both its interrogations of key players and its final report lay a strong emphasis on cost overruns, disappointing results in terms of ridership and limited effectiveness on environmental and other objectives. In addition, and more serious in the eyes of popular representatives, there was widespread concern about the way in which the Chambers of Parliament had been inadequately informed about changes to the estimates in the course of the planning, budgeting and implementation process. The new cost–benefit analysis described above played a minor role in these debates; this can be understood as most of the decision-making on the two mega-projects under public scrutiny originated long before the official adoption of CBA, exactly in the early 1990s when rigorous analysis was still badly lacking. In that sense, CBA can be seen as a major leap in the quality of decision-making and should be credited for that. However, the worries remain. An additional study conducted by Delft University of Technology on the 'Zuiderzeelijn', a railway link from the Amsterdam area through the polders to the (much less densely populated) North-East of the country, showed that until recently the decision-making process here evolved remarkably similarly to the two earlier ones (Tweede Kamer, 2004d). Moreover, in spite of obviously negative results in the CBA study, politicians and senior officials were inclined to ignore those results and proceed with the project because of previous commitments made to the Northern provinces. The major reason is that in April 1998, just before the elections, a promise was made by the then Dutch Cabinet to the Northern provinces to construct the Zuiderzeelijn. This commitment was later confirmed in the Coalition agreement of the subsequent government, but it did not include the specifications of the line. The political reliability (to stick to a promise made) was more important for most politicians than the negative results of the cost–benefit study, which was conducted only later. In fact, the phenomenon that political commitments lead to the depletion of public funds before analytical studies can become effective in the budgeting process, has for many years been known to be characteristic of Dutch decision-making on transport infrastructure (de Jong, 1999b).

The report of the Duijvestein-Commission has evoked a renewed debate on the desirability of the Zuiderzeelijn, the outcome of which is still uncertain. Disappointing to some, unsurprising to others, this example makes clear that improving the level of policy analysis does not automatically imply political conversion to opinions based on informed judgement. The impact of impact studies stands or falls with the way it is imbedded in the political interaction process and involved actors come to accept its outcomes. In other words, it is not just the political decision-making process that should be made interactive. If one wants analytical studies to have relevance in such a process, they need to be an integral part of it and political commitments should not be made before thorough analysis and a public debate about its results. The above-mentioned commission has given the issue of structuring the decision-making process some thought while taking into account political realities and has suggested a framework for decision-making. We agree with the committee that linking CBA in such a way to the political process might improve the impact of CBA on the quality of the decision-making itself as well as its process. Even though there is no such thing as perfection when it comes to decision-making on transport infrastructure, the attempt to approximate it is certainly worth the while, considering the enormous financial stakes.

ACKNOWLEDGEMENTS

The authors are indebted to Arjen 't Hoen of the Dutch Ministry of Transport, Public Works and Water Management for his comments on the draft of this chapter.

NOTE

1. In the remaining part of this chapter we will refer to the original Dutch language guide.

REFERENCES

Annema, J.A., C. Koopmans and B. van Wee (2002), 'Kosten-batenanalyse: ervaringen met de OEEI-leidraad. (Cost–benefit analysis: experiences with the OEEI

guideline)', in *Colloquium Vervoersplanologisch Speurwerk 2002: de kunst van het verleiden*, Delft: CVS, pp. 937–56.
Annema, J.A., C. Koopmans and B. van Wee (forthcoming), 'Evaluating the transport infrastructure: the Dutch experience with a standardised approach', Paper submitted to *Transport Reviews*.
Buck Consultants International (2002), *Evaluatie OEEI-leidraad (Evaluation of the OEEI guideline)*, Nijmegen: Buck Consultants International.
CPB, Ministerie van Verkeer en Waterstaat, Ministerie van Economische Zaken (2003), *Twee Jaar Ervaring met OEEI. De Discussie over Indirecte Effecten (Two years experience with OEEI. The debate on wider economic impacts)*, The Hague: Netherlands Bureau for Policy Assessment, in Dutch.
de Jong, W.M. (1999a), 'Cost-effective use of evaluation models: an empirical cross-national investigation', *International Journal of Technology Management*, **19**(3/4/5), 368–83.
de Jong, W.M. (1999b), *Institutional Transplantation: how to Adopt Good Transport Infrastructure Decision-making Ideas from other Countries*, Delft: Eburon.
de Jong, M. and H. Geerlings (2003), 'De opmerkelijke terugkeer van de kostenbaten-analyse in het centrum van de bestuurspraktijk', (The remarkable return of CBA in the core of governance practice), *Beleid en Maatschappij*, **30**(3), 166–78.
Eijgenraam, C.C.J., C.C. Koopmans, P.J.G. Tang and A.C.P. Verster (1999), *Evaluation of infrastructural projects: guide for cost–benefit analysis. Section 1: Main Report. Research programme on the economic effects of infrastructure*, Den Haag/Rotterdam: CPB Netherlands Bureau for Economic Policy Analysis, Netherlands Economic Institute.
Flyvbjerg, B., N. Bruzelius and W. Rothengatter (2003), *Megaprojects and Risk: An Anatomy of Ambition*, Cambridge: Cambridge University Press.
Hayashi, Y. and H. Morisugi (2000), 'International comparison of background concept and methodology of transportation project appraisal', *Transport Policy*, **7**, 73–88.
Heinzerling, L. and F. Ackerman (2002), 'Pricing the Priceless. Cost–Benefit Analysis of Environmental Protection', Georgetown Environmental Law and Policy Institute, Georgetown University Law Center, www.globalpolicy.org/socecon/encronmt/2002/CostBen2002.htm.
Janse, P., W.J. Dijkstra, J.M.W. Dings, G.P. van Wee, R.M.M van den Brink, C.J. Ruijgrok, H. Uitenboogaart, D.A. Hemstra and C. Conrelissen (2000), 'Milieuwinst op het spoor?. Synthese van onderzoeken naar milieu-effecten van het goederenvernrer per spoor', Delft/Bilthoven: CE, RIVM, TNO.
Kelman, S. (1981), 'Cost–Benefit Analysis: An ethical critique (with replies)', *AEI Journal on Government and Society Regulation*, January/February, pp. 33–40 and including replies printed in the AEI Journal, March/April 1991 issue.
Kopp, R.J., A.J. Krupnick and M. Toman (1997), 'Cost–Benefit analysis and regulatory reform: an assessment of the science and the art', Discussion Paper 97-19, Washington: Resources for the Future.
Mackie, P. and J. Preston (1998), 'Twenty-one sources of error and bias in transport appraisal', *Transport Policy*, **5**, pp. 1–7.
Ministerie van Verkeer en Waterstaat (1990), 'Tweede Structuurschema Verkeer en Vervoer. Deel D: regeringsbeslissing', (Second Transport Structure Plan, part D: decision of the governement). The Hague: Ministry of Transport and Public Works.

Ministerie van Verkeer en Waterstaat (2004), 'Aanvullingen op de Leidraad Overzicht Effecten Infrastructuur. Een samenvatting. (Additions to the guideline Overview Effects Infrastructure)', The Hague: Ministerie van Verkeer en Waterstaat, Ministerie van Economische Zaken.

Ministerie van Verkeer en Waterstaat & Ministerie van Economische Zaken (2000), 'Evaluatie van infrastructuurprojecten; leidraad voor kosten-batenanalyse, Onderzoeksprogramma Economische Effecten Infrastructuur, deel 1', (hoofdrapport) en deel 2 (capita selecta), Den Haag.

Ministry of Transport, Public Works and Water Management and Ministry of Economic Affairs (2000), 'Evaluation of infrastructural projects; guide for cost–benefit analysis. Section 1: Main Report, Section 2, Capita Selecta', Den Haag: Ministry of Transport, Public Works and Water Management.

Niemeyer, S. and C.L. Spash (2001), 'Environmental valuation analysis, public deliberation, and their pragmatic syntheses: a critical appraisal', *Environment and Planning C: Government and Policy 2001*, **19**, 567–85.

Posner, R.A. (2000), 'Cost–Benefit Analysis: definition, justification, and comment on conference papers', *Journal of Legal Studies*, **XXIX**, 1153–77.

SACTRA (1999), *Transport and the Economy, The Standing Advisory Committee on Trunk Road Assessment*, London: UK Department of the Environment, Transport and the Regions.

Scanlon, T.M. (1991), 'The moral basis of interpersonal comparisons', in J. Elster and J.E. Roemer (eds), *Interpersonal Comparisons of Well-Being*, Cambridge: Cambridge University Press.

Sen, A. (2000), 'The discipline of Cost–Benefit Analysis', *Journal of Legal Studies*, **XXIX**, 931–52.

Tweede Kamer (2004a), *Grote projecten uitvergroot; een infrastructuur voor besluitvorming*, vergaderjaar 2004–2005, 29283, nrs. 5–6, Sdu uitgevers, 's-Gravenhage.

Tweede Kamer (2004b), *Reconstructie Betuweroute; de besluitvorming uitvergroot*, vergaderjaar 2004–2005, 29283, nr. 7, Sdu uitgevers, 's-Gravenhage.

Tweede Kamer (2004c), *Reconstructie HSL-Zuid; de besluitvorming uitvergroot*, vergaderjaar 2004–2005, 29283, nr. 8, Sdu uitgevers, 's-Gravenhage.

Tweede Kamer (2004d), *Het project Zuiderzeelijn; toetsing met terugwerkende kracht*, vergaderjaar 2004–2005, 29283, nr. 9, Sdu uitgevers, 's-Gravenhage.

Tweede Kamer (2004e), *Grote projecten: Inzichten en Uitgangspunten; Achtergrondstudies*, vergaderjaar 2004–2005, 29283, nr. 10, Sdu uitgevers, 's-Gravenhage.

Tweede Kamer (2004f), *Hoorzittingen; verslagen, vergaderjaar 2004–2005*, 29283, nr. 11, Sdu uitgevers, 's-Gravenhage.

Van Wee, G.P., R. Thomas, W. Dunnewold and M. van den Heuvel (1994), 'Effecten van de Betuweroute op NO_x- en CO_2-emissies', (Effects of the Betuweline on NO_x and CO_2 emissions), RIVM Report nr 251701015. Bilthoven/Delft: Rijksinstituut voor Volksgezondheid en Milieuhygiëne/ Instituut voor Ruimtelijke Organisatie TNO.

8. Project appraisal and decision-making in practice: evidence from the Deurganckdock case in the port of Antwerp

Chris Coeck and Toon Tessier

INTRODUCTION

The renewed attention for the existing European Union policy on nature conservation increased the importance of environmental impact assessment (EIA) as an instrument for the evaluation of port projects. From the 1990s, substantial economic research has to be performed in order to decide on a project (such as a cost–benefit analysis and an investment analysis). In addition, an EIA needs to be carried out prior to the realization of major projects. More recently, transport policy of governments and ports in Europe has been based upon the creation of a sustainable situation, see also Gilman (2003). As Gilman (2003: 276) states, the 'objective of this policy is a new model which achieves effective protection of the environment alongside economic growth'. Here, traditional evaluation procedures need to be complemented with additional elements. Examples of government initiatives are the UK New Approach to Transport Appraisal or the Dutch OEEI guideline for assessing the merits of transport projects *ex ante*. As a result, the aim is to realize only those projects that have a positive effect on an environmental as well as an economic level. Antwerp is attempting to clearly integrate economic and ecological aspects. Central in the contribution will be the description of the Deurganckdock project, whose decision-making procedure is analysed.

In this contribution, the different phases in the project evaluation of the Deurganckdock are described together with possible lessons for the future. First, a short history leading to the realization of the Deurganckdock is provided. Next, the current situation is described and an evaluation of the policy options is carried out. Finally, the status of the environmental impact assessment procedure, the relationship with the European Birds and Habitats Directive and criticisms and remedies for future evaluation are provided.

A SHORT HISTORY OF THE DECISION-MAKING PROCESSES OF THE DEURGANCKDOCK PORT PROJECT

This section provides an overview of the historical steps and decisions taken with reference to the evaluation of a specific port project, more in particular the Deurganckdock port development project in the port of Antwerp.

The Deurganckdock project provides additional container terminal capacity on the Left Bank of the port of Antwerp. Different alternative locations for the project were studied in the Starting Note dating back to 1995. The choice of the preferential alternative was based upon a multi-criteria analysis performed by the Antwerp Port Authority and the Flemish Community. Here, different criteria were distinguished as selection criteria. Finally, alternative A7 was selected as the most optimal alternative, that is, a location south of the Doel village. As such, the environmental effects of this alternative were studied in detail in an environmental impact study.

Indeed, in 1997 an environmental impact assessment was performed. This report concentrated only on the selected A7 alternative. There was a substantial protest against the environmental impact statement by local communities, by the inhabitants of the village of Doel and by environmental groups. Although these groups joined forces, their protests were based on entirely different objectives. The local community aimed to protect the future of the Doel village. The environmental groups, on the other hand, concentrated their critique on a correct application of the Birds and Habitats Directive. Indeed, the 1997 environmental impact study provided no specific compensation for the Deurganckdock harbour development project. As the Deurganckdock is located in a Special Protection Area of the European Birds Directive, compensation of nature is legally necessary/compulsory in case harm is to be expected. As a result, the main criticism of the environmental movement was that adequate environmental compensation had to be decided on and carried out before infrastructural and construction works could start.

In the process of evaluation following the environmental impact assessment, different individual policy steps can be distinguished. The first step in the policy procedure dates from 20 January 1998 and consists of a Decision of the Flemish Government. This decision included not only the realization of the Deurganckdock but stated also that the long-term viability of the village of Doel could not be guaranteed. The decision stated that a strategic planning process needed to be organized in which all public actors are involved (in order to prevent ad hoc planning). However, NGOs were still not included in the strategic planning process. In order to compensate possible environmental harm caused by the construction of the Deurganckdock, a specific compensation area was proposed: the Bazel-Rupelmonde-Kruibeke area was designated as a special protection area to replace possible habitat loss.

Next, an agreement on the Principles of the Strategic Planning of Left Bank Developments was signed by all public actors. In this agreement, all public actors accepted to expand the port area (by constructing the Deurganckdock) into the Special Protection Area No. 3.6. In addition, the outer limits of further expansion programmes related to port development were accepted by all public actors including the Antwerp Port Authority, and additional compensation measures had to be developed, anticipating possible future habitat loss.

Following complaints of local NGOs and environmental pressure groups, the European Union addressed a number of letters to the Flemish Government (in December 1998 and February 1999). More in particular, seven different questions were asked:

1. Do the individual projects have adverse effects on the Special Protection Areas?
2. Is an impact assessment with specific reference to conservation goals and objectives of the Special Protection Areas performed on a project basis?
3. Is an adequate alternative assessment performed?
4. What is the overriding public interest of the Deurganckdock project?
5. Have all relevant mitigating effects been considered?
6. Is sufficient compensation for inevitable adverse effects provided?
7. What are the cumulative effects of this project with other already finished projects?

As no sufficient answer was provided to the European Union by the Flemish Government, there was ongoing protest by local environmental NGOs and the action committee Doel 2020 against the realization of the Deurganckdock port development project. As a result, additional letters of complaint were directed to the European Commission and judicial procedures were started before the Administrative Court of Justice.

Next, the Flemish Government achieved a renewed consensus in 2000. This decision was based upon four elements: (1) the suspension of the earlier decision of the viability of Doel, making a social guidance for inhabitants necessary; (2) a delay of the decision for the possible realization of additional port expansion plans following the Deurganckdock project until 2007; (3) a confirmation of the other limits of the (Left Bank) port expansion possibilities and compensation measures; and (4) the participation of all relevant stakeholders in a strategic planning process, aiming to realize a renewed consensus on port development, in total conformity with the Bird and Habitats Directive.

The next step in the political decision-making was made in January 2001, triggered once again by an EU letter to the Flemish Government. The European Commission was not satisfied with the reply of the Flemish Government on the earlier questions concerning the Deurganckdock. The European Commission stated that all alternatives under investigation were mainly alternative designs rather than alternative solutions for the economic problem of insufficient port and container handling capacity. Indeed, a major criticism was that the environmental impact assessment procedure only assessed the already chosen A7 alternative. The European Commission stated that this needed to be corrected. In addition, the compensation measures foreseen in the environmental impact assessment procedure were not well substantiated and the European Commission argued that possible cumulative effects were not properly assessed. In addition, an impact assessment for maintenance dredging was lacking and no transboundary effects (relation with projects in the Netherlands) were considered. Finally, the zero option or the optimization of existing facilities was also not assessed. As a result, substantial changes needed to be made in the scientific research and environmental appraisal leading to political decision-making in order to fully comply with the comments of the European Commission and its strict interpretation of the environmental impact assessment procedure and the Birds and Habitats Directive.

Ultimately, the next step in the Deurganckdock decision-making process was the ruling of the Administrative Court of Justice that resulted in putting the works on hold and temporarily suspending the Deurganckdock port development project. As a result, a new environmental impact study on the effects of the Deurganckdock had to be drafted. The Antwerp Port Authority took the responsibility to order this study in 2001. This environmental impact study contains an answer to the elements proposed by the European Commission by closely examining all comments and criticisms. The major new element of this environmental impact assessment is a thorough analysis of all habitats destroyed and all possible needs for mitigation and compensation measures, leading to a fully fledged, substantial and scientifically based compensation plan.

The mitigation efforts resulted in a revision of the construction plan for the Deurganckdock port development project. While the original plan resulted in a loss of 450 ha of farm land needed for the storage of dredging materials, the revised plan could reduce this direct effect by 90 per cent. As a consequence, compensation measures could also be reduced. However it was required that the plan was implemented prior to the start of the infrastructural works. The compensation plans were carefully selected and determined. A distinction between temporary and permanent compensation areas was made and necessary compensation areas were designated: in these areas the restoration of several types of habitat needed to take place. Finally, the compensation plan provided a forum in which the NGOs could participate. Indeed, they were actively involved in the selection of the compensation areas. However, two problems are considered as being instrumental to the 2001 EIA. First, the absence of conservation objectives was a disadvantage for the construction of a compensation plan. Indeed, in the absence of clear conservation objectives, all effects need to be considered. The second problem involved the use of immediately available and suitable areas for nature development inside the port area (because these areas happened to be the only ones available in the short run) and hence the creation of temporary compensation zones inside the port area with negative consequences for normal port operations. On the other hand, a number of compensation obligations had to be exported to other areas (outside the Left Bank area of the port of Antwerp). This effect often leads to a false interpretation of compensation: the necessary compensation is often considered as too excessive by different parties.

The final step in the evaluation and decision-making process of the Deurganckdock port development project was the acceptance of the environmental compensation plan by the Flemish Government on 6 October 2001, and the introduction of a *lex specialis* organizing the construction of the Deurganckdock (Decree of 14 December 2001). In this *lex specialis*, a central position was guaranteed for the compensation plan. Indeed, the provision of permits for the construction and the exploitation of the Deurganckdock was closely linked to the realization of different phases of the compensation plan. In addition, the compensation plan was considered as a protocol between public actors to share the responsibilities of the implementation: a management committee was installed, responsible for the follow-up and realization of the plan, monitoring by the Institute of Nature Conservation was organized and a clear overview of responsibilities was drawn up. In sum, the total cost estimate of the compensation plan reached 25 million euros. Clear responsibilities for the financing of each step of the realization were included: government were to pay for land purchase and the Antwerp Port Authority to finance the definite nature development projects. Maintenance and monitoring of the project were also an integrated part of the compensation plan.

As a culmination of the entire decision-making process, the Deurganckdock port development project has now been realized, including the requisite road and railway infrastructure projects. The first phase of the dock was finished in June 2005 and has been operational since

September 2005; the entire dock will be finished in 2007. The compensation plan is carried out in parallel: the construction permits necessary for the realization of the plan are provided according to a specific time schedule, and the Flemish Parliament has to provide its formal approval prior to the actual execution of projects.

The description of the entire decision-making process indicates that it was very difficult to find a balance between (1) the long-term economic necessity of port development; (2) the ecological obligations of European legislation and its consequences for port development; (3) the increased pressures of other planning processes on the port area; (4) the demands of the farmers' organization; and (5) the question of the future long-term viability of the local community of Doel. It was clear that a multiple stakeholder approach and an integration of several evaluation instruments was necessary. As a result, traditional EIA procedures need to be expanded and the strategic planning process adapted, in order to guarantee the possibility of a future development of the port of Antwerp.

THE EFFECT OF THE EUROPEAN BIRDS AND HABITATS DIRECTIVE

Lack of sufficient government funds and strong competition between ports induce public authorities to be more critical towards project proposals: public authorities should support only those projects that are economically viable and can be considered as suitable and feasible.

The European Birds and Habitats Directive urges authorities to use environmental impact assessment as an important tool for augmenting the legitimacy of the project, improving its quality, reducing the impact on the natural environment and enforcing the realization of recommendations to the point that they become an integrated part of the project itself. On port project evaluations, the Deurganckdock case proved to be the turning point in project evaluation methodology in Flanders. As a result, the port of Antwerp is a pioneer in strategic project evaluation.

Indeed, a consequence of the exemption procedure laid down in article 6§3 and article 6§4 of the Habitats Directive, while enforcing a thorough analysis of the environmental impact of a project, is a clear exposure of all the arguments leading to the selected alternative and a consideration of necessary mitigation and compensation measures as a supplement to the normal EIA requirements. This procedure evolved from being 'best practice' recommendations to plain necessities (if the aim is to realize the project without delay).

The Birds and Habitats Directive continues to be considered by different parties as an obstacle to a sound economic policy on port development.

However, at project level the exemption procedures laid down in both directives (art. 6) have forced port authorities and governments to improve the quality of the economic as well as the environmental assessment of port projects.

The 2001 version of the Deurganckdock environmental impact assessment initiated by the Antwerp Port Authority was in many respects an exercise that comes to terms with the combined necessity of these directives and the criticisms of the European commission on the environment impact assessment of 1997. It proved to be a new landmark and pioneering exercise in the environmental impact assessment practice in Europe.

THE STATUS OF EIA AS AN EVALUATION TOOL

Compared to earlier assessments of port development projects, the evaluation process of the Deurganckdock project was a first step forward. However, it also showed a number of structural deficiencies, which are not uncommon to the EIA practice (especially in the common EIA such as the 1997 version of the Deurganckdock project). In particular, five elements can be distinguished:

1. Contrary to earlier project evaluations, the selected layout of the project and the project definition was the result of a multi-criteria analysis (including environmental considerations) and discussions with environmental authorities such as the Institute of Nature Conservation. In the 1997 report only the preferred A7 alternative was studied;
2. Other stakeholders such as neighbouring communities and NGOs were initially not invited to take part in the decision-making process and in the project formulation phase. As a consequence, public debate and evaluation were absent and the environmental impact assessment process was not used as an effective evaluation tool. Until very recently, public consultation at an earlier stage of the EIA process was not obligatory;
3. Once the decision on the selected alternative was made and the project defined, the decision-making process became more formal. The project initiators did not use the 1997 EIA as an instrument for further improvement of the project and reduction or mitigation of possible impacts on the environment or the neighbouring villages. Absence of recommendations that resulted from the EIA are a clear indication of the fact that the report did not serve an actual evaluation function. The

2001 EIA did remedy this: based upon this EIA, detailed policy recommendations were drafted;

4. There were clear indications that the impact of the EIA was minimized and that any conclusions that could delay a decision and/or its execution or could increase the cost of the project were repressed. Although, as a result of the proposal, the village of Doel would clearly become isolated from the rest of the Left Bank, the 1997 EIA concluded that there was no 'immediate' problem. The same goes for the loss of habitats, although it was obvious that acknowledging this would have made things more difficult to decide for policy makers. Again, the 2001 EIA solved this problem;
5. At the time the 1997 EIA was drafted, there was poor knowledge of the European policy regulations on nature conservation, especially the European Birds and Habitats Directive. At the level of the initiators, the experts, as well as the responsible state agencies (including the ones that should enforce the regulations), the lack of knowledge was leading to serious misjudgements of the risks taken.

As soon as the European Commission started a judicial procedure questioning the legitimacy of the decision-making process related to the Deurganckdock port development project, the Antwerp Port Authority was amongst the first of the policy makers to become aware of lacunae in the project evaluation and attempted to adjust the outcome of the environmental impact assessment, leading to the revised version of the environmental impact study in 2001.

STRATEGIC PLANNING AS AN IMPROVEMENT TO THE EVALUATION PROCESS

At first, the Flemish Government had initiated the plans to build an additional dock to increase the container handling capacity in the port of Antwerp, as one single project. However, due to the extent of the project and its impact on the surrounding environment, they concluded that the decision-making process should be expanded to include the total Left Bank area and also the future of other functions, next to port development. Assuming that port expansion – especially the growing need for container handling capacity – would (sooner or later) lead to the conclusion that the viability of the local village of Doel would conflict with future port expansion, the Flemish Government decided to plan for a total resettlement of the local population of the village. Faced with even stronger opposition from the local community and criticisms of the legitimacy of port expansion in itself, the Flemish Government aimed to mitigate the consequences of these decisions by integrating the port expansion plans into a wider context of strategic planning.

As a result of the Flemish Government's decision, the realization of the Deurganckdock project was made dependent on the elaboration of a strategic plan for the Left Bank region. The strategic planning process and the principles for the development of the region (agreed upon by all partners) should help to create a more robust or less sensitive framework for current and future (port) projects.

In terms of evaluation instruments, the tool of strategic planning (process) is a clear improvement and a valuable tool for preliminary assessment of possible solutions. Ircha (2001: 126) states that strategic planning 'provides a vision or direction and develops specific goals, objectives and actions for achieving the desired vision. (. . .) Strategic planning seeks to identify the major factors affecting the port's future, including an appraisal of the port's external and internal environment'. Strategic planning therefore needs to be considered as a complement to or a framework for economic studies and environmental assessment.

Different advantages can be distinguished:

1. Considering the scope of a strategic plan, it becomes possible to create a public debate and tackle more fundamental issues, conflicts of interest and opinions that otherwise have the tendency to be ignored or repressed on the level of individual project evaluation.
2. The design of the strategic plan and the general evaluation become more integrated. Through the iterative (and interactive) process of strategic planning, the development plans are amended, adjusted and evaluated to be acceptable for all partners, or, at the least, participation in the planning process (and the resulting positive atmosphere) increases the will to resolve conflicts of perspective.
3. Once the strategic plan is accepted as a framework, it can serve as a stable environment for future decision-making processes such as a strategic environmental impact assessment on a plan level or on a number of the individual projects that are compatible with (or with parts of) the original project.
4. Evaluation and decision-making by means of an environmental impact assessment can become more efficient, but only under certain conditions:
   a. Discussions on basic issues (for example the outer limits of possible port expansion) should be resolved at the level of the strategic plan. The more fuzzy the plan is, the higher the likelihood that in a consecutive phase, when things become more specific, a number

of basic elements that are questioned will make future decision-making extremely difficult or even impossible.

b. A clear methodology and action plan to implement the agreement is strongly recommended. Implementation of the principles of a strategic plan, in compliance with regulations, still proves to be a complex issue that requires serious efforts by all partners as well as a loyal participation. There might be a paradox here: while the principles are the result of difficult negotiations, with all partners being satisfied with the outcome, very little attention has been paid to the actual implementation or execution of the principles.
c. Full acquaintance and compliance with existing regulations is necessary, for example the consequences of the implication of the Birds and Habitats Directive were not fully acknowledged during the first phase of strategic planning (1998–1999). Not taking these regulations into account would result in inapplicable decisions.
d. 'Surprises' are inevitable and may always spoil the outcome, but are controllable, for example, (1) new political decisions can undermine previous decisions; (2) new regulations can change the context of the decision-making process; (3) unforeseen impact at the time of the approval of the strategic plan with large consequences for the basics of the plan; and (4) 'faked' participation or participation with no intention to find a balanced solution in compliance with regulations.

CRITICISMS, OPPORTUNITIES AND LESSONS FOR THE FUTURE OF PORT PROJECT APPRAISAL IN PORTS

Contrary to economic studies such as social cost–benefit analysis, the Birds and Habitat Directive and the environmental impact assessment procedure have been (and still are) severely criticized as a framework for evaluating port projects. Many of these criticisms, however, are unjustified.

1. At some stage, it is argued that the regulations of article 6 of the Birds and Habitats Directive are too restrictive and do not always favour the best solution from an economic point of view. There is an obligation to proceed with the ecologically best solution. However, assuming the integrity of the Natura 2000 network is essential for a long-term sustainable economic development and assuming the fact that a certain project generates significant effects on the integrity of the network, it is reasonable to argue for the alternative that has the least environmental

impact. As such, damage to the integrity of Natura 2000 can be compensated or minimized.
2. Different authorities complain that the exemption procedure is difficult to apply correctly. Indeed, the exigency that compensatory measures should be realized simultaneously with the project or, better still, in anticipation of the destruction of habitats (thereby causing time delays) forms the basis for this critique. However, authorities have to realize that it is often a lack of knowledge of the regulation itself or even an unwillingness to accept all the consequences that causes this lack of time to anticipate possible habitat loss rather than the measures themselves.
3. Port authorities often complain about the choice and designation of the port areas as Special Protection Areas. However, the designation of these areas as Special Protection Areas is not performed arbitrarily. Estuaries and coastal areas have an important role in maintaining biodiversity of the Natura 2000 network. Regional and national authorities complain as well, but forget their responsibility in the designation process and the acceptance of the directives in the regulatory framework.
4. Many parties and individuals are frustrated with the procedures and obligations of the exemption rule in article 6§3 and article 6§4 of the European directives but forget that the procedure – being an exemption rule – was never meant to be simple and easy to comply with. If this was not the case, it would not take long for the exemption procedure to evolve towards being the rule.

However, the exemption procedure in itself also has some major deficiencies that could undermine its legitimacy as a proper evaluation tool. A critical assessment by the European Commission is triggered by complaints from environmental organizations that focus especially on large projects with an immediately perceived impact (even if the importance of the impact is not always proportional to the size of the project and degradation can occur very slowly). As a consequence, smaller projects and practices that are not tied to clearly definable projects and include many agents are often not considered 'dangerous'. In reality this is incorrect; for example, the intensification of agriculture was several times more damaging to protected habitats than the realization of a dock project. Two additional elements need to be underlined. On the one hand, the European Commission has no clear policy or strategy on the definition of the scope for selecting the ecologically optimal alternative: the opinion of the European Commission can be contaminated by the point of view of the complainants. On the other hand, the European Commission is hesitant to set out criteria for evaluating the conditions of article 6§4 that 'overriding public interest' is applicable. Member States and port authorities criticize the European Community Commission on the lack of a level playing field in this respect.

Overall, the international port authorities ask the European Commission to create a level playing field between competitive ports. The directives should be applied in an equal way throughout the European Union. Therefore, more guidelines are needed regarding how the directives should be implemented and used for project appraisal. However, the international port community and the responsible state agencies can evade most of the problems by preventing the exemption procedure of article 6§3 and all its hazardous implications.

This situation can be obtained by defining the maintenance or preservation objectives that have to be set out for the Special Protection Area under consideration. This has to be realized in such a way that at any time in the future, the integrity of the Natura 2000 network is maintained and the negative effects on the relevant habitats and wildlife remain below a significant level even when, at some point in the future, a specific (port) project would be realized.

From the point of view of a strategic planning process, this means that the evaluation procedure is turned upside down and consequently the planning process itself enters into a second phase. During the first phase, next to the assessment of the economic contribution and necessity, the environmental impact of a project is evaluated, with all the consequences in terms of habitat destruction and subsequent application of the exemption procedure and its related consequences (selection of alternatives, compensatory measures, and so on). Still, evaluation of the environmental aspects appear as a result of an evaluation procedure – either on the level of a plan or a project. During the second phase, the impact of what it means to maintain the integrity of the Natura 2000 network and its consequences on the possibility of economic developments is evaluated beforehand, that is the evaluation of these environmental aspects appear as a condition, a framework for further evaluation procedures. According to the port of Antwerp, this way of dealing sets limits on possible economic development. However, this loss is compensated in terms of long-term economic security: the port will be sure about the area that can actually be used for port development projects without any constraints or limits.

At present, the strategic planning process on the Antwerp port development is an example of this kind of 'second phase' evaluation of strategic planning. Here, the preservation objectives are set out based upon in-depth scientific research. Next, all necessary measures need to be taken in order to translate and realize these objectives. Finally, a nature development scheme will create a new framework against which new projects can be evaluated according to their impact on maintaining the preservation obligations of the Special Protection Area.

A strategic environmental impact assessment will define the environmental constraints, including the ecological needs for maintaining the function of the Special Protection Area in the Natura 2000 network. In such a strategic environmental impact assessment an assessment will take place of the future possibilities for economic expansion. The central question that needs to be answered in such a study is: 'How much "environmental space" remains for economic activities such as port expansion and agricultural activities?' Here, constraints on the ecological situation, mobility and the viability of local communities need to be taken into account as well. As a result, a detailed consultation of environmental NGOs, resident farmers and their organizations and other relevant (public and private) actors is indispensable for scenario building and evaluation in the first stage of the evaluation: if a particular port project complies with all criteria no significant impact can be expected on the environment.

To conclude, it can be stated that practice reveals that a co-habitation between economic development, ecological aspects, agricultural elements and a residential function will be central to any future evaluation of port infrastructural projects. Economic and environmental analyses will have to integrate these aspects in order to be fully compliant with societal reality. As a result, a multi-stakeholder evaluation in the strategic planning process is also indispensable for the functioning of the evaluation procedure and the decision-making process.

REFERENCES

Gilman, S. (2003), 'Sustainability and national policy in UK port development', *Maritime Policy & Management*, **30**(4), 275–91.

Ircha, M.C. (2001), 'Port strategic planning: Canadian port reform', *Maritime Policy & Management*, **28**(2), 125–40.

9. An application of stakeholder analysis to infrastructure development: the case of the 'DHL super-hub location choice'

Michaël Dooms, Cathy Macharis and Alain Verbeke

1. INTRODUCTION

Macharis (Chapter 5, in this volume) has explicitly used the 'stakeholder' concept within a multi-criteria analysis framework, an approach that has many advantages over conventional evaluation methodologies when assessing large-scale investment projects and policy measures. In this chapter, we apply this multi-stakeholder, multi-criteria analysis methodology (MAMCA) to the 'DHL super-hub location choice' case. The DHL case is particularly interesting as it involved several stakeholders with a variety of conflicting objectives. The MAMCA methodology consists of seven steps, as explained in Macharis et al. (2004), as well as Macharis (Chapter 5, in this volume).

In section 2, we shall discuss and apply to the DHL case each of the seven steps included in Figure 9.1. Section 3 provides a number of policy recommendations and identifies future research opportunities.

2. CASE STUDY: THE 'DHL SUPER-HUB LOCATION CHOICE'

2.1. Problem Description

In the course of 2003, the multinational logistics provider DHL announced it had plans to concentrate all its daily air cargo and express flights in one European location. DHL gave two main reasons for this concentration strategy. First, in 2003 DHL was the only global express courier company

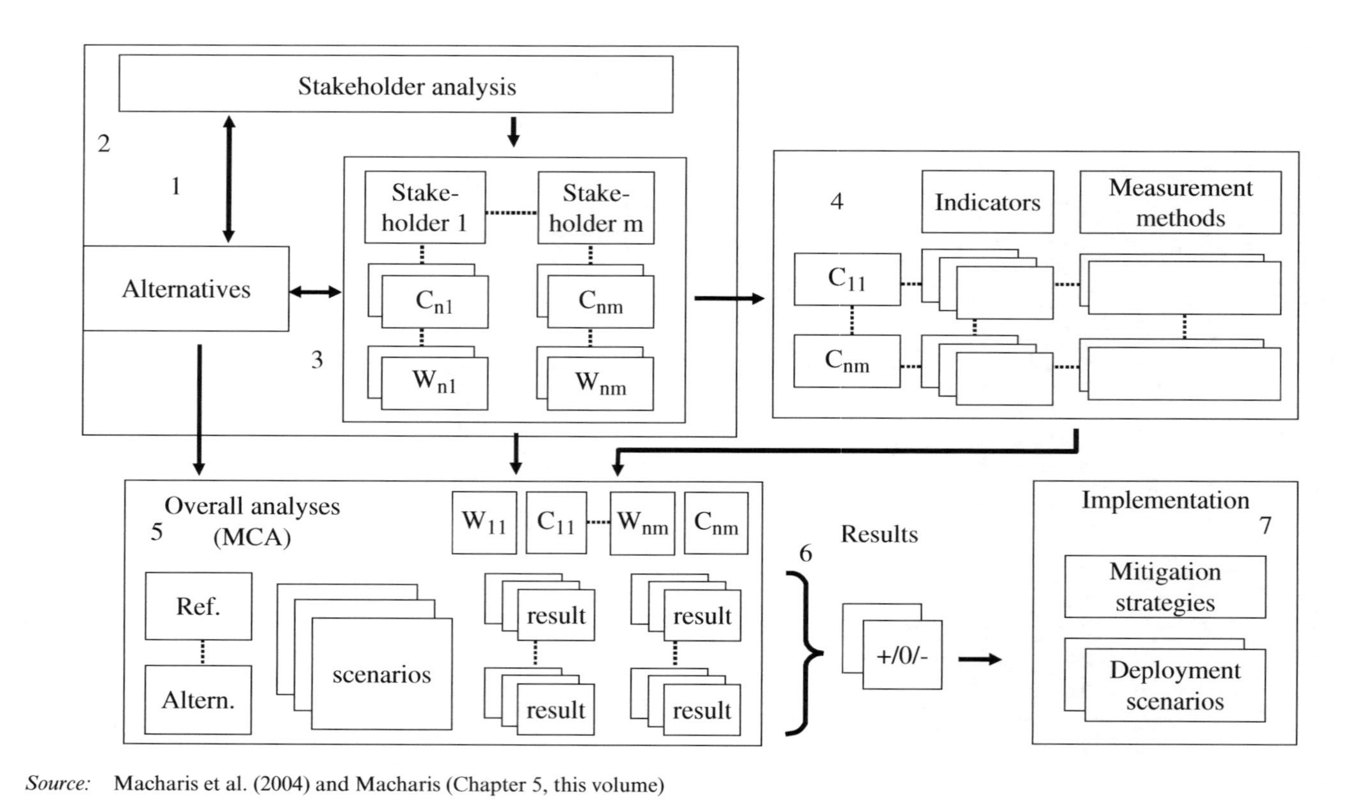

Source: Macharis et al. (2004) and Macharis (Chapter 5, this volume)

Figure 9.1 Multi-stakeholder, multi-criteria analysis (MAMCA) methodology

(the other global firms being UPS, TNT and Federal Express) working with a system of several sub-regional hubs, dispersed throughout Europe. DHL assumed that the regional concentration of activities in a single European super-hub was likely to bring substantial logistical cost savings. Second, the handling capacity at Brussels National Airport, which served as the main hub in the regional system, was expected to reach its saturation level in 2007, thereby imposing substantial new investments in handling capacity. Therefore, DHL sent a formal request for capacity expansion proposals to several European airports, including Brussels National Airport. If the pan-European super-hub were to be located at Brussels National Airport, this would imply a dramatic increase in night flights (from about 13 000 DHL night flights a year in 2003 to approximately 25 000–35 000 in the future, depending on the growth scenario). The DHL request for a proposal for new capacity at Brussels National Airport received substantial attention in the national press, especially given the large number of additional jobs that would be created in the wider region in the event of a DHL expansion in Brussels (Sleuwaegen et al., 2003). The employment data reported in the press were provided by the firm itself and by the airport infrastructure manager (BIAC – Brussels International Airport Company). At the same time, pockets of resistance against the DHL expansion arose in the local communities surrounding the airport, based on the alleged negative effects of night flights on human health, and the resulting increased healthcare costs, as well as lower worker productivity caused by a lack of peaceful sleep. In January 2004, the Belgian Federal Government announced that it would respond to DHL's request for capacity expansion in Brussels by September 2004. This response was supposed to include, in principle, a feasible extension plan at Brussels National Airport. In the event that a capacity expansion at Brussels National Airport would not be possible, an alternative location on Belgian territory would be proposed. This latter option quickly disappeared, however, as various feasibility analyses demonstrated, that the costs to build a new airport or to transform existing regional or military airports were too high. In addition, the administrative hurdles to overcome to allow DHL to function effectively in one of these alternative locations on Belgian territory were considered excessive in each case.

A capacity extension at Brussels National Airport proved to be the only feasible location in Belgium. However, such an extension also meant that the environmental permit given to the airport operator BIAC, set at a maximum of 25 000 night movements per year, would need to be renegotiated with the Flemish regional government, responsible for delivering environmental permits, so as to allow for more night flights. Furthermore, the Brussels regional government also needed to be involved, as each regional government determines the maximum noise levels tolerated on, or above, its territory. Though Brussels National Airport is physically located on the territory of the Flemish region, the aeroplane flight paths penetrate the Brussels Region, and a substantial number of night flights cross Brussels territory. As a result, the noise levels set by the Brussels government *would* determine to a large extent the feasibility of the extension at Brussels National Airport. The above suggests the need for an integrated policy approach by the Federal Government and the two other regional governments involved. In practical terms, the Federal Government acted as the sole political negotiator with DHL, but each decision it took would also need to be approved and implemented by the regional governments involved. Therefore, substantial decision power was actually held by the regional governments, namely the Brussels government in terms of setting the maximum noise levels and determining the maximum number of night movements above the Brussels region, and the Flemish Government, responsible for delivering the airport environmental permit.

The above decision-making complexities meant that in the time span of a few months, a number of important, interrelated decisions with long-term impacts had to be taken by different governments. Here, a number of partially conflicting objectives could be observed among the various stakeholders, namely:

- DHL's objective to function within the context of a stable regulatory framework that would allow the company to organize a sufficient number of night flights, as required by its business plan, and thereby ensure long-term growth, especially given the important capital investments in infrastructure to be undertaken by the company.
- The airport operating company's (BIAC) objective to achieve the same, stable regulatory framework, and to keep the extended DHL hub as a component of the airport's location advantages in attracting new cargo and passenger operators.
- The local community's objective to limit or eliminate entirely the DHL night flights, given the alleged health costs associated with night flights. The local community was represented by action committees, as well as elected representatives in the local municipal councils.
- The objectives of the different governments involved that included economic growth, reduction of ecological harm and a variety of policy objectives.

In order to support the decision process, two studies were commissioned by the province of Flemish Brabant, responsible for giving advice to the Flemish government on the environmental permit for the airport activity.

- A study on the economic benefits of the extension project;
- A study on the health effects (including health costs) of the extension project.

Both studies led to the identification of a number of economic benefit and cost categories, including both quantifiable and non-quantifiable impacts. Obviously, the parameters considered relevant and important were different for each stakeholder group, thereby imposing a stakeholder-based evaluation process. The project was highly controversial and there was a clear perception that decisions would not be accepted if stakeholders were not involved. In practical terms, the study required stakeholder input from DHL itself, from the airport operator BIAC, and from the 'government'. Given the conflicting objectives of the different governments involved, as outlined above, we constructed in this case a hypothetical government stakeholder that would be interested in balancing economic growth with ecological and social objectives.

The use of the MAMCA approach, given multiple sets of variables in different measurement units, and the presence of various stakeholders, seemed appropriate. In the following paragraphs, each of the seven steps of the methodology (see section 1) will be applied and discussed.

2.2. The Application of MAMCA

2.2.1. Step 1: Definition of the alternatives

The definition of the alternatives was driven by DHL's strategy regarding the choice of a new super-hub in Europe. From DHL's perspective, three strategies were considered as feasible and realistic.

We named strategic choice 1 the 'super-hub' choice, which meant the concentration of all European traffic at Brussels National Airport. In this case, an environmental permit allowing for 35 000 DHL night flights a year would be needed (approximately 140 each night). Cargo traffic volumes would rise to about 3000 metric tonnes a night.

Strategic choice 2 was the 'multi-hub' choice, which meant the concentration of all intercontinental traffic at Brussels National Airport, but with the continuous existence of capacity in other regional sub-hubs in Europe. In this case, an environmental permit allowing for 25 000 DHL night flights would be needed (approximately 100 each night). Cargo traffic volumes would rise to approximately 1875 metric tonnes a night.

Strategic choice 3 was the 'external super-hub' choice, which meant the relocation of the DHL hub from Brussels National Airport. This strategic choice implies that Brussels National Airport would be downgraded to assume the role of a spoke in the DHL network, and would only be used to serve the local market. This strategy would lead to a strong decline in night flights and traffic volume, compared to the actual situation (13 000 night movements a year and 1000 tonnes a night). In the extreme case, DHL would simply exit from Brussels (no night flights and no traffic volume at Brussels National Airport).

2.2.2. Step 2: Stakeholder analysis

In this case, we based the selection of stakeholders on their participation in debates regarding the future role of DHL in Brussels prior to the start of the research process. Within this stakeholder context, it is important to realize that two decisions had to be taken sequentially:

- First, the Federal Government would have to decide on the conditions for expansion (for example yearly number of night movements), and would need to communicate this decision to the other stakeholders;
- Second, and based on this first decision, DHL would have to decide on the location of its intercontinental hub.

In addition to the government (as a hypothetical, 'constructed' stakeholder) and DHL, two other stakeholders were included. The first was the airport operating company BIAC, which manages the airport, and has also a stake in DHL's ultimate location choice. The impact of DHL's choice on BIAC is both financial (in terms of investment and revenues) and on a more strategic level (for example positioning of the airport in the international airport network). Second, the local community needed to be included as a stakeholder, as night flights cause noise, leading to a possible decrease in quality of life. The last two stakeholders, though lacking formal decision power in the two key decisions noted above, had expressed their interest in the project. BIAC financed a study during 2003, which included a substantial section on courier company flights and night flights, as well as growth scenarios based on DHL's presence. The local community engaged in street protests, law suits against BIAC and the government, and made numerous appearances in the national press.

Based on the above, four main stakeholders were included in the evaluation: DHL, BIAC, the government and the local community.

2.2.3. Step 3: Define criteria and weights

The MAMCA decision tree, representing the criteria of each stakeholder, was the result of an interactive process that involved the province of Flemish Brabant (its input was considered to be the most relevant in constructing 'a' government interested in balancing economic, social and ecological considerations), DHL, BIAC and the researchers of a study on the impact of night flights on health costs (viewed as relevant to understanding DHL's effects on the local community and to some extent on the government). Each of the above actors was contacted separately to define specific stakeholder objectives/criteria. Here, the research team intervened to guarantee consistency in the overall decision tree, and to help the above actors in defining the criteria relevant to each stakeholder group (in other words, to help them answer the question: 'what needs to be measured or assessed?'). After the final decision on the criteria and their definition, the above actors also gave weights to the different criteria, using pairwise comparisons. After a methodological introduction by the research team, the choice of weights was left entirely to the actors above. In the case of the local community, we needed to assist the researchers involved in the health cost study in establishing the trade-off between the economic and health-related criteria.

2.2.3.1. Criteria of DHL DHL adopted three criteria to assess the alternative strategies. The first criterion is geographical in nature and measures how the different strategies contribute to the *proximity to the market.* For an integrator hub, location plays an important role, as a central position in the market is needed to operate efficiently (Rigas Doganis et al., 1999). The second criterion is related to *market share growth* in the logistics business. Each alternative strategy was likely to affect DHL's international competitive positioning, and hence its expected market share growth (or decline) vis-à-vis competitors. The third criterion measures how the different strategies contribute to the *internal logistical optimization* of the DHL network. This criterion plays an important role in terms of profitability, as the different strategies and the location of the hub strongly influence the synergy between the network and the different country operations. In other words, different locations and different growth strategies influence the logistical pathways (in terms of distances as well as the transport modes used) for the distribution of goods to the different countries affected, and hence, have a positive (or negative) effect on the total logistical cost of the firm.

2.2.3.2. Criteria of BIAC The airport infrastructure operator (BIAC) put forward five criteria in its decision-making process with regard to the DHL expansion.

The first criterion is *financial*, as all strategic alternatives influence the profitability of BIAC.

The second criterion takes into account the *diversification* of the traffic portfolio of the airport (cargo/passengers). In the highly competitive environment in which Brussels National Airport is situated, a balanced spread between cargo and passenger traffic allows demand shocks in air transport to be absorbed. Moreover, this balanced spread contributes to the attractiveness of the airport for suppliers of airport services, enhancing the diversification of the economic activity around the airport. The presence of suppliers of airport services in turn contributes to the attractiveness of the airport for new passenger and cargo operators. As a result, each strategy will contribute differently to the growth (or decline) of these supply effects.

The third criterion refers to the nature of the activities in the airport economic cluster, namely the presence of *high value-added activities* in the immediate environment of the airport. The presence of these activities contributes to the role of the airport as the source of high quality employment and value added, and supports BIAC in defending the airport activities vis-à-vis the local, regional and federal government.

The fourth criterion is related to *balanced growth*. This criterion takes into account internal aspects of the firm's activities (for example efficiency losses due to a mismatch between the short-term demand of capacity and the short-term supply of infrastructure and technical services), as well as external aspects, such as sudden changes in the regulatory framework concerning the airport activity which could lead to conflicts with the local community.

The last criterion shows the contribution of each strategy to the *positioning of the airport* in its international network. Each strategy contributes to the image of the airport, and plays a positive or negative role in attracting incremental traffic, thereby affecting the airport's competitive positioning.

2.2.3.3. Criteria of government The criteria of government can be split into two sets of objectives: socio-economic and ecological objectives.

The socio-economic objective of government can be split into three sub-criteria. The first sub-criterion measures the creation of *value added*, as an indicator of economic welfare. The second sub-criterion measures how the different strategies contribute to the creation of *employment*, one of the central objectives of government policy. The third sub-criterion refers to the impact of the different strategies on *regional competitiveness* of the Flemish and Belgian economy, in terms of cluster and agglomeration effects of high value activities in the industrial, logistics and ICT sectors.

The ecological objective measures the overall *health cost* for government associated with each of the strategies, as a result of changes in noise levels due to a growing (or declining) number of aeroplane movements.

2.2.3.4. Criteria of local community The criteria of the local community can also be unbundled into two main objectives. The first main criterion shows how the different strategies contribute to *local employment*. The boundary of what is 'local' was set based on the noise contour where night movements of 70 dB(A) and higher are measured. The second main criterion measures the different health impacts of each strategy, namely sleep disturbance, morbidity (diabetes, heart disease, alcohol abuse, depression), mortality, safety perception.

2.2.3.5. Decision tree Figure 9.2 shows the decision tree of the MAMCA with all stakeholders and their criteria.

2.2.4. Step 4: Criteria, indicators and measurement

Table 9.1 shows the different stakeholders as well as the criteria, and how these criteria were 'operationalized'. We indicate the nature of the criterion (quantitative/qualitative), the unit of measurement and the basis of the evaluation.

2.2.5. Step 5: Overall analysis and ranking

In this case study, the AHP method (Saaty, 1982) was used to perform the analysis and rank the alternative strategies. Based on the abovementioned criteria, pairwise comparisons were performed. In the cases of DHL and BIAC, stakeholder representatives made the pairwise comparisons themselves, as a substantial amount of commercially sensitive and

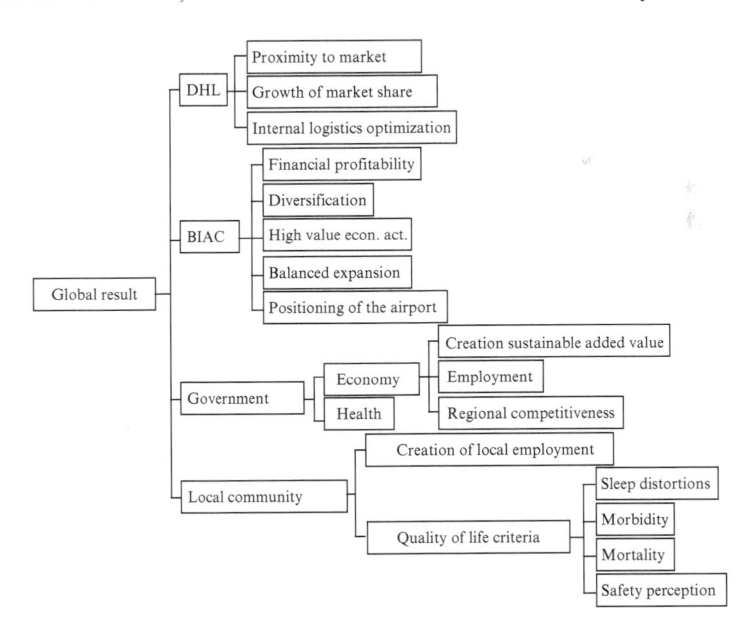

Figure 9.2 Decision tree

Table 9.1 Criteria, indicators and measurement

Stakeholder/criterion	Type of criterion	Unit of measurement**	Basis of the evaluation
DHL			
Market proximity	Quantitative	km	DHL calculations (internal)
Market share growth	Quantitative	%	DHL forecasts (internal)
Internal logistics optimization	Quantitative	euro	DHL forecasts (internal)
BIAC			
Financial	Quantitative	euro	BIAC calculation (internal)
Diversification	Quantitative	Value added / Employment	BIAC calculation (internal)
High value activity	Qualitative	/	Former studies (case studies based on questionnaires and interviews)
Balanced growth	Qualitative	/	BIAC technical service planning and calculation
Network position	Qualitative	/	BIAC assessment
Government			
Economic objective			
Value added	Quantitative	euro	Economic Impact Study
Employment	Quantitative	Number of jobs	Economic Impact Study
Regional competitiveness	Qualitative	/	Economic Impact Study (case studies based on questionnaires and interviews)
Health costs	Quantitative	euro	Health cost study

Local Community			
Local employment	Quantitative	Number of jobs	Economic Impact Study, DHL employment data
Health criteria			
Sleep disturbance	Quantitative	Number of people equivalent	Health cost study
*Morbidity**	Quantitative	Number of cases	Health cost study
Mortality	Quantitative	Number of people equivalent	Health cost study
Safety	Quantitative	Risk	Health cost study

Notes:
* Includes diabetes, heart disease, alcohol abuse and depression
** For DHL, the unit of measurement is indicative, as no documents were shown to the researchers, for reasons of confidentiality

confidential information was involved. In the case of the government and the local community, the pairwise comparisons were performed by the research team itself, based on the economic impact study and the study on health costs.

All pairwise comparisons were used as an input for expert choice, which reworks the pairwise comparisons into clear graphs and figures. These graphs and figures show how the alternative choices affect each stakeholder, and they also give an overall ranking.

2.2.6. Step 6: Results

In a first step, an equal weight was given to each stakeholder (see Figure 9.3 where the vertical gridlines show the weights). The sensitivity for changes in stakeholder weights was very high: a small positive change in weight in favour of DHL showed that the multi- and super-hub strategies would be much preferred as compared to the external super-hub. A small positive change in weight for the local community would rank the external super-hub as first alternative. This high sensitivity again showed the complexity of the decision problem. A balanced strategy, taking into account all stakeholder objectives, would be difficult to find.

Furthermore, the BIAC criterion related to the balanced expansion proved to be very important. A super-hub strategy was expected to result in short-term capacity bottlenecks, which would lead to inefficiencies, both for DHL and for BIAC. Based on information provided by BIAC's engineering department, we were able to determine that a full super-hub would only be operating efficiently from 2012 on, as the infrastructure and re-engineering

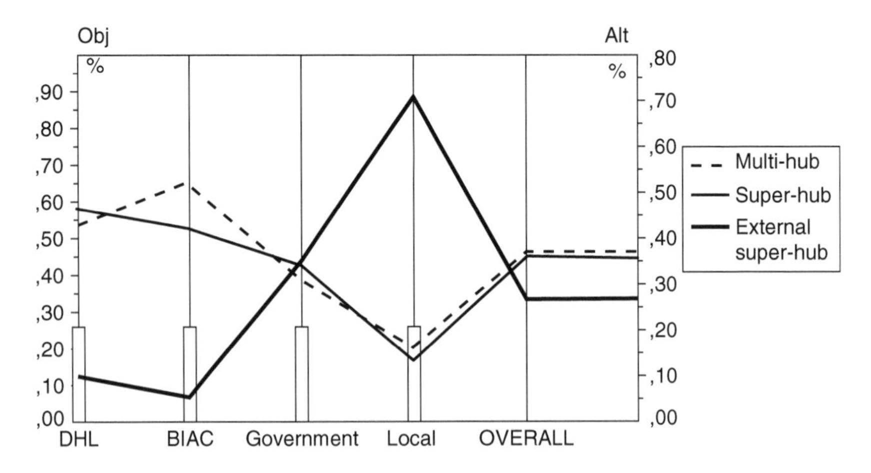

Figure 9.3 Overall result: horizon 2012

works at the airport would only be finished by 2012. As a result, what could be considered as the 'optimal' strategic choice could differ substantially depending on the time horizon considered, specifically an 8-year horizon (2012) versus a 20-year horizon (2023). This dynamic aspect was taken into account and the stakeholders whose preference was expected to change over time (that is, DHL and BIAC) were asked to make assessments on an 8-year horizon and a 20-year horizon. As a consequence, two overall analyses were performed, one having an 8-year horizon, another one having a 20-year horizon.

The results of the analysis with equal weights for all stakeholders showed that on horizon 2012, a multi-hub strategy is the preferred choice. On horizon 2023, a super-hub strategy appeared optimal as the infrastructural constraints would be removed, which makes a super-hub strategy more efficient for DHL as well as for BIAC. On the other hand, sensitivity remained very high to changes in the weights given to each of the stakeholders. The identification of the balanced growth criterion as an important driver of the overall preference in the mid-term, proved to be very valuable information for the community of stakeholders (more specifically DHL, BIAC, government) for implementation purposes. Figures 9.3 and 9.4 show the results on horizon 2012 and horizon 2023 respectively.

2.2.7. Step 7: Implementation

As mentioned in the problem description, government had to provide a legal-institutional framework with horizon 2023 capable of securing a

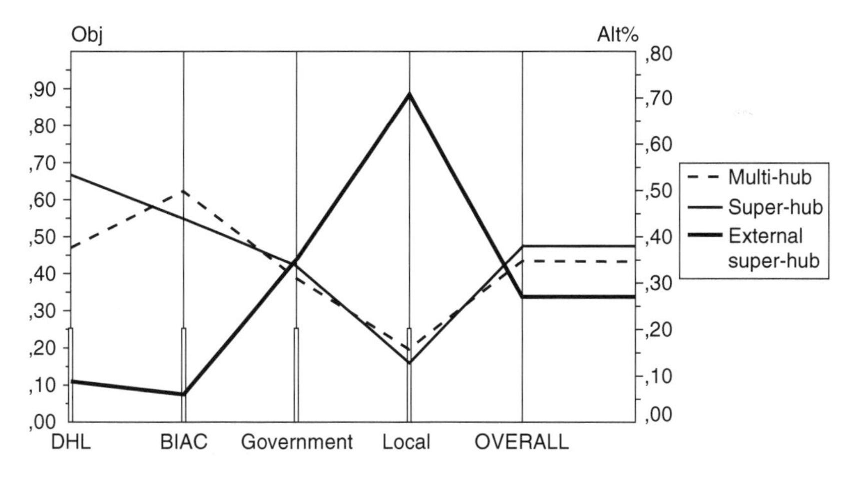

Source: Verbeke et al. (2004)

Figure 9.4 Overall result: horizon 2023

long-term growth of the activity, especially after 2012. If not, the hub activities of DHL would be relocated to another airport. In the mid-term, towards 2012, the multi-criteria analysis showed that Brussels National Airport could be used as a multi-hub in the DHL network. The negotiations between the Federal Government and DHL moved in this direction, as the short-term development to a super-hub would have led to a veto from specific stakeholders. A final agreement was reached between DHL and the Federal Government that included an alternative close to the multi-hub strategy as defined in the MAMCA (25 000 movements per year). However, implementation in practice still required changes in regional regulations on noise levels, as well as changes in the dispersion of night flights between the different regions. On that front, unfortunately, no agreement was reached during the implementation phase, leading to DHL's decision to exit from Brussels in 2008 (when new facilities in Leipzig, Germany would be ready). The lack of agreement by the regional governments (Brussels and Flanders) with decisions made by the Federal Government also shows that besides the temporal dimension in stakeholder management decisions (changing preferences in time), the geographical dimension plays a key role in implementation, especially for the stakeholder 'government' (changing preferences depending upon the geographic reach of the specific government involved).

3. CONCLUSION

In this chapter, the MAMCA method as described in Macharis et al. (2004) and Macharis (Chapter 5, in this volume) was applied to a case study, namely the 'DHL super-hub location choice'. This case study suggests that the MAMCA method contributes to the quality of the decision-making process in the realm of complex project evaluation on several levels.

First, the MAMCA method makes explicit the objectives of the various relevant stakeholders, thereby leading to a better understanding of the objectives of these stakeholders by all parties concerned. Allowing the stakeholders (be they representatives of business firms or government agencies) to reflect on their own objectives and involving them in the pairwise comparisons, also provides value added in the individual stakeholders' internal decision-making processes. The MAMCA approach forces them to reflect on what they really want and on the rationale for these wants. Moreover, the fact that the stakeholders know they are included in a comprehensive evaluation alters their way of thinking, and motivates them to make proper assessments. For example, the initial results obtained on the 'balanced growth' criterion led to a change of both DHL and BIAC with regard to short- and long-term preferences, and provided decision-makers at the government level with additional insights on the impacts of their decision.

Second, the MAMCA method shows the essential trade-offs made by all stakeholders, and makes these stakeholders more aware of the dynamic and spatial aspects of the societal decision-making process. The DHL case study showed that the temporal dimension plays a major role, as stakeholder preferences can change over time, especially when decision-makers are confronted with long-term impacts. The geographical dimension also plays a key role, in particular when implementing decisions, as some stakeholders (for example, individual governments and government agencies) may have fundamentally different attitudes or preferences according to the geographical location of their constituencies. This became clear when government eventually decided not to grant the environmental permit: the Brussels and Flemish regional governments could not agree on the night flights dispersion plan, despite an agreement within the Federal Government to allow expansion. One of the important lessons learned was that the present Belgian institutional model is not adapted to handle expansion plans of large multinational enterprises when significant interregional socio-economic and environmental impacts are involved.

This case study also suggests that further research is needed in order to develop the MAMCA method further and to include dynamic and spatial components in complex project evaluation, especially if the projects considered have long-term impacts on society.

REFERENCES

Doganis R. and Associates, The Aviation and Travel Consultancy Ltd, York Consulting Ltd (1999), 'The importance and impact of the express industry in Europe', study commissioned by the European Express Association (EEA).

Macharis, C., A. Verbeke and K. De Brucker (2004), 'The strategic evaluation of new technologies through multi-criteria analysis: the advisors case', in: E. Bekiaris and Y.J. Nakanishi (eds), *Economic Impacts of Intelligent Transportation Systems. Innovations and Case Studies*, Amsterdam: Elsevier, pp. 439–60.

Saaty, T.L. (1982), *Decision Making for Leaders*, Lifetime Learning Publications, Wadsworth: Belmont.

Sleuwaegen, L., K. De Backer, B. Van Pottelsberghe, S. Nysten, J. Gille and R.J. Molemaker (2003), 'Naar een nieuwe balans tussen economie en ecologie. Onderzoek over de economische impact van de luchthaven Brussel Nationaal voor de Belgische economie', (*Towards a new balance between economy and ecology. Economic Impact of Brussels National Airport on the Belgian Economy*), study commissioned by BIAC.

Verbeke, A., C. Macharis, M. Dooms and R. S'Jegers (2004), 'Economische impactstudie van de uitbreiding van de hubactiviteiten van het koeriersbedrijf DHL op de luchthaven van Zaventem', (*Economic impact study of the expansion of the DHL hub activities – Brussels National Airport: Final Report*), study commissioned by provincie Vlaams Brabant.

10. In search of the ideal institutional structure for decision-making on transport infrastructure: a conjoint analysis of expert opinions on hybrid forms of German, Danish and Dutch decision-making

Martin de Jong, Harry Geerlings and Eric Molin

INTRODUCTION

Decision-making on large scale infrastructure projects has figured strongly in the political and public debate in the Netherlands in the past 20 years. The most recent forum to address the topic has been the Temporary Commission on Infrastructure (TCI), commonly known as the Duijvestein Commission. This parliamentary committee was installed to investigate the reasons why huge cost and time overruns took place before and during the construction of rail projects and why responsible authorities were informed late or not at all about complications and disappointments during the process. Prior to this, decision-making on large scale infrastructure projects was extensively addressed in international – and certainly not least Dutch – academic publications on public policy and political science (cf. Reh, 1988; Taylor, 1992; Teisman, 1992; WRR, 1994; Leleur, 1995; Hendriks, 1997; Hendriks and Zouridis, 1998; WRR, 1998; Flyvbjerg, 1998; de Jong, 1999; Ministries of Transport and Economic Affairs, 2000; Woltjer, 2001; Flyvbjerg et al., 2002; de Jong and Geerlings, 2003; Stead and Geerlings, 2003). In the course of time, it looked as if all these debates had produced a sort of consensus on the design specifications for good decision-making. It included, for instance, the timely involvement of key interest groups and private citizens in the debate, proper preliminary research on important related aspects such as economic and environmental issues, consensus between the diverse tiers of government rather than confrontation, construction and maintenance costs remaining within acceptable boundaries, and transparency in the process leading to well-informed elected bodies.

It is generally assumed that thorough *ex ante* evaluation concerning economic and environmental impacts of infrastructure development, timely consultation of relevant pressure groups and citizens and a seamless and constructive communication between involved tiers of government are what is needed. If problems arise, the fixing should be sought in those aspects. Changing something about the latter characteristics could lead to an improvement in the quality of decision-making.

So, at first, it seems easy enough to envisage a new model. Closer scrutiny reveals, however, that these specifications can be interpreted in different ways and that attempts to meet them could lead to inherent contradictions in the model for a new decision-making structure. Acquiring insight into the value attached to each of the elements of the decision-making process is key in order to be able to choose a process enjoying wide support. To take this further, research has been conducted into the opinions of Dutch experts in the field. The authors have used the so-called conjoint analysis method (Louviere, 1988). In this method, all respondents are asked to come up with an integrated judgement on several alternative decision profiles.

Having knowledge only of the decision-making practice of one's own country at one's disposal severely limits the possibility of imagining completely different possible institutional worlds. To create variety in the different decision profiles, the institutional structures in some foreign countries have been studied. The profiles were drafted on the basis of an exhaustive analysis and comparison of the decision-making structures and practices in Denmark, Germany and the Netherlands. The findings revealed that the policy makers in these three countries endorsed the same design requirements but pursued them in different ways. The analysis indicated that the three countries differed mainly in the following areas:

- The role of cost–benefit analyses in the decision-making process;
- The role of environmental impact reports in the decision-making process;
- The way in which interest groups, such as environmentalists, the business community and others, are represented in the decision-making process;
- The degree to which central government, local authorities and private parties co-fund infrastructure and hence can exert an influence on the course of the decision-making process.

The different approaches to these four issues formed the basis for nine profiles that could be regarded as hybrid forms of the decision-making structures in the three countries.

The experts were asked for an overall assessment of each profile. As some of these aspects were more attractive than others, this meant that they had to trade off the aspects in the profile. Regression analysis was then applied to decompose the overall scores into the weights for each varied aspect. This method was far preferable to the individual approach applied in conventional assessment methods. By ascertaining the importance that the Dutch experts attached to each aspect of the decision-making structure, it would reveal what they considered the ideal structure.

This chapter explains step by step the background, the organization, findings and conclusions of the research. In the next section, the method, conjoint analysis, is described and the authors will indicate how it has been applied in the case at hand. It deviates strongly from the more qualitative and impressionistic research methods that have been used in the fields to date, such as unstructured interviews. This section also portrays how the four above-mentioned characteristics of the institutional structure ('attributes'), each with three possible scores ('values') have been established and how the experts have been approached and instructed. The authors present the outcomes of the survey in the third section, after which the fourth section discusses these outcomes in light of the current institutional structure in the Netherlands. The added value and limitations of applying conjoint analysis as compared to other research methods in this field are given in the final section.

CONJOINT ANALYSIS AND COMPILING THE DECISION-MAKING PROFILES

Conjoint Analysis

The introduction mentioned four elements of institutional structures and the way in which they appear in three selected countries (Denmark, Germany and the Netherlands). What we now need to find out is the value attached by the experts to each of these aspects with the ultimate aim of finding a model for an ideal decision-making structure. A more traditional assessment method would require each expert to accord a score to each separate aspect and to state the value that he/she attaches to each aspect. One of the flaws in this method is that when the respondents assess a single element they often make assumptions about the others. For example, if the experts are asked for an opinion on 'CBA decisive' some might assume from their knowledge of decision-making structures in other countries that the German decision-making structure is involved. In other words, their opinions on other elements of the German decision-making structure could influence their assessment of the single element 'CBA decisive'. Others who do not have this knowledge will not respond in this way, so that ultimately one does not exactly know what one is measuring. In addition, it has been demonstrated time and again in the past that a combination of the highest-scoring elements does not necessarily deliver the ideal alternative: apparently, it delivers a net total score which is more or less than the sum of the parts.

The disadvantages of traditional measurement are removed by conjoint analysis. In the literature on conjoint analysis the elements are called *attributes* and the values they can assume are called *attribute levels*. In the conjoint analysis the attribute levels were combined into profiles of decision-making structures. The respondents were asked to give an overall score for a complete decision-making profile. To do so they had to weigh attributes with attractive values against attributes with less attractive values. As the composition of the profiles varied systematically based on statistical designs, statistical analysis could be applied to determine which value the respondents attached to each attribute level (that is the score for each attribute level). This would then produce a model which could be used to predict the attractiveness of any given decision-making structure. The paragraphs below explain how this research was organized and conducted.

Determining the Decision-making Profiles

In order to compile the decision profiles, first the four attributes and their levels had to be determined, after which they could be combined into profiles. The four characteristics selected are shown in Table 10.1. This is not a complete list of all conceivable or possible institutional aspects, but rather a set based on the idea that most inspiration can be derived from differences between countries that are notably different and focusing on those differences. Table 10.1 shows these differences and how the countries have different scores for them.

- *What is the exact role of cost–benefit analyses in the decision-making process?* Are they omitted altogether or are they only conducted *ex tempore* by players who want to prove their own case, possibly against each other (informative)? Or are they conducted on a standard basis for each infrastructure project of any magnitude and are the authorities at least required to respond to them (advisory)? Or do they even play an important part in determining the outcomes of the decision-making process (decisive)?

Table 10.1 Scores of three countries on four decision-making structure attributes

Attributes of decision-making structure	Germany	Netherlands	Denmark
Influence of cost–benefit analysis on project approval	Decisive	Advisory	Informative
Influence of environmental report on project approval	Decisive	Advisory	Informative
Main funding organizations	Central and local government	Central government	Central and local government and private funders
Status of interest groups in the process	Recognized and committed partner	Advisory and non-committed partner	Independent and ad hoc discussion partner

- *What is the exact role of environmental impact reports in the decision-making process?* The categories for the cost–benefit analyses, namely informative, advisory and decisive, apply here as well.
- *What status is allotted to interest groups, such as environmentalists, the business community and other special interest groups?* Are they incidental players who have no guaranteed place in the process, but can still drop in on the decision-making arena when it suits them (ad hoc and independent partner)? Are they standard discussion partners, who cannot play a clear hand when the chips are down and can easily distance themselves from the results (advisory, non-committed partner)? Or are they permanent discussion partners who attend each meeting and are prepared to concede some of their independence in exchange for true input and an effective veto power (permanent, committed partner)?
- *Who is/are the dominant source(s) of funding?* Central government alone? Or central government in conjunction with the local authorities? Or central government and local authorities in conjunction with private parties who then defray some of their surplus profits from the sale of designated sites to the very infrastructure projects due to be developed there?

One can conclude that this study deals with four attributes, each at three levels. Hence, a total of $3^4 = 81$ decision-making profiles were constructed.

It would have been impracticable to present the experts with all 81 possible profiles, as this would have required huge amounts of time and attention. To keep the profiles to a minimum, the smallest possible orthogonal fraction was selected. This meant that nine profiles were assessed. The main effects could be ascertained on the basis of these scores, that is the influence of each attribute level on the total score (regardless of the other attribute levels in the profile). To achieve this, it is necessary to assume that all interaction effects are equal to zero, that is that certain combinations of attribute levels contribute no more or no less to the total score than might be expected on the basis of the main effects. Whether this assumption is correct cannot be checked out in this particular configuration. However, according to Louviere et al. (1988), 85 per cent of all variation can be explained by the main effects, and the predictions which are based on main effects alone are relatively accurate even if the interaction effects do not actually equal zero. It should be borne in mind here that the latter applies only to predictions for non-extreme profiles.

The decision-making profiles were constructed with a table of orthogonal attribute designs, which dictated which attribute levels should be combined (cf. Steenkamp, 1985). One of the nine profiles turned out to be the Dutch decision-making structure. In addition, two 'hold-out' profiles were included in the study. These were extra profiles which were not used in the statistical analysis of the assessments that were conducted in order to compile the model, but rather for determining the accuracy of the predictions. The hold-out profiles in this study were the decision-making structures of Germany and Denmark. The predictive capability of the conceptualized model was tested by comparing the predicted scores for the hold-out profiles with the observed scores. The deviation between the predicted and observed scores would indicate the accuracy of the model.

Measuring

The nine profiles were then presented to the experts who were asked to assess their quality. Determining quality criteria for the assessment of institutional structures is no easy task. Take, for example, a political concept like democracy, which is subject to ambiguity and multiple interpretations. Democratic participation, for instance, a concept derived from political science, is highly ambiguous and multi-interpretable. Does democracy imply direct citizen participation? Is it a system where pressure groups strongly reflect the will of the people? Or does it refer to the universally acknowledged concept of electoral representation? Governance norms (transparency, openness, mutual trust, player satisfaction, flexibility, reliability, robust choices) are equally difficult to effectuate and are sometimes contradictory.

The authors therefore decided to look for openings in publications on project management (Wijnen et al., 2004). After all, these also address infrastructure projects. In these publications project managers are instructed to pay attention to five aspects of quality in infrastructure projects:

- Time: What is the total amount of time spent on decision-making in a project?
- Money: What are the total expenses on a project?
- Information: How adequate is the information supply during a project?
- Organization: How adequate is the organization of a project?
- Quality: What is the quality of the end product delivered by the project?

These aspects were adjusted so that they would fit in specifically with this study on decision-making in transport infrastructure. Obviously, the 'time' aspect is represented by the first criterion, 'speed of decision-making', while 'money' is covered by the second 'total costs of the project'. The transformation of the other three is more indirect. 'Information' becomes 'open information-sharing', as information alone is difficult to operationalize. 'Organization' becomes 'acceptance of final decisions', because good organization in this domain normally amounts to timely involvement of the other players in the right way. If the organization is 'good', other players besides the overall process manager are involved in the right way at the right time, and acceptance of the decision-making process and the product increases. By far the most difficult aspect was 'quality', which is not only multi-faceted but typically subjective. This was interpreted in two ways: the respondents were asked (1) to gauge the quality of the infrastructure that would eventually emerge from the decision-making process and (2) to assess the quality of the variant as a whole.

The respondents were asked to indicate how much change could be expected in the five quality aspects if the profiled decision-making structure were introduced. They could express this on a five-point scale from -2 to $+2$, in which 0 indicated no change compared with the current decision-making structure in the Netherlands. After they had indicated the anticipated change in the five quality aspects the respondents were asked to award an overall score for the decision-making profile. This score was to be expressed on a scale of 0 to 10. An example of a decision-making profile with the accompanying scores is provided in Table 10.2.

The nine decision-making profiles were incorporated into a questionnaire. This included an explanation of the assessment tasks and a list of all the attributes and attribute levels, so that the respondents had an idea of the variants they could expect. The Dutch situation was then offered as a reference profile against which each of the nine variants was to be compared. The respondents were then asked to assess the nine profiles plus the German and the Danish profile in relation to five quality criteria. Finally, as a kind of dessert, each expert was asked to compile his own profile (Profile 12) and to assess it in the same way as the others. They were then thanked for their assistance and told that they would be notified of the results.

Although the questionnaire was not excessively long and all the experts were well versed in the subject matter, a lot was still being asked of them. First, they had to understand the ideas behind the study. Then they had to take the time to visualize the decision-making structure for each profile and the workings of the process as a whole. Finally, they had to figure out how all of this impinged on each of the quality criteria. It was therefore crucial to find the right candidates, to explain the concept clearly and to adopt a flexible approach to the way the respondents wanted to fill in the questionnaire. The respondents were selected on the basis of two criteria. In the academic category almost all Dutch academics were approached who were known to be working on this subject. For the other categories the participants in the 'Almere-Bollenstreek Corridor' study were approached (Almere-Bollenstreek

Table 10.2 Profile 1 complete, for assessment

Attributes of the decision-making process	Variant 1
Influence of cost–benefit analysis on project approval	Advisory
Influence of environmental assessment on project approval	Decisive
Main funding organizations	Central government, local authorities and private funders
Status of interest groups in the process	Recognized and committed partner

How far do you think this variant will change the following aspects?			
Speed of decision-making:	much lower	−2 −1 0 1 2	much higher
Acceptance of final decisions:	much lower	−2 −1 0 1 2	much higher
Costs of the project:	much lower	−2 −1 0 1 2	much higher
Open information sharing among parties:	much lower	−2 −1 0 1 2	much higher
Quality of the final infrastructure product:	much lower	−2 −1 0 1 2	much higher
What overall score do you give this variant of the decision-making process?			

is an area where the desirability of investment in infrastructure and spatial development was explored at the time of writing). The participants in this network come from diverse organizations. The respondents filled in the questionnaire during a personal interview with one of the researchers.

MAIN RESULTS OF THE QUESTIONNAIRE

Eventually, the questionnaire was distributed to exactly 50 respondents. During the processing phase 47 of these were found to be complete. These 47 respondents were all well-acquainted with the subject of decision-making on transport infrastructure. They were split into six sub-categories (1) academics, (2) state civil servants, (3) regional civil servants, (4) civil servants from independent government bodies, (5) consultants, and (6) interest groups involved in the area. This was necessary in order to gauge the influence of vested interest in the desired changes.

Table 10.3 shows that the largest groups were academics and state civil servants. Respondents who could, theoretically, fall into several categories were allocated according to their first employer. For example, university lecturers who did consultancy work were allocated to 'Academics'.

The background and workings of the questionnaire were explained personally to all the respondents before they filled it in. At first, most of them found the subject and the approach somewhat complicated and had to concentrate long and hard. But their enthusiasm soon increased once they got into the swing of things.

Relevant Findings about the Profiles as a whole

A number of observations can be mooted on the basis of the findings. The most striking observation is that, on average, the Dutch model scored

Table 10.3 Categories of respondents

Group	N	%
Academics	13	27.7
State civil servants	13	27.7
Regional civil servants	9	19.1
Independent civil servants	3	6.4
Consultants	5	10.6
Interest groups	4	8.5
Total	47	100

higher (6.08) than the German model (5.79) and even the Danish model (5.55). The average score for the individually chosen ideal models was around 8, while the average score for Profiles 1–9 was 5.57. Profiles 10 (Denmark), 11 (Germany) and 12 (ideal model) were omitted from this part of the analysis. We can conclude from this that the Dutch model scored higher than most of the other models, including the German and the Danish one, but that there is definitely room for improvement.

To understand how these results came about it is best to look at the scores for the various decision-making attributes in relation to the overall score. With this in mind, an individual regression model was drafted for each respondent, in which the dependent variable was the overall score and the independent variables were the coded attribute levels. It deserves mentioning here that for each respondent nine profiles have been scored, which implies that the estimated model for all respondents is based on 47 * 9 = 423 observations.

The estimated part-worth utilities and the constant are shown in Table 10.4. A full description of the attribute levels can be found in Table 10.1. The first column in Table 10.4 presents the results for all the respondents. Each of the remaining columns presents the results for the different categories of expert (independent civil servants, interest groups, consultants, regional civil servants, state civil servants and academics). The results in Table 10.4 can be read as follows. The constant reflects the mean overall score given to the nine decision profiles. This implies that all respondents have, on average, rated the nine decision profiles with the score of 5.6, meaning 'barely sufficient'. The other numbers indicate the changes that occur in the valuation if the attribute level concerned is part of the decision profile. For example, in the first column the levels of the attribute cost–benefit analysis have the following values: informative −0.06, advisory 0.30 and decisive −0.24. This means that a decision profile with an informative CBA is valued 0.06 lower than the average. A decisive CBA lowers the valuation even more (0.24), whereas having an advisory CBA increases the score of a decision profile by 0.30 (almost a third of a unit measurement). A more descriptive interpretation would be that experts generally prefer an advisory cost–benefit analysis, are loath to a decisive one, while an informative position for cost–benefit studies is awarded an intermediate position.

Table 10.4 also shows whether a part-worth utility significantly differs from zero at the 0.05 level or at the 0.10 level. It should be noted that only the coefficients for the first two levels of each can be tested for significance. The reason is that only two coefficients per attribute can be estimated; the third coefficient is derived from the first two. Because effect coding was applied, the part-worth utilities of the level of each attribute sum to zero.

Table 10.4 Report scores according to expert category and attribute

	All respondents	Independent	Interest Groups	Consultants	Region civil servants	State civil servants	Academics
Constant	5.57**	5.88**	5.61**	5.28**	5.56**	5.76**	5.43**
Cost–Benefit Analysis							
Informative	−0.06	−0.13	−0.19	−0.08	0.04	−0.20	0.08
Advisory	0.30**	0.29	−0.03	0.72**	0.11	0.26	0.42**
Decisive	−0.24	−0.16	0.22	−0.64	−0.15	−0.06	−0.50
Environmental Impact Analysis							
Informative	0.00	0.01	0.06	0.04	0.07	0.06	−0.13
Advisory	0.20**	0.49	−0.03	0.38*	0.04	0.33*	0.12
Decisive	−0.20	−0.49	−0.03	−0.43	−0.11	−0.39	0.01
Main Funder(s)							
Central gvt.	−0.13	−0.55*	0.31	−0.09	−0.15	−0.13	−0.18
Cent. & local gvt.	0.11	0.54*	−0.19	0.24	0.26*	0.19	−0.13
Cent. & loc. gvt. & private sector	0.02	0.01	−0.11	−0.15	−0.11	−0.06	0.30
Interest Groups							
Ad hoc	−0.39**	−0.05	−0.44*	−0.08	−0.22	−0.42**	−0.66**
Advisory	0.14	0.06	−0.11	0.50**	0.00	0.27	0.05
Recognized	0.26	−0.01	0.56	−0.42	0.22	0.15	0.61

Notes: ** significant at 0.05 level; * significant at 0.10 level

Given that the number of respondents in each category was very small, the figures should be regarded as indicative rather than representative for the category as a whole.

It may be concluded from Table 10.4 that the relative satisfaction with regard to the Dutch profile is primarily related to a preference among the majority of the respondents for an *advisory role for evaluation methods*, exactly the situation in the Netherlands: environmental impact reports and cost–benefit analyses are obligatory; the decision-makers must acquaint themselves with the results, but may deviate from them provided they have sound reasons for doing so. This ensures the continuation of political primacy. The German system, in which the results of such studies are more binding on the players, met with strong disapproval from many people, while ad hoc environmental impact reports – as in the case of Denmark – were regarded as too slapdash. Most of the experts took the view that the Dutch solution was a happy medium: systematic advice is valuable and necessary, but it must not have too strong an influence on the course of events.

The financial relationships tell a different story. *A scenario with central government as the dominant financier was more or less rejected*, even though this is normal practice in the Netherlands. Interestingly, the scores for the first nine profiles suggest that the preferred option is one in which funding is shared between central government and local authorities, while in the ideal variant the preferred option is more often one in which funding is shared by central government, local authorities and private financiers (see below). There is no obvious explanation for this, though it does appear to be 'the done thing' nowadays to promote the involvement of private parties in infrastructure projects. Interestingly, this preference was most prevalent among academics and independent civil servants. These two groups are entirely responsible for the margin in favour of the variant that includes private funders. Be that as it may, it is still patently clear that the vast majority of the experts would like to see a much broader basis for funding. In this regard the Dutch profile is inferior to the German and Danish profiles and two thirds of the other profiles.

As far as the fourth attribute is concerned, the status of interest groups in the process, there is a particularly strong aversion to ad hoc consultation. Ad hoc consultation with interest groups scores by far the worst out of all the decision-making attributes across all the profiles. *An advisory and non-committed role and a recognized and committed role by interest groups are both more preferable – and particularly the latter*. What this amounts to *in concrete terms* is that the respondents were generally satisfied with the advisory – but ultimately uncommitted – role of interest groups in the decision-making process, but would like the ties to be stronger. This would pave the way for a scenario which is more than just a talking shop and actually leads to joint decisions and shared responsibility. This aspect of the German model met with strong approval – notably among the academics and representatives of the interest groups. State and regional civil servants were also in favour but to a lesser extent, while the independent civil servants were neutral and the consultants were strongly opposed. These findings are particularly interesting in view of the fact that the interest groups may have a lot to gain from this set-up and the consultants a lot to lose. The opinion of almost all the other categories ranged from moderately to strongly positive, so that, on balance, it may be concluded that the experts actually would be in favour of a shift towards a corporatist or 'polder' model. A carefully chosen selection of these interest groups, such as the business community and the environmentalists, should be given the power of veto in the decision-making, and the government should respect as far as possible the outcome of the negotiations between the parties.

Finally, it needs to be emphasized that this last decision-making attribute had by far the strongest influence on the overall scores that the respondents awarded to the profiles. In that respect it is the most important attribute of the four in the assessment.

Relevant Outcomes for the Individual Quality Aspects

Apart from an overall assessment for each decision profile the interviewees have also evaluated each profile regarding five other quality aspects. The extent to which scores on these aspects shift as compared to the current Dutch situation will be dealt with in this section.

Out of the four attributes there was actually only one which the respondents believed to have a substantial influence on the speed of the decision-making: the status of the interest groups in the process. By and large, they reckoned that a 'looser' structure would speed things up, while a definitive status for interest groups would slow things down. What this boils down to, in the light of the previous paragraph, is that such a definitive status would have a positive effect on the overall report score, though the speed of the decision-making would slow down. Interestingly, this view is not shared by the academics, who could foresee no effects at all, while the interest groups – in contrast with the rest – believed that corporatist relations would actually speed things up. It is, unfortunately, impossible to discern just how far these views are based on vested interest or on experience.

Although the influence of the attribute 'status of interest groups' is also greatest in the quality aspect *acceptance of final decisions*, all the attributes exert some influence here. In general, the respondents felt that an advisory role for evaluations would have the most favourable effect on the acceptance of final decisions and the same applied to the co-funding of projects by

Table 10.5 Effect on quality aspects

	Speed	Acceptance	Costs	Information	Quality
Constant	−0.12**	−0.16**	0.03	−0.04	−0.10**
Cost–Benefit Analysis					
Informative	0.03	−0.05	0.22**	−0.01	−0.07
Advisory	−0.04	0.24**	0.11	0.12*	0.14**
Decisive	0.02	−0.19	−0.32	−0.11	−0.08
Environmental Impact Analysis					
Informative	0.05	−0.09	−0.32**	−0.01	−0.10
Advisory	0.07	0.15**	−0.17**	0.10	0.05
Decisive	−0.12	−0.05	0.50	−0.09	0.04
Main funder					
Central gvt.	0.06	−0.18**	0.05	−0.16**	−0.12*
Central & local government	−0.05	0.19**	0.04	0.07	0.09
Central & local gvt. & private funders	−0.01	−0.01	−0.10	0.09	0.03
Interest groups					
Ad hoc	0.17**	−0.53*	−0.14*	−0.41**	−0.19**
Advisory	−0.01	−0.09	−0.06	−0.07	0.00
Recognized	−0.18	0.62	0.20	0.48	0.18

Notes: ** significant at 0.05 level; * significant at 0.10 level

central government and local authorities (see Table 10.5). The respondents were unanimous in their opinion of how the recognition of interest groups would affect the decision-making process: the influence on acceptance would be sizeable and positive. In other words, if the business community, the environmentalists and other interest groups were co-responsible for the decision-making and the outcome of the negotiations, the legitimacy problem would be more or less solved.

A totally different picture emerged for *costs*. Here the influence of evaluations is actually stronger than for the other two decision-making attributes. The financial relationships have only a marginal effect (the involvement of private parties would lower the costs to some extent, even though the regional civil servants thought differently) and the recognition of interest groups would push up the costs. Far stronger, however, are the effects of making cost–benefit analyses the determining factor in sanctioning infrastructure projects: the costs would decline significantly. The reverse applies – even more strongly – to environmental impact reports: if these were a decisive factor in a project, they would, according to the respondents, lead to significantly higher costs. On the other hand, if these evaluations were actually to carry less commitment than in the current advisory scenario in the Netherlands, then an informative environmental report would save costs, while an informative cost–benefit analysis would raise the overall costs for infrastructure projects.

The aspect *open information sharing* tends in the same direction as acceptance of final decisions: the influence of the evaluations is relatively small and an advisory role is preferable for environmental impact reports (if present) as well as cost–benefit analyses. State-dominated funding would act as a constraint on communication, but co-funding by different layers of government would be favourable. Involvement by private funders would have virtually no effect. Here, the fourth decision-making attribute, the status of pressure groups, emerges again as by far the strongest, even stronger than acceptance. The representatives of all the categories agreed that if interest groups were officially recognized in the process and were required to commit, then the information-sharing between the parties would improve dramatically. On the five-point scale the score for a variant with recognized partners in relation to openness rose by as much as 1.14 among interest groups and regional civil servants and by 0.78 among the academics, the highest scores recorded in the whole study. The conclusion is crystal clear: a corporatist model would create more trust in the communication between the partners in the decision-making process.

The findings for the final infrastructure product are far less striking than for acceptance and openness but they tend in the same direction. Advisory evaluations have a slightly positive effect on the quality of the product while a dominant central government has a negative effect. Though the scores for recognition of interest groups are less impressive than for openness, the most pronounced scores, interestingly enough, came from exactly the same three groups (interest groups 0.31, regional civil servants 0.27, and academics 0.35).

The Ideal Decision Model

According to the model, the decision-making structure that should get the highest overall score would be constructed as follows: the environmental impact assessment and the cost–benefit analysis would both be advisory, central government and local authorities would share the funding and the interest groups would be recognized and committed. Table 10.6 presents an estimation of how this pans out in relation to the quality aspects.

The respondents felt that in order to increase the speed of the decision-making a much looser structure was needed, rather like the one in

Table 10.6 The ideal decision-making structure according to the model (overall scores)

Attributes of the decision-making process	Attribute levels
Influence of cost–benefit analysis on project approval	Advisory (as in the Netherlands)
Influence of the environmental impact report on project approval	Advisory (as in the Netherlands)
Funding and coordination	Central government and locals authorities (as in Germany)
Status of interest groups in the process	Recognized and committed partners (as in Germany)

How far do you think that this variant would change the following aspects?		
Speed of decision-making:	lower	(−0.32)
Acceptance of final decisions:	much higher	(0.87)
Open information-sharing:	much higher	(0.73)
Total costs of the project:	neutral	(0.09)
Quality of the final infrastructure product:	much higher	(0.55)
Overall score for this variant:	highest	(6.44)

Denmark, but this would also trigger unacceptable adverse effects on most other fronts. To lower the costs, the role of the cost–benefit analysis should be decisive and the role of the environmental impact report should be brought back to informative, but these changes would also spark primarily negative effects.

Profile 12, the ideal model, was compiled by asking the respondents to mould their ideal characteristics into their own ideal variant. The 47 respondents submitted a total of 21 different variants, three of which were by far the most popular. Curiously, the profile that was predicted on the basis of the analytic data was not among them. Indeed, it was chosen by only one of the 47 respondents. The most popular candidate was the variant in which both evaluation methods are advisory, the projects are co-funded by central government and local authorities and interest groups have an advisory and non-committed status (8 votes). This variant is fairly similar to the current scenario, except for the sweeping financial decentralization. The variant in which both evaluations are advisory, the funding is shared by central government, local authorities *and the private financiers* and interest groups are recognized and committed, received 7 votes. This, we could say, is a model that makes heavy demands on process, but is also highly versatile. It is a combination of Dutch (advisory methods), Danish (everybody pays a share) and German elements (recognition and commitment for partners), which would entail profound interventions in the current situation. The bronze medal went to a model in which the evaluation methods are again advisory, everyone pays a share, and the interest groups are advisory and non-committed (5 votes).

What stands out in these results is that co-funding by the private sector suddenly figures strongly, even though in the assessment of the nine profiles that counted in the statistical analysis, it was clearly inferior to profiles that included public–private partnerships. A possible explanation is that in the current public and political debate, private funding enjoys quite some interest and popularity. As a consequence, respondents giving socially desirable answers are more likely to include it in their ideal institutional structure.

Finally, the respondents were firmly of the opinion that their ideal variant would lead to improvements in all the quality aspects: in acceptance, openness and quality of the infrastructure product this effect is considerable, in speed and costs it is limited, but positive nonetheless. This comes across as somewhat contrived, as the respondents generally applied the decision-making attributes in such a way that acceptance, openness and quality of the product were maximized, possibly at the expense of speed and costs. It would be very optimistic to expect the personally chosen ideal structure to bring about improvements in all these aspects.

Predictive Capability of the Conjoint Model

A conjoint model is capable of predicting the attractiveness of every decision-making structure that is defined in the attribute levels from the experiment. But this automatically raises the question: what is the level of accuracy? To address this question, the decision-making structures of Germany and Denmark (Profiles 10 and 11) were included in the questionnaire as hold-out profiles, that is the model was used to predict the scores for these two profiles. A comparison between this prediction and the recorded scores provided an indication of the accuracy with which the model can predict scores for new observations.

The average recorded score for the decision-making structure in Denmark was 5.55 while the model predicted 5.14. Hence, the prediction was too low by 0.41. For Germany the average recorded score was 5.79 and the prediction 5.49. Hence, the prediction was too low by 0.30. On average, the model underestimated the average overall score for these two hold-out profiles by 0.35, which is not at all bad. Moreover, the direction of the changes and the ranking of the countries were both predicted correctly. The model can also accurately predict the direction of the change (higher or lower). We can therefore also conclude that the drafted model can predict scores for new observations with a reasonable degree of accuracy. This inspires confidence in its predictive capability.

CONCLUSIONS AND DISCUSSION

Citizens and organizations involved in decision-making on transport infrastructure are exigent and rightly demand high quality for their money. When the time comes to implement these ideas, consensus is easier said than done. This is chiefly because the aspects that the parties need to agree on are, to some extent, contradictory. The wishes of politicians, pressure groups and private citizens may be diametrically opposed to the results of a broad-based evaluation. In many domains the private parties may only be prepared to contribute if they are allowed to coordinate part of the decision-making process, but the public parties are anything but amenable to such demands. If cost-effectiveness is to be guaranteed in a project, there is no way that all the wishes of the local authorities can be accommodated, but this can ultimately seriously disrupt the relationships between central and local government.

The research shows that the respondents are relatively satisfied with the current decision-making structure for transport infrastructure in the Netherlands, particularly the advisory role of analyses and reports. Environmental impact assessments and cost–benefit analyses should be mandatory; persons in authority should have knowledge of them but not be bound by the results. Ad hoc studies, on the other hand, carry too few obligations, while the vast majority of the respondents were strongly opposed to reports with a decisive character. Nevertheless, there is clearly room for improvement in the current structure: for one thing, the financial relationships are far too centralized. Local authorities and perhaps the private sector should become major co-financiers. It might also be worthwhile to accord interest groups a more definitive role in the discussion process. Acceptance of final decisions, openness in information-sharing and quality of the final infrastructure product would, in any case, probably benefit from this. The experts were ready to accept that this might slow down the decision-making a little. There would be scarcely any effect on the costs, as they would be affected more by the role of the analyses and reports. And no one wanted to see any changes on that front.

It is common practice in administrative and policy studies to conduct qualitative research when investigating complex and multi-faceted policy issues in which the players have different interests and perceptions. Such research often takes the form of open-ended interviews, case studies, close observation or combinations of all three. Recently role-play has gained in popularity, computer-supported and otherwise.

The general opinion about quantitative analysis is that the researchers are not (sufficiently) capable of relaying the nuances and subtleties in exchanges of opinion, changes of preference, unpredictable interaction processes and the multi-dimensionality of policy problems. There is a lot to be said for this view. However, in this chapter, conjoint analysis – a research method that lends itself to processing quantitative data – is used for the first time in this field. Conjoint analysis is frequently used to measure preferences in concrete, visible domains, such as the purchase of property or public transport services, but it has never been applied to more abstract subjects, such as expert opinions on institutional structures and their impact on the quality of decision-making. It is certainly conceivable, even probable, that individual analysts have been aware of various of the above-mentioned observations, but the degree to which they were shared by the wider community of practice has never been verified, nor have qualitative methods made this possible.

No doubt, complexities were simplified in the operationalization. After all, a cost–benefit analysis has more modalities than the three described above, and the situation in Denmark involves a lot more than just the systematic application of public–private partnerships in infrastructure projects. Nonetheless, the findings from this study conducted among 47 respondents have proven robust, and the respondents had a good general understanding of the material. The findings are also meaningful. They provide a clear picture of the strengths and weaknesses in the current Dutch system and point it in the right direction: keep policy analyses advisory, decentralize financial relationships and give interest groups a more definitive status in the decision-making process. The authors believe that conjoint analysis is a valuable addition to the arsenal of research tools in public administration and political science, and have shown that it can lead to new insights into complex decision-making on major infrastructure projects.

REFERENCES

de Jong, W.M. (1999), *Institutional Transplantation; How to Adopt Good Transport Infrastructure Decision-making Ideas from other Countries?*, Delft: Eburon.

de Jong, W.M. and H. Geerlings (2003), 'De opmerkelijke terugkeer van de kostenbaten-analyse in het centrum van de beleidspraktijk', *Beleid en Maatschappij*, **3**, pp. 166–78.

de Jong, W.M. and H. Geerlings (2004), 'Wat kan Nederland leren van de Deense infrastructuurplanning?', *Bestuurswetenschappen*, **58**(3), 193–216.

Flyvbjerg, Bent (1998), *Rationality and Power; Democracy in Practice*, Chicago and London: University of Chicago Press.
Flyvbjerg, Bent, Nils Bruzelius and Werner Rothengatter (2002), *Megaprojects and Risk: An Anatomy of Ambition*, Cambridge: Cambridge University Press.
Hendriks, F. (1997), *Het Verhaal van twee Steden*, Leiden: DSWO Press.
Hendriks, F.A.M. and S. Zouridis (1998), 'Beslissen over infrastructuren', *Bestuurswetenschappen*, **52**(3), 150–66.
Leleur, S. (1995), *Road Infrastructure Planning; a Decision-Oriented Approach*, Lyngby: Polyteknisk Forlag.
Louviere, J.J. (1988), 'Analyzing decision making: metric conjoint analysis', Sage University Paper, Series on Quantitative Applications in the Social Sciences, No.07-067, Sage Publications, Beverly Hills.
Ministries of Transport and Economic Affairs (2000), 'Leidraad Onderzoeks-programma Economische Effecten Infrastructuur', The Hague (in Dutch).
Reh, W. (1988), 'Politikverflechtung im Fernstrassenbau der Bundesrepublik Deutschland und im Nationalstrassenbau der Schweiz, eine vergleichende Untersuchung der Effizienz und Legitimation gesamtstaatlicher Planung', *Beitrage zur Politikwissenschaft*, **37**, Frankfurt am Main: Peter Lang.
Stead, D., H. Geerlings and E. Meijers (eds) (2000), 'Policy integration in practice: the integration of land-use planning, transport and environmental policy making in Denmark, England and Germany', Delft: DUP Science.
Steenkamp, J. (1985), 'De constructie van profielensets voor het schatten van Hoofdeffecten en interacties bij conjuncte meten', *Jaarboek van de Nederlandse Vereniging van Marktonderzoekers*, pp. 125–55.
Taylor, B.D. (1992), 'When finance leads planning; the influence of public finance in transportation planning and policy in California', UMI Dissertation Service, California.
Teisman, G. (1992), *Complexe Besluitvorming; een Pluricentrisch Perspectief op Besluitvorming over Ruimtelijke Investeringen*, The Hague: VUGA.
Teisman, G. (1997), *Creatieve Concurrentie; een Innovatieplanologisch Perspectief op Ruimtelijke Investeringen*, Nijmegen: KUN.
Weggeman, J. (2003), *Controversiële Besluitvorming; Opkomst en Functioneren van groen Polderoverleg*, Utrecht: Lemma.
Wetenschappelijke Raad voor het Regeringsbeleid (WRR) (1994), 'Besluiten over grote projecten, Rapporten aan de regering no. 46', The Hague: SDU Uitgeverij.
Wetenschappelijke Raad voor het Regeringsbeleid (WRR) (1998), 'Ruimtelijke ontwikkelingspolitiek, Rapporten aan de regering no. 53', The Hague: SDU Uitgeverij.
Wijnen, G., W. Renes and P. Storm (2004), *Project management*, 18th edn., Utrecht: Het Spectrum.
Woltjer, J. (2001), *Consensus Planning: the Relevance of Communicative Planning Theory in Dutch Infrastructure Development*, Aldershot, UK: Ashgate Publishing Limited.

Conclusion: evolution towards integrated project appraisal

Chris Coeck and Elvira Haezendonck

The description of the use of different instruments for transport project evaluation is a very appealing and even tempting theme. It is interesting to ascertain the relevance and usefulness of the conclusions of the evaluation based upon different instruments and their impact for policy making. Indeed, an analysis of sustainable transport and mobility in Europe is a very real and even 'hot' topic. In recent history, numerous institutions, consultants and research centres have devoted attention to mobility research. As the different contributions in this book reveal, the AIPE has succeeded to combine theory and practice of state-of-the-art experts on this subject. As such, the contributors provide an insight into a wide array of aspects related to mobility research and to more institutional aspects of transport project appraisal. This book will prove to be a benchmark in the transport evaluation literature. The contributors concentrated on their knowledge and expertise in economic evaluation of transport projects. In this conclusion, the different elements that stressed the institutional aspects in economic evaluation and the related problems and impediments will be described. In addition, a general conclusion or trend revealed in the different contributions of this book will be provided.

Economic appraisal of transport and mobility projects is crucial and instrumental for policy making. It provides policy makers with essential information on the welfare effects and the economic contribution of individual projects and on the conditions in which different projects are formulated. Economic theory and practice suggest that evaluation combines a number of elements. More in particular, institutional aspects such as societal values and the opinion of multiple stakeholders need to be taken into account when performing optimal project appraisal.

The demand for transport has increased over the years at a much higher pace than GDP or than the growth of industrial production. As the financial means of government are limited, intended investments in infrastructure will not be able to follow the pace of transport growth. At EU level, the increasing demand for transport also reveals a growing awareness of the negative external effects of transport and the resulting search for sustainable mobility and transport solutions. As a result, traditional evaluation methods have to be reconsidered and restyled based upon the most recent evolutions and trends.

In general, infrastructural transport projects can be assessed based upon their profitability, their economic costs and benefits or on their contribution towards specific investors' goals. Today, these projects also need to be evaluated in the light of their contribution to both societal welfare, value added, return to government and general well-being. In this context, a multiple stakeholder analysis and in general an appraisal based on multiple criteria is considered a very appropriate evaluation tool. The different contributions in this book document this trend.

The book also focuses on the institutional aspects of transport in project evaluation. It attempts to answer different questions, such as: (1) Why do institutional aspects need to be introduced and included in transport project evaluation? (2) What aspects or elements need to be included? (3) What methods can be used in order to incorporate the institutional aspect into transport project evaluation? and (4) What is the legitimacy of stakeholders towards this kind of appraisal?

Different policy documents reveal that the European Union, as an important supra-national institution, is concerned with the evolution of mobility in general and with proper transport project evaluation in particular. The White Paper on Transport Investment Projects suggests for example that when evaluating these kinds of projects essentially an environmental impact assessment (EIA) needs to be performed. Within the TEN-T network and with the White Paper it is attempted to promote sustainable development and to decouple transport growth and GDP by rebalancing the modal split and improving quality and safety. As such, 30 transport axes are selected across Europe and 29 priority projects are implemented. However, an EIA needs to be performed in any case.

The contributors to Part I of this book concentrate on the necessary evolution towards an integration of institutional aspects of transport projects in the evaluation practice. Different perspectives on the evaluation of transport projects are provided. However, an overall attempt was made to identify the different institutional aspects of the assessment of large-scale transport investments. Vickerman, De Brucker and Verbeke indicate that traditional economic evaluation and common welfare economics are characterized by a number of disadvantages and boundaries. A more institutional approach to transport economics and especially economic evaluation is suggested throughout this part of the book. This entails an evolution towards a more integrated project appraisal, in which different tools and instruments are combined into a comprehensive whole. As a result, an overview of the positive and negative effects can be constructed and the collective benefits of increased efficiency and effectiveness can be identified. In this respect, it is also essential to indicate the 'musts' and 'wants' related to transport infrastructure projects in order to be able to calculate the individual effects related to project implementation. Moreover, Part I provides an in-depth analysis of the instruments commonly used in transport project evaluation. Economic project evaluation of any type is a process with different and distinct steps: knowledge of a specific step influences the following and sometimes even the preceding phases of the evaluation process. Conceptually, nine research or evaluation steps have to be followed in any institutionalized project evaluation (see for example the Dutch OEEI guideline): (1) an analysis of the problem setting; (2) a definition of the project; (3) an identification of the project effects; (4) an identification of the relevant exogenous developments; (5) a valuation of the project effects (direct, indirect and external effects); (6) a prognosis of project costs; (7) an application of different evaluation techniques; (8) performing a risk and sensitivity analysis; and (9) the preparation of decision-making and implementation. Here, it can be concluded that social cost–benefit analysis (SCBA), socio-economic impact analysis (SIA) and multi-criteria analysis (MCA) have to be considered as complementary instruments for economic evaluation. All these instruments provide policy makers with useful, relevant and necessary information for decision-making. Once again, modern evaluation demonstrates a shift towards a multiple stakeholder evaluation. Finally, Part I sheds a light on legal issues concerning transport project evaluation by describing ad hoc procedures for project evaluation.

In Part II, a number of modern practices and new approaches for project evaluation are illustrated. The framework and guidelines for large-scale project evaluation in the Netherlands are documented and evidence from the evaluation of the Westerscheldt project was described. The main conclusion of this contribution is that even a strict application of the guidelines for *ex ante* project evaluation will not always result in a direct political commitment or a formal decision-making trajectory. Basically, an important conclusion from the theoretical perspectives in Part I is confirmed: a combination of different perspectives in project evaluation is necessary and will increase the social commitment of the relevant stakeholder groups. As such, this will lead again to the necessity of a multiple actor or multiple stakeholder approach. Part II also features an empirical study of one of the most recent port projects in Western Europe, particularly the Deurganckdok in the Port of Antwerp. The practical applications of port project evaluation indicate once again that in fact a combination of different evaluation techniques is used for evaluating the project: EIA, SCBA and integrated strategic planning are used as main instruments. The application of common EIA practices presents a number of structural deficiencies. Here, it can be observed that economic evaluation is embedded in strategic planning of port zones. As a result, strategic port planning is more and more considered as a useful tool for the preliminary assessment of possible solutions. The correct application of EU directives and, in particular, taking into account the limitations of for example the Birds and Habitats Directive is crucial for the future development possibilities of a port. As the described projects suggest, there are a number of problems in relying on the EU exemption procedure. According to the authors it is more advisable to ensure that preservation goals and objectives are met *ex ante* in order to prevent the use of the exemption procedure. As a result, nature development and future economic development will go hand in hand.

As the different contributions indicate, the context of evaluation focuses on applying a multiple perspective and multiple stakeholder approach. In this respect, a wide array of opinions need to be taken into account. More in particular, economic goals, theoretical propositions arising from project expectations or general scientific knowledge, stakeholder claims and societal and cultural values need to be fully integrated in transport project evaluation.

In practice, this element is acknowledged: recent port projects are evaluated based on a theoretical mix of instruments using social cost–benefit analysis, environmental impact assessment and economic effects analysis but also introduce elements central to numerous stakeholders. These elements will focus more on the natural environment or the well-being of, for example, the inhabitants of the surrounding villages. More specifically, multiple stakeholder evaluation will attempt to translate basic values, beliefs and needs of citizens into the policy framework and contributes to the legitimization process of project evaluation.

To conclude, it has to be stated that evaluation practices cannot be considered as a mere series of rational economic activities, but have also to be seen in terms of applying a social reality. Transport project evaluation has to be a product of the necessity to combine economic evaluation with a direct participation of multiple actors or stakeholders in terms of formulating basic needs and values. When these elements are fully taken into account, a bright future exists for integrated economic appraisal of transport projects as a tool for policy decision-making.

Index